S0-BZB-237

Blacks and Whites in Christian America

Religion and Social Transformation

GENERAL EDITORS: ANTHONY B. PINN AND STACEY M. FLOYD-THOMAS

Prophetic Activism: Progressive Religious Justice Movements in Contemporary America
Helene Slessarev-Jamir

All You That Labor: Religious Activists and Theological Ethics in the U.S. Living Wage Movement
C. Melissa Snarr

Blacks and Whites in Christian America: How Racial Discrimination Shapes Religious Convictions
Jason E. Shelton and Michael O. Emerson

Blacks and Whites in Christian America

How Racial Discrimination Shapes Religious Convictions

Jason E. Shelton and
Michael O. Emerson

NEW YORK UNIVERSITY PRESS
New York and London

NEW YORK UNIVERSITY PRESS
New York and London
www.nyupress.org

© 2012 by New York University
All rights reserved

References to Internet Websites (URLs) were accurate at the time of writing. Neither the author nor New York University Press is responsible for URLs that may have expired or changed since the manuscript was prepared.

Library of Congress Cataloging-in-Publication Data
Shelton, Jason E.
Blacks and Whites in Christian America : how racial discrimination shapes religious convictions / Jason E. Shelton and Michael O. Emerson.
p.   cm. — (Religion and social transformation)
Includes bibliographical references (p.   ) and index.
ISBN 978-0-8147-2275-6 (cl : alk. paper) — ISBN 978-0-8147-2276-3 (pb : alk. paper) — ISBN 978-0-8147-2278-7 (ebook) —
ISBN 978-0-8147-2277-0 (ebook)
1. African Americans—Religion. 2. Race discrimination—Religious aspects—Christianity. 3. Race discrimination—United States. 4. Black theology. 5. Protestant churches—United States—Doctrines. 6. Faith.
I. Emerson, Michael O., 1965– II. Title.
BR563.N4S49 2012
280'.408900973—dc23   2012016651

New York University Press books are printed on acid-free paper, and their binding materials are chosen for strength and durability. We strive to use environmentally responsible suppliers and materials to the greatest extent possible in publishing our books.

Manufactured in the United States of America

c 10 9 8 7 6 5 4 3 2 1
p 10 9 8 7 6 5 4 3 2 1

To Sarah—this is no ordinary love.

—J.E.S.

Al mio pisello dolce, l'amore della mia vita.

—M.O.E.

Contents

Preface: Religion and Race   ix

1   Why Do African Americans Pray So Often?   1

2   So Rooted a Past: Slavery and African American
    Protestant Religious Tradition   31

3   The Apostles' Creed: Racial Similarities in
    Commitments to Core Christian Tenets   48

4   Learning and Burning: Racial Differences in
    "Academic" versus "Experiential" Models
    of Christianity   57

5   Religious Convictions: Everyday Faith-Based
    Actions and Beliefs   86

6   Shaded Morality: Not So Black and White   111

7   Far-Reaching Faith: Evidence of an Inclusive
    Religious Doctrine   133

8   Reconciling the Race Problem: Identity Politics and
    the Gulf between Black and White Protestants   168

    Epilogue: The Race Problem and Beloved Community   199

    Appendix A: Sampling Procedures /
       Sample Characteristics   209
    Appendix B: Descriptive Tables   215
    Appendix C: Interview Guides   235
    Notes   239
    References   253
    Index   271
    About the Authors   279

Preface
Religion and Race

Religion and race differences have remained major sources of conflict since our nation's founding. Not only were there profound religious tensions among the early European settlers, but also between them, African slaves, and Native Americans. Today—nearly 250 years after America's birth—there are still deep-seated religious tensions across members of different racial groups. There are also racial tensions among followers of the same faith.

In this book, we examine the intersections of religion and race among a specific set of believers: black and white Protestants. More specifically, we assess racial differences in how black and white Protestants think about and practice their religious faith. As one might expect, we uncover profound faith-based similarities and entrenched differences. We explain these differences by focusing on African Americans and describing what we call the *building blocks* of black Protestant faith.

Before going any further, we must establish several important points. First, we are trained as sociologists, not as theologians or historians. Most of the existing research in this area has been produced by the latter groups, rather than the former. Sociologists systematically analyze beliefs and behaviors across groups of people. Consequently, we draw on established social science research methods—such as nationally representative surveys, focus groups, and in-depth interviews —that allow us to compare and contrast black and white Protestant's attitudes, activities, and emotions.

Second, this book is purposely written to be accessible to a general audience. Although we are social scientists, we did not write this book exclusively *for* social scientists. People across a wide range of backgrounds are interested in the intersections between religion and race. We have taken steps to ensure that this book is as reader-friendly as possible—regardless of whether the reader is a university professor, a deeply committed Christian, or a casual observer.

Jason Shelton principally authored this book, so any shortcomings in it are principally his. For all that is positive about this work, we wish to thank Craig Dykstra and Chris Coble at the Eli Lilly Endowment. Their efforts were critical in securing the generous funding for the Portraits of American Life Study (PALS), which was crucial in making this book possible. We would also like to thank Jennifer Hammer, our editor at NYU Press, for sharing her insights and expertise. Jennifer has been a staunch supporter of this project from the very beginning. We can confidently say that this book would not be as robust without her assistance.

We thank the thousands of study participants who volunteered their time in order to participate in our surveys, focus groups, and in-depth interviews. We gladly recognize several anonymous book reviewers who helped to improve the work, as well as colleagues who provided helpful feedback after we presented chapters of this book at the following conferences: the 2011 "Race and Power Mini-Conference" that took place during the annual meeting of the Southern Sociological Society, the 2011 annual meeting of the Southern Conference on African American Studies, the 2011 annual meeting of the American Sociological Association, and the 2009 annual meeting of Society for the Scientific Study of Religion. We would also like to thank staff and participants at the 2010 Summer Seminar "The Power of Race in American Religion" at Calvin College. George Wilson of the University of Miami deserves special recognition for proofreading several early drafts of this manuscript, and Christy Davis at Executive Services transcribed many hours of in-depth interviews and focus groups. We would also like to thank colleagues, administrators, and assistants at the University of Texas at Arlington (UTA) and Rice University. Jason Shelton is especially grateful for the extraordinary institutional support that he has received from UTA. Research funds embedded within his Stars Plus Package were critical to completing this project.

Finally, this book could not have been written without love, support, and tolerance from our families. They put up with us writing and researching for long days and nights, at inconvenient moments, and during times when they would rather have been making memories and enjoying our company. Michael Emerson would like to thank Sweet Pea, Ace, Juice, Three Scoops, and Soap Soap.

Jason Shelton would like to thank his parents Iris Lynn Bailey and Eugene Shelton, Jr., for their unconditional love, nurturing, and support. He is also indebted to his brother, Eric, his grandparents, aunts (especially Beverly) and uncles (especially Michael), godfather, in-laws, Mrs. Shirley Adams, and Henry Arthur Callis. He is most especially thankful for his amazing wife, Sarah, and their two wonderful daughters, Layla and Chloé.

1

Why Do African Americans Pray So Often?

Long before we got serious about writing this book, we had concluded that black Christians more often publicly display their religious faith than white Christians do. Two observations shaped our beliefs about this. First, we stopped counting the number of times that we had seen a black athlete, actor, or musician give glory to God after winning the Super Bowl, an Emmy, or an American Music Award. It happened so often that it seemed customary. However, we both admitted that we still take notice when white athletes or artists do so (especially non-country-music singers).

Second, when asked the everyday obligatory question "How are you?" we noticed that many African Americans respond with "I'm blessed. And you?" It is worth noting that we are just as likely to hear this reply on a Wednesday afternoon as we are a Sunday morning. Moreover, the "And you?" reply is a thinly veiled test of one's faith; it often inspires a public discussion over God's impact on a person's life. These testimonials can take place at any moment, in any setting from sanctuaries to subway trains, from Bible study groups to ball games.

Just to be clear, we are not saying that white Christians do not thank God in secular public settings or that they do not have their own faith-based adages (some might even respond with some variation of the expected reply, such as "I'm blessed by The Best. And you?"). But in our view, it seemed as if these small but noticeable differences were motivated by a distinct sense of Christianity among blacks rather than whites.

We did not get serious about writing this book until we experienced an awkward situation that forced us to deliberately engage the fault

lines between religion and race. The following encounter supported
our speculations about the unique manner in which African American Protestants go about their religious faith.

We had narrowed our search for an administrative assistant down
to three people and had begun the final step of interviewing our top
candidates. Sharon[1]—a tall, 30-something-year-old African American woman—was one of the final three. Her interview took place on
a rainy Houston day, so we let her know that it was okay if she needed
some extra time to freshen up before our meeting. The interview
went pretty well. It was only awkward because Michael and I both in-
stinctively knew that one of our other candidates was a better fit for
the position.

Maybe Sharon sensed this. In our final moments together, she told
us that she was "so nervous" about the interview that she had spent the
additional time before our meeting praying in the bathroom. "I had to
talk to the Lord," she said with a smile. "I needed some extra strength!"
We all shared in a good laugh. But then she went on to tell us how
she prays several times a day, just about anywhere and everywhere and
whenever she feels the need to "call on the Lord." Sharon volunteered
all of this information and even gave specifics—despite this being an
interview for a secular job at a secular institution. Before leaving, she
openly thanked the Lord for getting her to our offices safely and asked
for His "mercy" in getting back home.

After the interview, Michael and I talked about Sharon at length. I
told him that as far as I could tell, many churchgoing African Americans approach their religious faith in the same way that Sharon does.
"Black folks pray all the time," I said. "It's just what we do." I followed
up this observation with a question: "How many white Sharons are out
there?" I was curious to know whether he believes that whites often
call on the Lord in a public bathroom or pray several times a day. I
figured that he would have a better idea than I do, since I am black
and he is white. Michael stopped and paused. "Probably not too many,
perhaps a few evangelicals."

That got us thinking: Do black Christians pray more often than
white Christians do? And if so, why do African Americans pray so
often? Conventional wisdom presumes that despite minor cultural dif-

ferences, members of the same universal religion do not radically differ in their religious practices and convictions. This is largely because
"universal religions" (such as Christianity, Islam, Buddhism, and Judaism) are thought to have the same core beliefs and practices, no matter
where a follower is located on the globe. Moreover, these universal religions, according to their own teachings, all ideally work to be vessels
for bringing people together, building consensus, and inspiring camaraderie among their followers. If black Christians consistently pray
more often than white Christians do and have distinctly faith-based
reasons for doing so—and if this difference is merely one of many significant racial differences—then Christianity's "universal" standing
would seem untenable. Indeed, it would suggest that different groups
think about and practice Christianity in perhaps fundamentally different ways.

In this book, we find out if there is any validity to our informal observations regarding *racial differences in how black and white Christians go about their religious faith*. This book has three goals. First, we
bring together important ideas that are disseminated across the extensive literature on black religion. Second, we advance a new set of
principles—what we describe as *building blocks*—for understanding
the distinctive way that African Americans think about and practice
Christianity. While some of our building blocks are familiar to scholars of black religion, we advance original contributions as well as new
takes on established ideas. Third, and most important, we empirically
assess the merits of these building blocks by way of rigorous research
methods (surveys, focus groups, and in-depth interviews). This final
contribution is what truly sets this book apart from the rest—our
analysis of cutting-edge data sources allows us to move beyond theory and conjecture. We provide empirical evidence that supports our
arguments in the form of statistical findings and emergent patterns
from dialogue with everyday Christians. But there is no need to fret:
we present what we find in plain English, in a way that is accessible to
all our readers (that is why we ask those readers who are fluent in the
language of statistics to please consult our appendices).

To be sure, the answers to such interesting and important questions
as "Why do African Americans pray so often?" shed much-needed

light on issues relevant to race relations among black and white Christians in the United States. At stake is not just knowledge for its own sake but rather *knowledge relevant to the political, social, and religious functioning of this nation.* For instance, the findings presented in this book suggest that Rev. Dr. Martin Luther King's vision of the "Beloved Community"—a spiritually based gathering of people from all walks of life motivated by goodwill, reconciliation, and justice—will remain unachievable until Christians engage in honest and forthright dialogue on the respective roles that racial oppression and privilege have played in shaping commitments to dissimilar models of Christianity. Efforts aimed at improving race relations will have limited success until social scientists, religious leaders, and the wider American public recognizes that there are profound similarities—and most especially differences —among blacks and whites with respect to how they think about and practice their religious faith.

What Is This Book About?

We argue that the cumulative effects of past and present racial discrimination and inequality have strongly influenced how African American Protestants go about their religious faith. The legacy of race-based oppression and privilege has helped to fuel differences in black and white Christians' *religious sensibilities* (i.e., the scope and content of faith-based actions and beliefs). As a result, African Americans remain strongly committed to a unique form of Protestantism that was born out of—and continues to protect them against—the historical consequences of racial stratification in the United States. Identity politics—that is, political beliefs and actions that are associated with a group of people that someone identifies with—drive significant racial differences among everyday black and white Protestants with respect to their faith-based thoughts and practices. Blacks and whites not only approach faith matters differently, but faith *matters* differently to blacks and whites. This is mainly because African Americans tend to lean on their faith as a supernatural call for help to protect against the consequences of historical and contemporary racial discrimination and inequality.

We offer a new framework for understanding how racial group membership color-codes religious sensibilities among Christians. One of our key contributions is the establishment of the *five building blocks of black Protestant faith*. These touchstones address the nature of black religion by capturing the fundamentally distinct, dynamic, energetic, and at times intricate manner in which African American Protestants go about their religious faith. Scholars across various fields of study have made significant contributions to the vast literature on racial group membership and religious identity among blacks.[2] Although some features of our five building blocks of black Protestant faith are common to the study of black religion, we present fresh theoretical insights and fill some of the conceptual gaps in time-honored ideas. Moreover, the five building blocks of black Protestant faith are clear and straightforward. The African American Protestant religious tradition is steeped in a rich and dynamic history that is multifaceted. Our building blocks help to clarify confusion (among both scholars and the wider American public) over the connections between religion and race among Christians, and they elicit take-home points that are useful, easily understandable, and applicable to everyday life.

Furthermore, we supply greater empirical precision and specificity than has been previously attained. The overwhelming majority of studies in this line of research are theoretical and/or historical. Our research methodology allows us to move beyond prior research by *testing* the extent to which black and white Christians differ in their religious sensibilities. This book includes a critically important comparative aspect: we directly assess black and white believers across a range of important dimensions of religious identity, such as how often they pray and attend worship services. Each of our five building blocks of black Protestant faith is simple, logical, and most important, testable. Hence, we are able to document the depth of faith-based similarities and differences—as well as to discover complexities and nuances—that lie beyond the reach of speculative analyses. In sum, these two major contributions (our comprehensive theoretical/conceptual approach and our comparative empirical analysis) allow us to present a more exhaustive and decisive investigation of the links between racial group membership and religious identity among Christians than any other study to date.

We are not the first scholars to note a difference in how black and white Christians go about their religious faith. For instance, a recent Pew Research Center poll of 36,000 Americans revealed that racial group membership has at least some influence over faith-based thoughts and practices. Findings from the survey show that blacks do, in fact, report praying more often than nonblacks do.[3] Furthermore, a greater percentage of African Americans than nonblacks attend worship services frequently and also report being an official member of a religious congregation.[4] While these findings are important, they do not tell us *why* African Americans pray or attend church services more often than nonblacks do. The "why" component of this issue is paramount; it potentially taps into deep-seated historical and contemporary tensions at the root of race relations in America.

For some time now, many scholars of black religious studies have argued that African American Christians undertake a distinct approach to their religious faith. In particular, these intellectuals have maintained that black Christians' beliefs and actions are strongly influenced by *liberation theology*[5] and a distinct *theology of suffering and evil.*[6] The former posits that Christ's message should not be separated from but rather should be used to alleviate social, political, economic, and racial problems in society. The latter addresses a unique set of issues pertaining to how believers—most particularly the downtrodden—reconcile their faith in Christ alongside the consequences of inequality. (We will address liberation theology and the theology of suffering and evil in detail at various points throughout this book.) Both of these impressive bodies of work argue that the dynamics of power and racial stratification in America have fostered theological and doctrinal chasms between black and white Christians.

The five building blocks of black Protestant faith—and their supporting evidence—bolster these claims. More specifically, they provide support for noted scholars C. Eric Lincoln and Lawrence Mamiya's influential (though untested) assertion that a *black sacred cosmos* lies at the center of the African American religious experience.[7] Lincoln and Mamiya describe this defining feature of black religion in the following insightful way:

> The black sacred cosmos or the religious worldview of African Americans is related both to their African heritage, which envisaged the whole universe as sacred, and their conversion to Christianity during slavery and its aftermath. It has been only in the past twenty years that scholars of African American history, culture, and religion have begun to recognize that black people created their own unique and distinctive forms of culture and worldviews as parallels rather than replications of the culture in which they were involuntary guests. . . . While the structure of beliefs for black Christians were the same orthodox beliefs as that of white Christians, there were also different degrees of emphasis and valences given to certain particular theological views. . . . The direct relationship between the holocaust of slavery and the notion of divine rescue colored the theological perceptions of black laity and the themes of black preaching in a very decisive manner, particularly in those churches closest to the experience.[8]

In this passage, Lincoln and Mamiya assert that while African American Protestants are committed to core Christian tenets (i.e., "orthodox beliefs"), they have also developed their own racially specific approach to and understanding of Christianity. The authors go on to pronounce that a "meaningfully different cultural form of expressing Christianity is found in most black churches, regardless of denomination, to this day."[9]

Lincoln and Mamiya's widely respected work should be viewed as a starting point rather than an ending. Although they painted the broad strokes, Lincoln and Mamiya left it to future studies to fill in the details regarding the formation and composition of the black sacred cosmos. In our view, the following are just a few of the critical questions that their book inspired yet remain unanswered: What exactly is "African" about the African American Protestant religious tradition? What are the "different degrees of emphasis and valences" that black Christians accentuate but white Christians do not? What specifically are the "meaningfully different cultural form[s]" that distinguish black Christianity from white Christianity?

The five building blocks of black Protestant faith advance our understanding of the black sacred cosmos's shape, content, and structure. They not only address the aforementioned questions (as well as others) but help with clarifying the distinct manner in which African American Protestants go about their religious faith. The five building blocks of black Protestant faith are not mutually exclusive but rather are closely connected and often overlap as well as reinforce one another. Moreover, these five features of the uniquely African American model of Christianity operate at the *group* level—when blacks and whites are compared in aggregate: they are not applicable to and should not be imputed on all black *individuals*. Lastly, racial differences in religious sensibilities primarily result from the dynamic interplay between cultural and structural factors (we explain this in detail over the duration of this book). Neither African Americans nor whites are biologically or genetically programmed to think about and practice their religious faith in any way; they *learn* to think about and practice (or not) and make choices about their religious faith over the course of their lives. The five building blocks of black Protestant faith are as follows:

1. *Experiential building block*: black Protestant faith is active and experiential; it is less concerned with precise doctrinal contours than is white mainline or evangelical Christianity.
2. *Survival building block*: black Protestant faith is critical to survival and helps individuals cope with suffering associated with everyday trials and tribulations.
3. *Mystery building block*: black Protestant faith is mystical and expresses an appreciation for the mystery in life; it includes folklore and cultural components deriving from the African Diaspora, the consequences of racial inequality in America, and non-Christian religions.
4. *Miraculous building block*: black Protestant faith is confident and comprehensive; the miraculous is ordinary and the ordinary is miraculous.

5. *Justice building block*: black Protestant faith is committed to social justice and equality for all individuals and groups in society.

Our goal in this book is clear: to help Americans of all backgrounds
better understand the links between race, religion, and identity politics. We provide an accurate, rigorous, and careful analysis of often
conflicting, complicated, and controversial issues influencing how
racial group membership color-codes faith-based thoughts and practices in the contemporary United States. We focus on religious identity among African Americans, and our driving theoretical and methodological contributions involve explicating and evaluating the five
building blocks of black Protestant faith.

In accomplishing this goal, we undertake the most comprehensive
and systematic investigation of African American religious actions
and beliefs to date. Relatively few studies have carried out a rigorous
empirical (i.e., quantitative and/or qualitative) examination of this
topic.[10] We rely on widely accepted social science research strategies
that are transparent. Our analysis of contemporary survey data and in-
depth interviews with everyday Christians provide us with a unique
opportunity to bridge the impressive theory-based and historical literature with modern research techniques.

Let us be clear: our intentions in this book are not to reignite or fan
the flames of historical tension between black and white Christians. To
the contrary, our purpose is the exact opposite: to expose and explore
the combustible causes of faith-related racial firestorms so that they
might finally be extinguished. This is the best way to ensure lasting
progress with respect to improving race relations among blacks and
whites in general, working for racial equality, and paving the way for
Dr. King's vision for the Beloved Community.

Why Black and White Protestants?

In this book, we compare and contrast faith-based thoughts and
practices among black and white Protestants. However, our theoretical, methodological, and interpretive analysis focuses on African

Americans. We chose this approach for several reasons, including (a) the unique role that religion has played in buffering blacks from racial hostility, (b) the fact that blacks are more willing to talk about racial differences in religion than are whites (we will have more to say about this topic later), and (c) there are far fewer empirical studies of religiosity among blacks than among whites.

We examine faith-based similarities and differences between black and white Protestants for three reasons. First, black and white Protestants have a longstanding, contentious history in North America that dates back nearly 400 years. Second, the vast majority of blacks and the majority of Christian whites in the United States are Protestant. At least 70% of African Americans and 51% of whites claim to be affiliated with a Protestant denomination; 23% of whites and only 6% of blacks claim to be Catholic.[11] Furthermore, less than 14% of all Asians or Latinos are Protestant. While at least 67% of Latinos are Catholic, half of all Asians are neither Protestant nor Catholic. Lastly, studies have shown that most Asian and Latino Christians are relatively recent arrivals to the United States with diverse national origins, immigration contexts, and conversion histories.[12] The rich racial, ethnic, and religious backgrounds of Japanese, Chinese, Korean, Mexican, Cuban, and Dominican Christians, for example, are well beyond the scope of the present study.

Research Methods

We discern the five building blocks of black Protestant faith by way of quantitative and qualitative research strategies. Our primary data source is the 2006 Portraits of American Life Study (PALS). This innovative, nationally representative sample of U.S. residents contains the most comprehensive survey modules to date regarding beliefs about core Christian theological tenets, religious practices and convictions, and attitudes about contemporary race-related issues. A second quantitative data source is the 2006 General Social Survey (GSS), an annual opinion poll that asks a nationally representative sample of Americans about various topics, including religion and race. Our final data source is a series of forthright qualitative interviews with people in the pews, small-group sessions with churchgoers, and meetings with high-ranking religious clergy. The PALS and the GSS were designed to include both time-tested and cutting-edge sampling procedures. This combination of conventional and advanced data collection techniques ensures that the study participants enrolled in these surveys accurately reflect the larger American population (see appendix A for more information on sampling procedures, sample characteristics, data coding, and analysis procedures). The everyday people included in these surveys come from various walks of life. They live in all regions of the United States, in small towns, major metropolitan areas, suburbs, and inner cities. Furthermore, the respondents in these surveys are older and younger people, men and women, rich and poor, those with a college degree and those who did not finish high school, and of course, they racially categorize themselves as black or white. In short, the research teams responsible for developing these surveys undertook comprehensive and demanding procedures in order to provide as much assurance as possible that their study participants are the same average, everyday Americans that you, your family, and your friends probably are. As a result, based on appropriate statistical tests, we are confident in generalizing our survey findings to the wider American population.

Of course, many popular and scholarly texts have already examined the connections between racial group membership and religious identity among Christians.[13] However, our analysis moves beyond differences in culturally based praise and worship methods such as preaching styles, music ministries, and what some people affectionately describe as "dancin' in the aisle." In this book, we examine religious identity among African American Protestants on a more profound theological and doctrinal level. We investigate the prevalence of faith-based actions and beliefs across numerous facets of religious life.

Some of the topics addressed in this book include levels of commitment to core Christian tenets—those consistent with the Apostles' Creed—such as beliefs about creation and the existence of Heaven and Hell. Other assessments concern religious convictions such as whether black Protestants are more likely than whites to view God as a "personal being" or "impersonal spiritual force" and if there are racial differences across beliefs that are closely associated with Christianity (such as angels and miracles) as well as religious-related beliefs that are typically not associated with Christianity at all (such as astrology and reincarnation).

We also test to see whether there are significant racial differences in the frequency of religious actions such as church attendance and reading the Bible, as well as the extent to which blacks and whites espouse dissimilar beliefs about the Bible (such as whether it should be interpreted literally or figuratively). Results from these analyses help to clarify whether African American Protestants place a stronger emphasis on certain faith-based thoughts and practices than whites do, or vice versa.

Furthermore, we analyze faith-based beliefs about morality such as whether "God's law" is the basis of "right and wrong" and whether it is "sometimes okay to break the rules if it works to your advantage." Our analyses of morality are especially critical because they allow us to assess the extent to which racial group membership color-codes Christians' views on righteousness and virtue.

Popular media outlets and scholarly publications have detailed the ardent and impassioned manner in which white evangelicals go about their religious faith.[14] Therefore, for our most specific comparisons, we restrict our analyses to black Protestants and white evangelicals—whose common heritages derive from the Great Awakenings of previous centuries in American life. This is important because recent studies by sociologists of religion confirm that there are significant racial differences among blacks and whites with respect to how denominational affiliations shape faith-based thoughts and practices.[15] In short, denominational affiliations appear more important in shaping religious identities among white Protestants than among black Protestants.

This is not to say that denominational differences are not meaningful to African Americans. The majority of black Protestants attend predominantly African American churches that are Baptist, Methodist, or Pentecostal.[16] Strong theological and doctrinal differences exist across these denominations (not to mention differences within them by subdenomination). However, the fact that African Americans are *black* tends to take precedence over their individual denominational affiliations. Most scholars agree that the impact of denominational differences is small when compared to more consequential underlying similarities linked to past and present inequities associated with racial minority status. The findings presented in this book support this conclusion.[17]

We limit our analysis to similarities and differences between black Protestants and white evangelicals when this is the most appropriate and interesting comparison. Results from these procedures are especially critical: they further attest to the centrality of race within a subset of black and white believers who, at least from the outside, appear similarly fervently committed to their Christian religious identities. What does it mean if the average black Protestant—who might be Baptist, Pentecostal, or Methodist—prays and attends worship services more frequently than the average white evangelical does? We attempt to attach meaning to these differences.

The final set of items that we examine assesses the extent to which black and white Christians differ in their beliefs about racial problems and racial reconciliation. Public opinion research has long established that blacks and whites espouse contrasting beliefs about the causes of and solutions to our nation's historic "race problem."[18] Moreover, a handful of studies have shown that blacks' and whites' beliefs about how to solve the "race problem" are often intensified in the religious realm.[19]

Consequently, we also compare and contrast black and white Protestants' views on individual versus structural solutions for ameliorating racial inequality. Some of the hot-button topics addressed include whether the U.S. government should develop and implement racially specific policies such as affirmative action and reparations for slavery. Our findings for these aspects of *identity politics* tell us whether black and white Protestants are on the same page regarding strategies for bridging racial divides. This portion of the book further enhances our awareness of the potential pathways and roadblocks to faith-based racial reconciliation.

Our Quantitative Analysis

In this book, we make use of both descriptive and multivariate statistics (again, don't worry, you don't have to know statistics to read or understand this book). Descriptive statistics provide readers with a general "description" of the topic under analysis (such as the percentage of people who say that they pray at least once a day). Multivariate statistics are more sophisticated in that they provide much more specific information on the topic under analysis (such as the likelihood that a person who makes more than $100,000 a year and has an advanced degree prays at least once a day).

The handful of survey-based studies in this area tends to make use of descriptive rather than multivariate statistics. Our utilization of both methods is vital; they allow us to paint a more precise picture concerning the extent to which racial group membership color-codes the manner in which blacks and whites go about their religious faith. An exclusive reliance on descriptive statistics can be misleading since they do not account for important background information (such as a person's income and education level).

For example, regarding the aforementioned Pew Research poll, 59% of black Protestants reported attending church services at least once a week, while 50% of nonblack Protestants reported attending weekly (this latter statistic must be interpreted with caution since it includes data for whites as well as other nonblack groups).[20] Polling data from the PALS and the GSS are consistent with this finding. We found that 45% of black Protestants in the PALS say that they attend church at least "once a week," while 37% of white Protestants say that they do so (see appendix B, descriptive table B.1A). Similarly, 44% of black Protestants in the GSS report going to church at least once a week, while 33% of white Protestants say that they do so (see descriptive table B.1B). Taken together, across all three of these nationally representative surveys, it appears as though African American Protestants attend worship services more frequently than whites do. Note that in each of these surveys, a greater percentage of blacks report attending services more than once a week as compared to nonblacks in general or whites in particular.

But can these descriptive findings withstand more rigorous tests of scientific scrutiny? For instance, will blacks continue to attend worship services more often than whites do after accounting for relevant background factors such as income, education, age, gender, and region of residence? Studies have shown that each of these variables plays a statistically significant role in shaping faith-based thoughts and practices.[21] If there is no meaningful difference between blacks and whites after accounting for these factors, then it could be that one or more of the aforementioned variables (such as age or education, for example) accounts for the percentage gaps in church attendance between blacks and whites. However, if we find a statistically significant gap between blacks and whites—even after accounting for the background factors—this tells us that the percentage differences between blacks and whites cannot be reduced to other variables such as income, gender, and region of residence. In other words, if the difference between blacks and whites holds constant after adjusting for these potentially explanatory factors, then the difference between blacks and whites is statistically meaningful and operates independently from the other variables.

In returning to our example of racial differences in church attendance, it turns out that black Protestants continue to go to church more frequently than white Protestants even after adjusting for relevant background factors. While education, age, gender, and region of residence play a significant role in shaping how often Protestants attend worship services, the finding for African Americans is highly statistically significant and is by far the strongest in magnitude of all variables in the model. This result holds constant across both the PALS and the GSS (see the corresponding multivariate tables D.1A and D.1B in appendix D).[22] In fact, the similar finding for blacks in both surveys is striking. These results further attest to the statistical accuracy and generalizability of our survey findings.

Still, we decided to take our analysis a step further. How do black Protestants specifically compare with white evangelicals on the frequency of church attendance? Results from both surveys show that the average African American Protestant attends worship services more often than the average white evangelical does (the corresponding "special" multivariate tables are also presented in appendix D). This finding is particularly meaningful considering these groups have deep historical roots in the Great Awakenings. The role that racial group membership plays in color coding church attendance can neither be ignored nor reduced to the other factors.

Our descriptive analysis of the PALS data also shows that a higher percentage of black Protestants than of white Protestants report having an official church membership (see descriptive table B.1C). Remember that the Pew poll reported this result as well. Does this finding hold even after accounting for racial differences in church attendance? Yes. In fact, the difference between blacks and whites only grows stronger in magnitude and more highly significant when restricting our analysis to African American Protestants and white evangelicals.

Our Qualitative Analysis

Thus far, our descriptive and multivariate analyses have shown that black Protestants are more likely than white Protestants to regularly attend worship services and to report being an official member of a religious congregation. Why would this be so? We realized early in the process of researching this book that statistics alone could explain neither the rich complexity nor the real-world consequences of our findings. The results for church attendance, church membership, and prayer (which mirror the findings already presented but are discussed in greater detail later in this book) impressed on us the need for engaging in dialogue with everyday Christians.

Therefore, we complement our analysis of survey data with one-on-one interviews and focus groups with 30 Christians representing the three largest African American Protestant denominations. Our small, nonrandom snowball sample of black believers should by no means be viewed as a definitive or conclusive qualitative inquiry. Nevertheless, we were astonished by the remarkable intellectual consistency with which our interviewees answered the questions that we asked them. Qualitative researchers often say that it is okay to stop conducting interviews once you no longer learn any new information from the people with whom you have spoken. In other words, there is no need to recruit new people for your study once an obvious pattern of responses has emerged, and when the most recent people you have interviewed do not say anything that dramatically differs from those whom you have already interviewed.

That is exactly what happened with this study. Despite our small sample size, we decided to stop recruiting people for interviews because a distinct pattern had become apparent among our earliest and most recent participants. This is especially important considering that the people of faith whom we talked to are members of both big and small churches in and around Cleveland, Dallas–Fort Worth, Los Angeles, and New York City. The 14 in-depth interviews that we conducted with high-ranking clergy—including senior pastors well as other influential members of the pastorate—took place on the interviewees' terms. They dictated the time, location, and duration of the meeting (which typically lasted about an hour and a half). We interviewed pastors during the morning, noon, and night in their church offices, homes, or favorite local restaurant. The remaining study participants enrolled in hour-long focus groups that were typically conducted following Sunday worship services or Bible study groups (the in-depth pastoral interview and focus group interview guides are presented in appendix C).

We did not intend to conduct the overwhelming majority of our interviews with African Americans. At the outset, we aimed to conduct interviews with a similar number of black and white Protestants. We realized that some of the topics to be discussed in these interviews (such as race relations, prayer, and church attendance) could potentially make some study participants feel uncomfortable. That is why we decided that Michael Emerson would mainly interview the whites, and Jason Shelton would mainly interview the blacks.

However, we quickly found that many whites were averse to participating in a study about race relations among Christians. Furthermore, many whites were puzzled to hear of our survey finding that racial group membership influences people's faith-based thoughts and actions. We made it clear to all potential respondents that their participation was anonymous and confidential and that they did not have to answer a particular question if they did not want to. Our university protocol required us to let potential respondents know that there were no correct or incorrect answers and that each participant would be compensated at least $40 for sharing their time and thoughts. Most important, we let all potential participants know that we would not ask them any questions about how they *personally* go about their religious faith (although they were free to share this information). As survey researchers, we were most interested in hearing their opinions about why one group of Christians (African Americans) answered a survey question one way, while another group of Christians (whites) answered it another way.

Even so, many whites still expressed great consternation about our study. For instance, a white woman who participated in a focus group was forthcoming in her confusion about a survey finding that people who say that their race is "very important" to them also tend to pray more than other people. In an irritated tone she said, "I'm really shocked at that statement, that people who pay more attention to their race tend to pray more. That blows me away. But it should be the opposite. I . . . I mean . . . I can't quite put it together, but that doesn't jibe right with me because Christians shouldn't even be looking at race."[23]

This was precisely the "off-the-record" sentiment conveyed by a white male Methodist pastor who declined to participate in our study. Like many whites, he let us know that he "does not see color" but rather ministers to all people regardless of race or sexual orientation. Yet he told us that his participation in our study would require him to do something that he "simply" does not do: "think about people in categories." At the end of our conversation, he informed us that earlier in the day he had faxed our interview guide to his church's lawyer, who subsequently advised him not to participate.[24]

Our experiences with recruiting blacks to participate in the study dramatically differed from our experiences with whites. Only one African American pastor whom we approached about participating in the study declined to be interviewed (he said that we would not "understand" him since we were trained as sociologists and not theologians). Blacks were also eager to participate in our focus groups—so eager that we had to turn people down so as to ensure that the groups remained manageable. Moreover, the vast majority of our interviews with African Americans were lively, informative, and energetic. In fact, our African American informants—both the pastors and the focus group members—provided rich and defined data that fit squarely in line with longstanding arguments advanced by leading scholars in black religious studies. Consequently, we deemed it intellectually appropriate and worthwhile to secure an interview with a foremost contributor to the scholarly literature on black religion. An interview of this sort would serve as a meta-analysis for contextualizing, synthesizing, and cross-referencing the findings from our survey and personal interview data.

Dr. James H. Cone was the last participant whom we interviewed for this study. Dr. Cone is the Charles A. Briggs Distinguished Professor of Systematic Theology at Union Theological Seminary, which is affiliated with Columbia University in New York City. He received his master of divinity degree from Garrett Theological Seminary in 1961 and his Ph.D. from Northwestern University in 1965. Dr. Cone is an ordained minister in the African Methodist Episcopal (A.M.E.) Church, the first Protestant denomination founded by African Americans. He has authored 12 books and more than 150 research articles and has been invited to speak at more than 1,000 colleges and universities across the globe. Dr. Cone is best known for penning the following classic texts: *Black Theology and Black Power* (1969), *A Black Theology of Liberation* (1970), *God of the Oppressed* (1975), and *Martin and Malcolm and America: A Dream or a Nightmare?* (1991). Each of these books has been translated into nine different languages. Dr. Cone's latest book is titled *The Cross and the Lynching Tree* (2011). Many people (both inside and outside the academy) consider him *the* most influential scholar of black theology living today.

Dr. Cone granted us the special consideration of waiving his anonymity and confidentiality. We are therefore able to attribute quotations directly to him. Dr. Cone brings decades of experience and insight to our study. Not only do we view him as a data source in and of himself, but his interpretation of our survey findings suggests that the logical consistency of African American viewpoints largely remains uniform regardless of whether an interview took place in a storefront, megachurch, or a hallowed hall of academia.

But for the Grace of God

We agree with Lincoln, Mamiya, Cone, and many other scholars of black religion who argue that in the United States, racial group membership and religious affiliation are so deeply interconnected that they cannot be separated without losing knowledge vital to our understanding of Christianity. Our survey findings for church attendance, church membership, and prayer support this conclusion. Findings from our in-depth interviews and focus groups reinforce this claim as well.

For instance, Rev. Washington, the senior pastor at a neighborhood Baptist church in Cleveland,[25] linked African Americans' unique approach to Christianity with racial stratification in the United States. Notice that in his statement, Rev. Washington references the "social gospel" and the "evangelical gospel." The former refers to the worldly, people-oriented dimensions of Christianity that can help with solving social problems in society. In contrast, the latter refers to the Biblically based dimensions of Christianity that are critical to attaining one's personal salvation:

> Well, I think that first of all there are different experiences that African Americans have had in American history, such as slavery and discrimination, in which the church religious bodies were complicit and white Christians were complicit in it. This led to African Americans starting their own churches, which reflected their own historical background; so the rituals, the symbols, the worship design, the music, the preaching, the prayers, all of that, . . . how they interpret the Bible, their theology—all of those things were *theirs.*
>
> I think another issue between a very large percentage of black Christians and white Christians is the social gospel versus the evan-

gelical gospel. It has been suggested throughout history that white Christians tend to be more doctrinaire and black Christians tend to be more practical oriented, which is why you get the social gospel.

Rev. Washington's statement describes how the legacy of racial discrimination and inequality in the United States encouraged the onset of dissimilar faith-based actions and beliefs among black and white Christians. In fact, he—like many of the pastors whom we talked to —contends that the dynamics of race-based oppression and privilege are the driving force behind the racial difference in religious sensibilities. As we will soon detail, most of our interviewees believe that white Christians are more attentive to the fundamentals of Christian doctrine while black Christians are more concerned with the practical application of the faith to their everyday lives.

We asked Rev. Washington to clarify exactly what he meant by the term "experiences." This seasoned pastor with a scholarly demeanor replied, "I mean slavery. We're still living with the scars of slavery. I mean discrimination. I mean this whole matter of depersonalizing people, just stripping them of their identity and even in some instances destiny—all of the things that happened to black people and continue to happen to black people in America today."

Rev. Washington's feelings are by no means rare or unique. In fact, *all* 14 of the African American pastors we spoke to specifically referenced slavery or issues related to racial discrimination at some point during the course of their interview. This is important because none of the questions in our interview guide specifically references these topics. Our study participants evoked these concepts—slavery and racial discrimination—on their own intellectual volition, without prompting from us.

Findings from our in-depth interview and focus group data suggest that beliefs about slavery, racial discrimination, and inequality are a critical component of the African American Protestant religious tradition (these sentiments are consistent with our *Mystery building block of black Protestant faith*). Take, for instance, this powerful revelation from Rev. Edwards, a young Pentecostal pastor focused on "building up" the size of his small congregation in Cleveland:

We [African Americans] have dealt with things through our existence where the only help we had was God. We were set aside—anything that you can conceive of negatively that happens to a group of people basically happened. We survived through it all; we made it. Women survived rape; we survived beatings. I read that 10 million slaves made it to America, but there were 13 million in all. So 10 made it, but there are 3 in the sea somewhere. We have had to come through all of that, and I think now when our race looks at it and we see how blessed we have become, we attribute that to God. We didn't get out of slavery on our own.

More often than not, the portion of the interview in which our interviewees mentioned slavery, racial discrimination, or inequality was packed with tension and antipathy. However, these moments could also be quite humorous. A fun-loving yet quirky focus group participant at a Pentecostal church in Los Angeles literally brought the room to laughter-produced tears with his response to the aforementioned question about racial identity and prayer. After patiently waiting his turn to speak, he leaned back, looked toward the ceiling, placed his hand on his forehead and sarcastically said, "Uuuuhmmmm . . . We've been catching hell for about . . ." He couldn't even finish the statement. The laughter in the room had overwhelmed his otherwise booming voice. Everyone knew what he was doing: using humor to make a serious point about the connection between prayer and racial identity. He was finally able to make his point a few minutes later, after folks in the room had gathered themselves:

Five hundred years, five centuries of slavery, Jim Crow, the Civil Rights Movement, the whole nine yards—so we [African Americans] had to depend on a power greater than ourselves because that is the only way we kept our sanity. We were being lynched and everything else. We had to depend on somebody other than ourselves to keep our heads together to keep surviving. So we were in church every Sunday. We were crying out for God to help us. And that's one of the reasons why I personally believe that we [African Americans] are more keen on being in church and being more religious and studying the Bible. Our faith in God is what got us through slavery.

While the subject of slavery, racial discrimination, or inequality became a topic of discussion during all of our interviews, not all of our study participants said the same things about how these issues shape religious sensibilities among black and white Christians. In fact, as we will see, there is important intellectual, attitudinal, and emotional variation among them. For instance, Rev. Shannon, a self-described "womanist" A.M.E. assistant pastor (*womanism* is a faith-based perspective positing that some ideological elements of feminism and black liberation theology should have a place within the African American Protestant tradition), emphasized that a person's social status can play a critical role in shaping his or her religious beliefs. According to her, race, economics, politics—and most important, *power*—each influence people's faith-based thoughts and practices:

I think that black and white Christians recognize that there is one God. We recognize there is one Jesus, and I think that as Christians we understand there is one Holy Spirit that's the Trinity in three persons. Our faith helps us to see our theology through those eyes and to call ourselves Christians.

But how we look at that and what it means to us and how . . . [*Her thought trails off.*] I think that our social status and our economic status weigh into our theological beliefs, tremendously, and I think that's why there's a difference in how white people look at their theology. White people are looking at their theological belief system through their economic and social eyes. Black people are doing the same thing. We are looking at our theology, our belief system, through our economic and social eyes, but we're *oppressed*. So we have heavier reliance on our theology to carry us through. We don't have the advantage of asking somebody to help us out financially. I mean, when you run out of food stamps you're going to have to figure out something else to do. So we look at our belief system, our theology, through our social and economic and our political eyes. And a white person does too. There's the three: the social, the economic, and the political. But they have always had the *power*. So if you already got the power, you may not have to look at your theology and your God in the same way because you've got the power.

Rev. Shannon's comment suggests that having a privileged position on the status ladder can strongly impact how a person thinks about and practices his or her religious faith. She is trying to tell us that the circumstances of individuals' lives can literally determine what they see (or at least what they think they see) out in the social world. This perception—of being near the top, middle, or bottom of the social ladder—in turn affects how individuals and groups go about their religious faith.

The basic thrust of Rev. Shannon's point—that the worldly social dynamics of race, economics, culture, and politics strongly influence people's faith-based thoughts and practices—was a common sentiment expressed by our interviewees. Both the preachers and the people in the pews made it clear that they were aware that African Americans continue to lag behind whites across many quality-of-life indicators such as income, education, occupational status, health, and family-related issues. While our respondents differed in the extent to which they believe that blacks themselves are responsible for these cleavages, virtually all of them recognized that structural factors beyond individual initiative—such as racism and classism, for example—play a significant role in explaining racial differences across many important spheres of American life (we address the ideological debate over *individualism* and *structuralism* in chapters 4 and 8).

Rev. Johnson, a widely respected senior pastor at a large Baptist church in the Dallas–Fort Worth area, said that he did not realize how important the status ladder was in shaping one's religious faith until he invited a white preacher to his church one Sunday. His comment addresses the links between everyday practical concerns and the institutional centrality of the black church:

Dr. Jeffery Hunter of [a Christian college] spoke at our church several years ago. He's a white preacher, and he was listening to the songs that our choir sang. And he made an interesting observation, and that is, a lot of songs our choir sang, they had to do with "the rent is due," "I need money to get my hair fixed"—they sang about a God that has to do with personal issues. And he said to me, "You would never hear that in a white church." I didn't think about it until he said it, because I have visited a lot of white churches.

In black churches, we sing and testify and talk about a God that I expect to show up and deal with my problems *today*. I'm looking for hope and answers and encouragement *right now*, today, for my concerns.

He [Dr. Hunter] said that whites keep it a little more generic and intellectual. Whites would not bring God down to precisely address the fact that you and your husband are breaking up, and you don't have money to pay your rent tomorrow. He said those kinds of songs, testimonies, and issues are rarely dealt with publicly in a white church.

So that's why I think African American Christians rely on the church. That is what we do; that has been our tradition. We couldn't afford psychology or psychiatry. We didn't know what a "therapist" was. So the church became . . . [*His thought trails off.*] I'm shocked at the number of people who call my office looking for a lawyer. They will call my office and say, "Recommend one" [*laughs*]. We get a lot of calls, and I'm thinking, "Why are you asking me for a mechanic? A doctor? A lawyer? The funeral home?" [*laughs*]. But all those questions come right here to this church because the church is expected to help people. That has been our history and tradition as African Americans.

We found this sentiment—that black Christians pray to and recognize a God that they believe can and will "show up" when needed—to be an important feature of black Protestant faith (it is consistent with our *Survival* and *Miraculous* building blocks). Real-world stressors and pressures such as paying the rent, feeding one's family, paying the electricity bill, getting or keeping a job, and even affording a trip to the beauty salon or barber shop are common concerns for African American Protestants. In the minds of many of our study participants, the legacy of racial discrimination and inequality has a lot to do with these everyday trials and tribulations.

So why do African Americans pray and attend worship services so often? The answer is closely related to the fact that many African American Protestants believe that they as individuals and blacks as a group would not have made it in this country *but for the grace of God*. That is essentially what Rev. Edwards and Rev. Shannon meant by their statements that African Americans "didn't get out of slavery on our own" or that blacks need a "heavier reliance on our theology to carry us through." Blacks recognize and ask for God's help so frequently because they are thankful for still being here, despite all of the big and small historical and contemporary challenges that they have faced in the United States.

This sensibility was best clarified by Pastor Thomas, the ranking minister at a large A.M.E. congregation in New York City. He described how a popular gospel song captures the theological underpinnings and basic teachings of the African American Protestant religious tradition:

My wife and I were at a banquet recently, and someone at the piano started playing a song—Marvin Sapp's "Never Would Have Made It." Somebody at our table joked that the song has been like number one on gospel and R&B charts forever.

We started laughing about how simple the song is. I could have written that song! [*laughs*]. But seriously, it raises three themes that you'll hear in most black churches every Sunday. First, "I never would have made it. I can't make it without God. I would have lost it all, but now I see that you were there for me." "I couldn't have made it without God" is one theme. Second, another theme is that "in my worst situation, God is there with me, and even though I maybe didn't recognize it at first, I now realize that whatever I'm going through God is with me." And third, "I'm wiser, stronger, I'm doing better—so much so that those trying experiences don't destroy us but actually makes us stronger, wiser, better."

And so those themes are central in African American churches, and it's all related to having that connection and relationship with God. So reading the Bible, praying—"I've got to pray because I got to. I need God to help me through what I'm going through."

This pastor, like so many of the African American Protestants whom we talked to, believes that blacks would not have "made it" but for the grace of God. (By the way, Marvin Sapp's song has maintained a significant presence on the gospel music charts for several years now.)

So what does Dr. James Cone, one of the foremost scholars of black religion in the United States, have to say about all of this? Does he think that there is any validity to claims made by the African American Protestants that we interviewed? Most certainly. In fact, Dr. Cone believes that there is a clear link between the legacy of racial discrimination and how African American Protestants go about their religious faith. His views corroborate the initial findings that we have discussed thus far:

> Blacks are searching for meaning. They are searching for purpose because they don't see it obviously allowed and expressed in the society. And when you live in a society which does not grant you meaning, from a human point of view, but considers you less than human, then you have to look beyond the values in the society for a meaning which that society cannot control. And that's where religion comes in. And that's where imagination comes in. Religious imagination empowers black people to know things about themselves in an ultimate sense that cannot be controlled and defined by the people who oppress them.
>
> See, faith emerges because there are contradictions in the world which people can't quite explain. So faith emerges in a community because they need resources to cope with the world they're living in.
>
> And black people got a whole lot of contradictions [*laughs*]. I mean, slavery, oppression, lynching, unemployment, prisons—just a whole lot of contradictions . . . [*His thought trials off.*] What do you do when you see your community cracking up, and you've got to respond to tragedy, but you have little material resources to respond?

Overview of the Book

The remainder of this book is devoted to developing, explaining, and substantiating our argument concerning the *five building blocks of black Protestant faith.* We argue (and show) that these five postulates go a long way toward explaining racial differences in religious sensibilities among black and white Christians. In accomplishing this goal, we fill a major hole in the existing scholarly literature by detailing the form, content, and structure of the *black sacred cosmos.* The distinct manner in which African American Protestants go about their religious faith will become evident.

Before proceeding, however, we must make three points abundantly clear. First, as previously stated, one of our primary contributions is a comparative statistical analysis of black and white Protestants. In our final chapter, we devote some attention to examining the impact of denominational differences among members of the same race. Nevertheless, a comprehensive test of contrasting religious sensibilities among black Methodists and black Pentecostals, for instance, or white Baptists and white Lutherans largely lies beyond the scope of the present study. Hopefully scholars will consider addressing this important and undoubtedly complex issue in the near future. Second, there are limits to survey research. As social scientists, we are bound by the scholarly expectation not to theorize or interpret beyond our actual data. Consequently, we do not attempt to read our respondents minds or psychoanalyze their responses. Religious beliefs are often deeply personal, subtle, and nuanced. We explain our survey findings at face value because it would be intellectually inappropriate to do so in any other way.

Last, and most important, our analysis highlights racial differences that are more often than not driven by African Americans' religious sensibilities. Blacks should by no means be viewed as "deviant" because they pray and attend worship services more often than whites do or because they prescribe to certain faith-based beliefs. That there are differences between blacks and whites does not mean than one or the other is deficient or operates at a faith-based deficit. In fact, we argue that black Protestants *and* white Protestants think about and practice their religious faith in often unique and distinct ways.

This book proceeds in a stepwise fashion; each chapter addresses a specific feature of our *five building blocks of black Protestant faith.* In the coming chapters, we assess a wide range of faith-based similarities and differences with respect to black and white Protestants' religious sensibilities. Some of our results are easily explainable. However, others are not. In fact, the pastors whom we interviewed expressed deep reservations about two very important survey findings that concern beliefs about God and the afterlife.

We will continue sharing relevant commentary from Rev. Washington, Rev. Edwards, Rev. Shannon, Rev. Johnson, and Pastor Thomas (as well as introduce others to the dialogue). Data from our in-depth interviews and focus groups remain a critical component of most chapters in this book. We will also continue to share Dr. James Cone's expertise and analysis. His renowned acumen brings further clarity, context, and insight to the topics under discussion.

The next chapter of this book is a necessary, focused review of the role that slavery played in shaping the African American Protestant religious tradition. With assistance from Derek Hicks, a professor of religious studies and theology, we spotlight the structural and cultural factors that gave rise to and reinforced racial differences in religious sensibilities among black and white Christians. Moreover, we establish that *liberation theology* and the *theology of suffering and evil* are widely accepted and deeply rooted themes among scholars of African American religious studies.

We continue our analysis of national survey data in chapter 3. Here we examine whether black and white Protestants report contrasting beliefs about the importance of God in their personal lives and whether there are racial differences in commitments to core Christian theological tenets.

In chapter 4, we establish our theoretical framework for understanding racial differences in religious sensibilities by further developing an idea that we introduced earlier in this chapter: many of the high-ranking clergy members whom we interviewed believe that whites are more concerned with the precise doctrinal fundamentals of Christianity, while blacks are more concerned with the practical application of their religious faith to their everyday lives.

Our analysis of racial similarities and differences in faith-based actions and beliefs continues in chapters 5 through 7. In these chapters, we examine black and white Protestants' commitments to religious convictions such as beliefs about the Bible, the frequency of reading the Bible and prayer, and the extent to which our respondents claim to have doubts about their faith. We also assess beliefs about morality, including attitudes about whether God punishes people for their sins and whether blacks or whites are more likely to lean on their religious faith when "facing major problems" in life. In chapter 7, we analyze commitments to religious beliefs that are closely associated with Christianity (such as the beliefs in angels and miracles), as well as those that typically are not associated with Christianity (such as reincarnation and astrology). The intriguing findings presented in this chapter make it abundantly clear that the African American Protestant religious tradition is simultaneously theologically *broad and definitive* in its attentiveness to Christianity.

Chapter 8 establishes the wide and deep gap between black and white Protestants' beliefs about the causes of and solutions to contemporary racial inequality. For instance, there are major attitudinal differences regarding (a) the individual and structural roots of racial inequality in America and (b) beliefs about the U.S. government's role in bridging racial gaps in society. In this final chapter, we discuss the results of this study within the context of faith-based efforts aiming to achieve racial reconciliation. Our quantitative and qualitative results suggest that contrasting commitments to identity politics severely limit prospects for racial reconciliation among black and white Protestants.

2

So Rooted a Past

Slavery and African American Protestant Religious Tradition

with Derek S. Hicks

Between the Christianity of this land, and the Christianity of Christ, I recognize the widest possible difference—so wide that to receive the one as good, pure, and holy, is of necessity to reject the other as bad, corrupt, and wicked. . . . The Christianity of America is a Christianity, of whose votaries it may be truly said, as it was of the ancient scribes and Pharisees, "They bind heavy burdens, and grievous to be borne, and lay them on men's shoulders, but they themselves will not move them with one of their fingers. All their works they do for to be seen of men." . . . They attend with Pharisaical strictness to the outward forms of religion, and at the same time neglect the weightier matters of law, judgment, mercy, and faith.

> —Frederick Douglass, "Slaveholding Religion and the Christianity of Christ" (1845)

Human recovery from the grip of oppression is a messy affair.[1] Suffering leads people of faith to ask difficult questions about God. Questions about black Christian faith have always necessitated an understanding of African American experiences, including slavery, segregation, and the prevailing systemic issues continuing to carve a crater between the haves and the have-nots. What is the relevance and impact of Christianity for those—as the influential African American theologian Howard Thurman described it—with "their backs against the wall"?[2]

The merging of religion and human recovery involves real human experiences. For example, Derek Hicks, the principal author of this chapter, recounts two instances of religion's impact on the human condition. The first event takes us to Los Angeles. In one week, two close friends of his were violently murdered in his neighborhood. At both funerals, he found himself embracing the mothers of his friends. Both times he was struck by the mothers' responses to such enormous loss. Each mother expressed a sentiment, while laced with lament and overwhelming pain, of renewed and even recharged strength, faith, and hope in a God who had the power to heal their despair. They equally saw this experience of loss as a watershed moment of faith: the God they had so earnestly prayed to on behalf of their sons had now changed their lives in a transformative, if unexplainable, way. The prayers of these women to their God did not cease with the loss of their sons; they, in fact, became more frequent, more fervent. In full acknowledgment of the issues plaguing their community in that Watts neighborhood, they chose to emphasize that direction and strength could be gained from God. What explains the kind of faith displayed by these mothers, holding ever faster to God when their sons had just died nonsensical deaths?

The second event came at a triumphal moment in Derek's life. At his college graduation, amid the glee of his family who had made the trip from Los Angeles to Louisiana for the ceremony, his grandmother began to weep. When asked why she was crying, she declared, "I spent many a night on my knees for this moment." In that simple statement, she expressed the role of prayer in navigating him through his college years to the happy ending of his graduation. Despite life's setbacks, she was convinced that her daily prayers fueled his accomplishment—one of the first in his family to achieve a bachelor's degree. What is the nature of this souled-out expression of faith through prayer? What is it about the faith of African Americans (its uniqueness is analyzed and discussed throughout this book) that leads to an engaged, active expression even when the odds are stacked against them? What anchors

this faith? How do we explain the mothers' and grandmother's enduring faith in a God who will "make a way out of no way"?

This chapter examines the historical underpinnings of African
Americans experience with Christianity. More specifically, we explain how the oppressive social and political circumstances of slavery molded blacks' knowledge and understanding of their religious
faith. The African American Protestant religious tradition is inextricably tied to the consequences of chattel slavery (outright ownership
of people and their offspring), the postbellum and Reconstruction
era, Jim Crow segregation (a racial caste system that operated in the
southern United States between 1877 and the mid 1960s), the reality of
postslavery domestic terrorism in the form of lynching, the civil rights
struggle, inequality, and continued forms of racial segregation. In
many ways, African American Christianity takes on a distinct nature
and function. We highlight several "dramas"—with origins in slavery
—that set the tone for a distinct form of Christian experience.

This religious experience should not, however, be conceived as
something other than Christian or American. Black Christians, in very
American fashion, have brought together various cultural norms and
traditions, whether connected to West African Yoruban traditions or
normative Protestant Christian practices (as well as others). Through
Christianity, African Americans have been equipped with tools and
a language for the purpose of overcoming adversity. In this chapter,
we lay out various historical moments—and their consequences—that
gave rise to a particularly "black" form of Christian experience, setting
forth the claims made in the chapters that follow.

*The Historical Drama of American Protestant Christianity and the
Experience of Chattel Slavery*

The swell and enthusiasm surrounding the religious revival of the
antebellum Great Awakenings suggest the possibility of a common
Christian heritage between blacks and whites in the United States. Yet
dueling social positions of antebellum whites and blacks set the tone
for the complex look, feel, and texture of American Christianity. On

one stage, we find the *planter class*—the white landowners, competitive capitalists, and aristocracy with sovereign authority and institutional support for the enslavement of Africans (and soon, the planter class expanded to include others who were racially defined as "white"). For them, the notion of *manifest destiny*—the belief that the United States was destined to expand across North America—set the tone for a Christian ideology intimately tied to notions of power and empire. Their perceptions of "freedom" in the New World instilled within them a vigorous desire to secure and develop their own land flowing with milk and honey.

On another stage, we find the African *slave class*, for whom Christianity takes on another dynamic. Whereas their captors and enslavers were driven by a desire to find new space to live fuller and freer lives, enslaved blacks faced the horrors of the forced relocation from Africa to the Americas. Once across the Atlantic, they found their lives in complete upheaval.

For Africans, the various destructive phases of enslavement gave rise to the cultural content that drives their distinct Christian thought and practice. Among these principal phases, we highlight the efforts (a) to socially and Biblically justify chattel slavery, (b) to justify the dehumanization of blacks and making their bodies into commodities, and (c) to address the inherent challenges of forging a sense of community based on the merging of many distinct African cultures. These dramas form the basis for a distinct Christian expression.

Justifying Enslavement and the Making of Bodies into Tools

The justifications for enslaving human beings were comprehensive. This precisely explains why slavery was ultimately *institutionalized*. By this we mean that it was sanctioned and supported by political and legal initiatives in society, therefore becoming sewn into the American social fabric. The backdrop of justifications for slavery required claims that Africans were "unenlightened" and that their biological composition made them suitable for hard labor. Theologically, several arguments surfaced during the antebellum period. Biblically, God's Old Testament commands for Israel to "take servants" and New Testament epistles calling for slaves to "obey their masters" were often used by whites to establish that blacks could fittingly serve as slaves.

Early theologians helped to create a justification for slavery along Biblical lines. On the basis of supposed differences in God-given intellectual and physical abilities, several early theologians argued that enslaved blacks simply lacked the necessary control over themselves, their thoughts, beliefs, and passions.[3] According to these thinkers, the slave system was a benevolent tool that would actually help to improve on the morally, culturally, and intellectually depleted African.

Further cementing the religious justifications were Biblical interpretations of the so-called *Curse of Ham*. When tied to black bodies and moral makeup, this myth provided yet another validation for enslavement. As the Biblical account goes, after Noah drinks wine from his vineyard, he falls asleep "uncovered" in his tent. Ham disgraces his father, Noah, by looking on his nakedness and telling his brothers Shem and Japheth about what he saw. Conversely, Shem and Japheth cover their father's nakedness without looking at him, which at that time was the respectable thing to do. Upon awakening, Noah censures his son Ham for his disgraceful act. The resulting curse itself declared that Canaan, Ham's son, would be in bondage as a servant to his brethren. This Biblical interpretation offered a position that Ham's despicable act prompted the swift, decisive, and appropriate action (and that others who exhibited similar behaviors would be punished in the same way). According to American religious historian Stephen Haynes, Ham's behavior simultaneously exhibited clear signs of both dishonor and disorder.[4] The result: blacks were connected to Ham for their propensity for similarly uncontrolled actions and also to Canaan, the one to whom the curse was actually aimed, as a justification of their enslavement. Although to most people today this would be a reach, in earlier times such a connection was sensible.

The glue of the mythical Curse of Ham sticks to blacks because of the belief that Ham possessed a darker skin color. While the Biblical record did not support an interpretation that negatively categorized a people based on skin color,[5] that Ham was "black" was for many people in antebellum America a legitimate Biblical conclusion. Even Edward Blyden, a black clergyman, wrote in 1869 that it was not to be doubted that "the black complexion of some of the descendants of Noah was known. Ham, it would seem, was a complexion darker than that of his brothers."[6] Whether legitimate or not, many people at that time believed that Ham was "black." Accordingly, both blacks and whites during the 19th century adopted a notion of Ham being the ancestor of the black race, thereby justifying black slavery. Notably for African Americans, the mythical Curse of Ham was an issue of identity and belonging. By way of Ham, some blacks felt they could be identified in the Bible as being a people. Thus, on the one hand, they were descendants of an ultimate heathen. But on the other hand, they were simultaneously a people of Christian identity, accepted and loved by God.[7]

With justifications firmly entrenched in the antebellum planter-class culture, black's *bodies* were corralled and made into commodities for exploitative use. The justifications for slavery made the use and maltreatment of these bodies more palatable to even the broader society. Black bodies were thus seen as detestable and uncontrollable "others." The chattel slave system offered the best way to control and perhaps even to civilize the supposed savagery and licentiousness of the African population.

Enslavement and the Challenge of Forging Community

Historian Michael Gomez presents an extremely useful study that brings attention to the inherent difficulties enslavement posed for merging multiple cultures. According to Gomez, we can view slave insurrections as attempts to gain freedom by bridging differences among the slaves with respect to origin, status, and culture through religion.[8] Those believers with a shared social experience could come together around not simply a single mode of belief and object of faith but also the aim of liberation. Thus, *liberation became a norm that fueled Christian faith for the enslaved.*

Cultural Formations in African American Christian Experience

The God invoked by slaves was connected to culture. Both West African and North American religious traditions influenced their perceptions of God. Black church studies professor Henry Mitchell argues that there was a "powerful early influence of African traditional religion and culture on the belief and practice" of enslaved blacks during the early formulations of the black church. Rejecting the argument that little or no African culture survived the "Middle Passage," Mitchell connects traditional African religious customs and practices with later manifestations of black church worship styles and rituals in America. For example, intermingled within the early Christian practices of blacks was a cultural tradition of *conjure*. Conjure is often associated with "root magic" or other forms of cultural expression.[9]

Henry Bibb, an escaped slave from Kentucky, identified a way in which West African cultural tools were used for daily life maintenance. He stated that many slaves held in bondage believed "in what they call conjuration, tricking, and witchcraft" and that through such practices they could "prevent their masters from exercising their will over their slaves."[10] Bibb's account reveals the tactical aspects of black religious life. The aim of conjurational action was to transform social reality, to improve life for African Americans. So, while Christian faith guaranteed the future benefits of Heaven, conjuring aided blacks in facing daily struggles for dignity. African American practices of conjure were intended to "cure" or "revise" conditions of violence and racial oppression. Quite simply, utilizing a faith-based cultural toolkit, blacks sought to deflect poor treatment and abuse.

The Bible has offered African Americans what religious scholar Theophus Smith describes as "prescriptions for reenvisioning and, therein, transforming history and culture."[11] Practices of conjure as a means of transforming reality come together with the use of the Bible as a magical formulary and tool. For Smith, the Bible-conjure connection is the primary way we can understand black spirituality. Therefore, African American Christian expression should not be understood in strictly evangelical terms. (As we will see in forthcoming chapters, our theoretical, statistical, and interview data clearly shows this to be the case.)

While cultural practices may help us understand the enslaved African and African American's approach and style of living their Christian faith, we are left with a question: Why was Christianity itself appealing to them in the first place? Why would so many people in bondage find something of substance in what many saw as the "white man's religion"?

The Appeal of Christianity to the Enslaved and Their Own Worship Style

With the onset of the first Great Awakening in the mid to late 1700s, many whites and blacks in North America converted to Christianity. According to historian and religious scholar Albert Raboteau, the Great Awakening represented "the dawning of the new day" in the history of the conversion of slaves to Christianity.[12] Massive black Christian conversion was made possible because of an emphasis on the *emotional experience over doctrine*. Appealing to enslaved African Americans were revivalist sermons that raised their level of joy in experiencing the fellowship with the God who loves them too. As the full tide of the awakenings swept over the colonies, both whites and blacks were among those engulfed by religious excitement.

The appeal of Christianity to enslaved blacks had both spiritual and social dimensions (and these two dimensions were often intertwined). To enslaved blacks, Christianity offered hopes of a raised social status and eventual freedom from bondage. Their hopes were connected to Biblical themes and stories. Particularly appealing was the Exodus story, in which, with God's help, the Israelites are led by Moses out of slavery. For them, the Exodus theme raised expectation but also had the power to galvanize fragmented communities. In Jesus, many blacks saw a co-suffering servant who was ultimately victorious over evil and suffering. For them, Jesus's labor on the cross and resurrection signaled the possibility of real freedom from tyranny.

However, early African Americans found the emotional excitement of the revivals during the Great Awakenings most attractive. While many plantation churches offered worship opportunities to whites as well as to enslaved blacks, a unique spiritual expression blossomed among many enslaved blacks, in which they found spiritual solace in secret worship meetings.[13] Often termed the "Invisible Institution," these meetings served as a safe space for blacks held in bondage to preach, sing, and fully express themselves with their co-laborers. The preacher encouraged them with uplifting Biblical stories. During these moments, slaves would share stories of both dread and longing as they sought a fuller expression of life and human dignity. Despite the risk of being beaten, slaves would meet in secluded places they called "hush harbors." In other instances, they would meet in various slave dwellings. Always careful to keep these worship meetings a secret, they would turn over a large iron pot to "catch the sound." Whether placed in the center of the room or at the front door, the sound-dampening pot served as either a symbolic or literal tool to maintain secrecy.

Regarding these secret slave-only religious fellowships, former Virginia slave Peter Randolph stated, "Not being allowed to hold meetings on the plantation, the slaves assemble in the swamp, out of reach of the patrols." With respect to what happened in the meetings themselves, he recalled,

They first ask each other how they feel, the state of their minds, etc. . . . Preaching . . . then praying and singing all around, until they generally feel quite happy. The speaker usually commences by calling himself unworthy, and talks very slowly, until feeling the spirit, he grows excited, and in a short time, there fall to the ground twenty or thirty men and women under its influence. . . . The slave forgets all his sufferings, except to remind others of the trials during the past week, exclaiming: "Thank God, I shall not live here always!" Then they pass from one to another, shaking hands. . . . As they separate, they sing a parting hymn of praise.[14]

For enslaved blacks, carving out a distinct religious life was inextricably tied to their experience of oppression. Decades of social, political, cultural, and physical maltreatment greatly shaped the way enslaved blacks viewed God, notably over and against the way the white planter class perceived the same God. We might therefore conclude that the content and object of one's faith, even about one's God, is driven by experience.

Double Evocation, One God: Dueling God Concepts in Antebellum America

History presents few ironies quite like how various communities have evoked or called on God. In Christianity, God is ultimate and transformative. God can aid people in life maintenance or help them to overcome great challenges. Conversely, through God—or, at least, *in the name of God*—power is wielded, opposing armies are destroyed, lands and peoples are conquered, and lives are forever altered. Rooted in a desire to be fully counted as part of the human family, both slaveholders and slaves evoked God for one very important attribute: *power*. That is, each community fashioned their God for a particular and empowering function. Their distinctive desires of God had similar ends in mind: social advancement, communal harmony, and a fuller sense of human freedom. Each side had a unique view of God, and that view was connected to their innermost desires.

The Slaveholder's God

Because of the many paradoxes of slaveholding Christianity, it takes up an interesting space in North American evangelical history. Despite the swell of religious fervor among whites and blacks alike during the Great Awakenings, the racial stratification order remained the same. Revivalist George Whitfield (a white man) hinted at this in his recounting of a revival in 1740: "Near fifty negroes came to give me thanks for what God had done to their souls."[15] The scene of enslaved blacks giving thanks directly to Whitfield cannot swiftly be separated from the social context. It is possible that this exchange simply reflects the extent to which oppressed blacks could look beyond the human flaws associated with the culture of domination, with which Whitfield was associated. Yet Whitfield's recollection of the event is made in full consideration of blacks' subjected positions in society. He recounts gratitude paid to him alone. He may not have perceived that they were simply being respectful of his position as a clergyman. Rather, noteworthy here is that the object of thanks for the saving of black souls was the man, Whitfield. Giving *him* thanks directly (as opposed to directly thanking God) created the perception among the slaveholding class that they had even some authority in matters of eternal salvation. Thus, even in Christian conversion, a slave's fate was subject to the authority of whites. The finite slave masters' connection to an infinite God only begins to reveal their concept of the divine. For whites, God granted ultimate authority, a manifest destiny, in all matters of life. Certain then in their belief that God had created them superior to people of African origin, slave masters questioned whether blacks were created in the image of God.[16] For them, God was Himself the ultimate slave master, having condemned by decree the African to servile state.[17]

The God of the Enslaved

Historian Winthrop Jordan writes that if it was difficult for Negroes to become men of affairs in this world, it became increasingly easy, after the watershed of the Great Awakening, for them to become men of God.[18] But in what way was God useful for a people with so few options for a full expression of life? A Biblical interpretation rooted in their unique experiences became an important tool for early blacks. In the Bible, African Americans sought expressions and themes that would counter the God of slaveholding Christianity. They believed instead that God was a liberator and "worth giver." As theologian Riggins Earl writes,

> Slaves believed that God had transformed them into new beings with a radically different mission in the world—a mission that required them to live counter to plantation values. First, converted slaves believed that their status of new being in Jesus interiorly distanced them from the psychological abuse of slavery. It gave them the needed transcendent means of getting a critical perspective of both their masters

and themselves. Second, slaves believed that their definition of conversion gave them a radical sense of God having disengaged them from the world for the purpose of calling them to radically engage it. This twofold perspective of new being and purpose gave the slaves a sense of divine worth in a world that negated their self-worth.[19]

Notice Earl's identification of the slaves as "transformed into new beings" in accordance with their position as believers in God. As a result, slaves could view their world differently.

Slaves' belief that conversion gave them a "radical sense of God having disengaged them from the world for the purpose of calling them to radically engage it" brings to mind the notion that slaves, through God, were equipped to confront their slave masters. In this sense, the slaves were equipped by God to aggressively seek better life options. In isolated cases, even some whites acknowledged this sense of religious empowerment of the slave. Former slave William Hayden recalled a conversation he overheard between his former master and another planter regarding Hayden's religious empowerment. In reference to Hayden, the planter informed his former master, "He appears too independent to serve—you must put another brow upon him. . . . He's entirely too free with the tongue."[20] To put "another brow" on him was to strike or hit Hayden with enough force to make his head swell. The goal was to inflict enough pain to ward off any slave's efforts at independence.

Former slave James Albert Gronniosaw gave another example of this type of God-to-slave empowerment. Recounting his experience as a servant anticipating being harmed by whites who worked for his master, he asserted, "I was sure to call upon God to damn them immediately."[21] Implicit here is the perceived *privileged* position associated with a partnership with God while a person is yet in a state of enslavement. In speaking about his conversion to Christianity, Gronniosaw states, "Though I was somewhat enlightened by this information of my master's, yet I had no other knowledge of God than that He was a good Spirit, and created every body, and every thing.—I never was sensible, in myself, nor had any one ever told me, that He would punish the wicked, and love the just."[22] Formative images of a God concerned *with* the enslaved resulted in the religious practice of active protest. A strong strain of social justice beliefs impacted the slaves' religious worldview of God; thus, their belief in human action (through God) sustained them against the racist assaults of European slavers and their descendants in the New World.[23] This activity was exhibited in a clandestine form of faith in God. That is, as previously mentioned, enslaved blacks saw the necessity of secret practices of their faith, in which their own lives and stories could be valued in worship. Former slave Simon Brown highlighted this form of faith and worship practices:

> The folks would sing and pray and testify and clap their hands, just as if God was right there in the midst of them. He wasn't way off in the sky. He was a-seeing everybody and a-listening to every word and a-promising to let His love come down. . . . Yes sir, there was no pretending in those prayer meetings. There was a living faith in a just God who would one day answer the cries of His poor black children and deliver them from their enemies. But the slaves never said a word to their white folk about this kind of faith.[24]

Notice the partnership between God and the black slaves. The "living faith" of Simon Brown was connected to expectancy. *This was a faith distinct in nature and character from the slaveholders' faith in God. African American faith, therefore, took on a unique essence, with attention placed on the poor and oppressed as a motivating force behind an active partnership with God to bring about social change.* In the end, enslaved blacks called on a God who loved them and considered them worthy of every good and pleasant thing this life had to offer. This belief encouraged them to love the beauty of their own flesh and honor their own culture and humanity.

In the end, we have *formative dueling evocations of the same God.* And in both evocations, we find that God seems to favor, at least in the eyes of the faithful beholder, progress and success of the respective faith community. One could argue that what we have discussed simply identifies divine attributes of one God. However, we must acknowledge the way God distinctively functions in the lives of two separate communities during the period of slavery and bring into focus a conflicting arrangement God never intended in Christianity. As Emerson and Smith put it, blacks and whites were "divided by faith."[25]

Jesus as a Liberator

The God evoked by oppressed blacks was a God seeking their best interests. This God, through Jesus Christ, desired to release them from suffering and give them freedom. But why did this God allow enslavement in the first place? Why did African Americans have to endure hundreds of years of suffering and oppression and ridicule?

Black theology has sought to answer these questions by promoting *liberation* as God's primary work on behalf of suffering blacks. Dr. James H. Cone, a leading scholar of black religious studies (we first introduced him in chapter 1), has stated that the Jesus "of the Biblical and black traditions is not a theological concept but a liberating presence in the lives of the poor in their fight for dignity and worth."[26] The affirmative nature of Cone's words draws him to the ultimate conclusion that God is indeed on the side of the oppressed.

Slaveholding Christianity only resembled the faith's core tenets in *some* outward aspects. Slaveholding Christians knew how to "speak" the Christian language of love and righteousness and to present themselves as pious. However, they promoted the "letter of law"—which they believed called for black servitude. In response, many slaves, often putting their lives on the line, began searching for scriptures to seek an alternative view of God.[27] For them, Jesus Christ became a beacon of transformative hope, not just for future glory in Heaven but also for life management through dire circumstances on earth. Accordingly, the Jesus of "true" Christianity seemed to identify with the despised and disenfranchised. Black slaves worked to find a sense of liberation rather than submitting to the limiting conversion experience they were given. They discovered self-worth through a new relationship with God through Jesus Christ.

Dr. Cone is one of many scholars of black religion who argue that for African Americans, Jesus plays the crucial role of connecting oppressed blacks to actual liberation—making possibilities available to them for human fulfillment (he made this point crystal clear during the course of our interview). However, black slaves established Jesus's significance as a "liberator" long before any contemporary scholar did. Take, for instance, African American (or Old Negro) spirituals. The hope embodied in these popular songs and sayings by black slaves highlights the triumph of the cross among browbeaten souls. Black Christians' view of Jesus as the conquering Savior only strengthens their faith and confidence despite their suffering. Consider this:

Jesus said He wouldn't die no mo',
Said He wouldn't die no mo',
So my dear chillens don' yer fear,
Said He wouldn't die no mo'.

De Lord tole Moses what ter do,
Said He wouldn't die no mo',
Lead de chillen od Isr'el froo',
Said He wouldn't die no mo'.[28]

The constant refrain of Jesus never dying anymore underlines the momentous significance of the Christ Event, particularly for the oppressed.[29] Triumph on earth would forever be bonded to final victory of evil. Again we can see this resolve in the following spiritual:

Ride on, King Jesus,
Ride on, the conquering King.
O, ride on King Jesus,
Ride on.
No man can hinder thee.[30]

And we see it again in this one (with the resolve based on an association with Jesus Christ):

Ride in, kind Savior!
No man can hinder me.
O, Jesus is a mighty man!

No man can hinder me.
We're marching through Virginny fields.
No man can hinder me.
O, Satan is a busy man,
No man can hinder me.
And he has his sword and shield,
No man can hinder me.
O, old Secesh done come and gone!
No man can hinder me.[31]

In these verses (as well as many others), the model of the conquering Jesus is anchored to the hope of finally overcoming social evil, suffering, and oppression. This type of hope encouraged former North Carolina slave James Curry to conclude, based on his reading of the Bible, that "it was contrary to the revealed will of God that one man should hold another as a slave."[32] Driven by this interpretation of scripture (and as seen in the second and third spirituals), the oppressed saw themselves as partakers and colaborers in the work of securing freedom, an early form of *liberation theology*. Their hope was tied to the final triumph of Jesus Christ. As destructive as slavery was, Jesus —who had overcome equally terrible odds—was the primary power source for destroying the yoke of slavery.

Conclusion

The late religious historian James Melvin Washington, referencing the prayers of African Americans, stated that "prayer is an attempt to count the stars of our souls. Under its sacred canopy, an oratory of hope echoes the vast but immediate distances between who we are and who we want to be. This peculiar trek sentences its devotees to an arduous discipline."[33] This "trek" of faithful utterances to God, as it were, bespeaks the active nature of the African American Christian's prayer life. Fittingly, then, this chapter closes by returning to the question asked at the beginning of this book: "Why do African Americans pray so often?" Our central task within this chapter was to briefly investigate the sociohistorical origins of such a question. It is clear that for blacks, the trek of devoted prayer is inextricably tied to a Christian experience *rooted in slavery, suffering, active critical engagement with authoritative power, and overcoming.*

The historical and theological underpinnings examined in this chapter help to contextualize the forthcoming findings from our survey data and in-depth interviews. African Americans, whether construed as traditionally oppressed or even the objects of a violent episode of American history, have remained highly religiously active. Slavery and blacks' subsequent conversion to Christianity have encouraged them to ask difficult questions of themselves, their oppressors, and even the God they serve. They have critically reflected on their experiences and yet remained resolute that God can and will remove from them the stain of social death and pain. They are encouraged to seek from God all that the Bible has promised for God's people. As we move to subsequent chapters, we shall see how the *five building blocks of black Protestant faith* forged in the context of the 1700s and 1800s have continued to shape the *black sacred cosmos* and African American Protestant religious tradition to this very day. History has power.

3

The Apostles' Creed

Racial Similarities in Commitments to Core Christian Tenets

I believe in God, the Father Almighty,
Maker of heaven and earth,
And in Jesus Christ, His only Son, our Lord.
He was conceived by the Holy Ghost,
born of the virgin Mary,
suffered under Pontius Pilate
was crucified, died, and buried;
He descended into hell.
On the third day He arose again;
He ascended into heaven,
And is seated at the right hand of God the Father Almighty;
He will come again to judge the living and the dead.
I believe in the Holy Spirit;
the holy catholic Church[1]
the communion of saints;
the forgiveness of sins;
the resurrection of the body; and
the life everlasting.
Amen.

For nearly 2,000 years, Christians (especially in the Western tradition) across places, denominations, and cultures have subscribed to the Apostles' Creed. The creed exists in two forms; a shorter and longer version. The shorter version, often called the Old Roman

Form, can be traced back as far as 140 AD. The longer form, recorded above, took final shape somewhere between the 5th and 7th centuries. It is this version that is recited by Christians around the world today.[2] There are several Christian creeds, but it is the Apostles' Creed that is upheld as describing the core essential beliefs of Christians, no matter a believer's denomination or branch of the faith. Despite differences across times, places, cultures, races, ethnicities, nations, and traditions, the Apostles' Creed represents the closest universal statement of fundamental Christian beliefs.

We ask in this chapter whether black and white American Protestants differ in any core Christian tenets, using the Apostles' Creed as our guide. This is the place to start to be sure, given that there is a long-standing history of mistrust between these believers; at times, each has wondered whether the other is quite fully Christian. The authors of this book, and likely many of our readers, have heard members of one racial group question the other's commitment to Christianity. For instance, among blacks talking with blacks, Jason Shelton has heard people say things like, "Do they really believe in the same God? If they do, then how come there's so much racism in America?" or "They may believe in God, but they don't seem to rely on God's Power—they're too busy relying on themselves." Similarly, among whites talking with whites, Michael Emerson has heard people question whether African Americans can really be practicing Christians since they seem to focus on religious emotionalism rather than theological training. He's heard people say things like, "If they are Christians, why are so many black children born out of wedlock?" or "Why do they always seem to want the government to give them special treatment? God helps those who help themselves."

Given the questioning that often occurs in same-race groups but is rarely voiced in mixed-race groups, we explore whether there are racial differences in commitments to core Christian theological tenets. We seek to determine the extent to which black and white Protestants meaningfully differ from one another across fundamental Christian beliefs as expressed in the Apostles' Creed.

Core Christian Tenets

No Christian belief is more fundamental than the belief in God, the belief that a Supreme Being exists. The first four words of the Apostles' Creed are "I believe in God." So we were interested in analyzing the extent to which study participants agree or disagree with the following statement: "I definitely believe in God." More than 9 out of 10 black and white Protestants who participated in the Portraits of American Life Study (PALS) "strongly agree" that they believe in God. Only about 1 out of 100 at least "somewhat disagree" (see descriptive table B.3A). Still, the percentages are not exactly the same for the two groups. In our sample, it appears that black Protestants lean slightly more toward the nonagreement options *and* the "strongly agree" option than do white Protestants.

So can we conclude that black and white Protestants differ from each other on this question? We would be making at least two errors if we made such a conclusion at this point. First, we are only examining a sample of black and white Protestants, and samples can be wrong. What we really want to know is if black Protestants differ from white Protestants in general, not just if the ones in our sample do. Second, we want to know if the differences are likely attributable to racial group membership, not to differences in other factors. Consider two groups of 10 people each: one group is our black Protestant group and the other is our white Protestant group. Do they differ in their belief in God? Suppose we ask each of them if they believe in God and find, indeed, that the two groups differ. Let us say that our sample of black Protestants, on average, is more likely to "strongly agree" that God exists. If so, we would be tempted to conclude what seems obvious—that black Protestants are more likely to "strongly agree" that God exists than are white Protestants. But wait: our sample of black Protestants includes 8 females and 2 males, while our sample of white Protestants is the exact reverse, 2 females and 8 males. Studies have shown that females are more likely to "strongly agree" that God exists than are males.[3] Thus, once we account for this difference in the number of males and females, we find that black and white Protestants are equally likely to believe in God.

So in reality, do black and white Protestants differ in their belief in God? Our more sophisticated analysis shows that (a) after accounting for relevant background factors such as income and educational levels, church attendance, age, male-female ratios, and region of residence and (b) after we use appropriate statistics to test for differences not in the sample but in the entire population, the answer is no. Despite some small differences, black and white Protestants are identical in their belief in God. Furthermore, according to their responses, the overwhelming majority of black and white Protestants "strongly agree" that God exists.

The Apostles' Creed also affirms that God created the earth. The opening of the book of Genesis reports that God created the world in six days and rested on the seventh. Traditionally and currently, Christians have debated whether a day in this context means 24 hours or is instead representative of an unspecified period of time. We asked black and white Protestants their feelings about the following statement: "God created the world in six 24-hour days." About 19% of both black and white Protestants "strongly disagree" (see descriptive table B.3B). While it is possible that they disagree because they do not believe God created the world, the more likely interpretation (and the interpretation more consistent with the totality of our data) is that about 1 in 5 Protestants—be they black or white—clearly do not believe in the literal 24-hour-day theory. Conversely, about half of both black and white Protestants feel that the world was created by God in six 24-hour days. Moreover, about another 1 in 5 are simply unsure, saying they "neither agree nor disagree." While it appears that blacks in our sample are somewhat more literal in their understanding of creation than whites are (they appear more likely to "strongly agree"), we find that these believers do not meaningfully differ from one another once we apply the appropriate statistical controls and tests.

Also absolutely central to Christianity are beliefs about Jesus Christ, for whom the faith is named. We asked two survey questions about Jesus. First, we asked people to tell us which of the following statements best describes their belief about Jesus Christ: (a) he was "the Divine, only Son of God" (the orthodox position), (b) he was "a prophet of God but not God," (c) he was "a wise man or good moral teacher but not God," (d) he was something other than described in these first three options, or (e) he is someone the respondent has never heard of. As one might expect, the results reveal that only one of the thousands of Protestants that we surveyed said that she or he had never heard of Jesus (however, of course, several non-Christians did say this). The findings also show that about 9 out of 10 black and white Protestants took the orthodox position, which is most consistent with the Apostles' Creed—that Jesus was the Divine, only Son of God (see descriptive table B.3C). As with our previous findings, our multivariate results suggest that black and white Protestants do not differ in their beliefs about Jesus Christ. This finding is of tremendous importance. No matter what other differences may exist between black and white Protestants, they are in fundamental agreement about this fundamental tenet of the faith: Jesus Christ is to them in equal measure the Divine, only Son of God.

The Apostles' Creed and Biblical tradition teach that Jesus was crucified, died, and then on the third day was physically raised from the dead. Clearly, to assent to this position requires a faith in something that defies scientific law; it requires belief in what one is not able to see every day, such as a miracle or a supernatural power. We asked black and white Protestants their level of agreement with the following statement: "Jesus Christ physically rose from the dead." About 80% of our study participants said that they "strongly agree" (see descriptive table B.3D). Still, on this question, black Protestants appear to be slightly more likely to "strongly agree" than white Protestants are (85% to 79%). But this is only in appearance. When we account for differences in other characteristics (such as regular church attendance and gender), we find that black and white Protestants are identical in their belief about the physical resurrection of Jesus. Taken together, these results show that black and white Protestants report similar beliefs about Christ.

The Apostles' Creed and Biblical traditional also teach that both Heaven and Hell exist beyond the physical world and universe. Heaven is viewed as a place of eternal joy and glory, while Hell is a place of eternal suffering and misery. We posed the following statement to black and white Protestants: "I believe in Heaven where people live with God forever." More than 9 out of 10 black and white Protestants in the PALS at least "agree" (see descriptive table B.3E). Furthermore, more than 3 out of every 4 black and white Protestants at least "agree" that "there is a Hell where people experience pain as punishment for their sin" (as seen in descriptive table B.3F). So while most black and white Protestants believe there is a Heaven where people live with God forever, a few less believe there is a Hell where people suffer (not a pleasant thought). It is worth noting that black Protestants appear more likely to "strongly agree" with the statements about Heaven and Hell than white Protestants are. But as before, this is only in appearance. Correcting for differences in relevant background factors tells us that black and white Protestants do not differ in the likelihood of believing in Heaven and Hell.

Finally, the Apostles' Creed ends by stating, "I believe in . . . the life everlasting." We found that more than 85% of black and white Protestants believe in life after death (see descriptive table B.3G). However, contrary to what we have seen before, it appears that white Protestants are slightly more likely to believe in the afterlife than are black Protestants. And also contrary to what we have seen before, when we account for other important characteristics and apply the correct statistical tests, we find that white Protestants in fact are *more likely* to believe in life after death than are black Protestants. In fact, we found what is often called a *suppressor effect*. That is, the slight difference found in table B.3G understates the degree of difference between black and white Christians on this belief. Our multivariate findings show that once we control for differences across relevant background factors such as age, income, education, church attendance, and region of residence, the opinion gap between black and white Protestants widens significantly. This finding holds constant when we restrict our analysis to black Protestants and white evangelicals.

This latter result is important because it foreshadows elements of our *Experiential* and *Mystery building blocks of Black Protestant faith*. While it appears that black Protestants are less orthodox on this portion of the Apostles' Creed than whites are, what we find and discuss in chapter 7 will suggest a different interpretation, one that enhances our understanding of the unique form, composition, and structure of the *black sacred cosmos*.

Religious Centrality

Apart from the apparent anomaly of belief in the afterlife (which we will see in chapter 7 does not hold), we have established that black and white Protestants do not meaningfully differ in their commitments to Christianity's core tenets. In fact, these believers are indistinguishable with respect to almost every fundamental belief. But we cannot stop there. We must ask another important question: How important is religious faith to people? If groups differ dramatically on the centrality of faith in their personal lives, then it makes less sense to compare them on what they actually believe. This is because religious beliefs can and do have a dramatically different meaning and impact on different followers of the same faith.

For instance, imagine two groups who both believe that rocks, when aligned just so, have magical healing powers. The first group believes this, but when asked in a survey, they overwhelmingly tell us that this belief is "not at all important" in their lives. However, the second group, who also believes in the magical healing powers of correctly aligned rocks, tells us overwhelmingly that this belief is "extremely important" to them. Since the power of the rocks is clearly more important to members of the second group, they have monthly rock-aligning ceremonies, books, seminars, and instructional videos on how to harness their power for healing. In contrast, members of the first group are not interested in consulting these materials. Yes, members of the first group believe that correctly aligned rocks can heal, but no, this belief is not very important to them. Why would this be so? It is because upon further investigation, we find that the first group mostly looks to doctors and medicines when they are in need of healing. So it turns out that what is important to them is the training of doctors, research dollars for finding better medicines, and rules and regulations to govern the practices of the medical industry.

This example illustrates that religious beliefs can and do animate people's actions. But to do so, a person's beliefs generally have to be *important* to him or her. How important is religious faith to the black and white Protestants analyzed in this study? We asked the following question: "How important is *God or spirituality* in your life?"[4] We gave those whom we interviewed five options for their response: "not at all important," "somewhat important," "very important," "extremely important," and "by far the most important part of your life." We found that nearly 80% of both black and white Protestants feel that God or spirituality is, at the least, "very important" (see descriptive table B.3H). Moreover, for about 3 out of 10 members of each group, God or spirituality is "by far the most important part" of their life, but slightly more black Protestants say this than do white Protestants. So do black and white Protestants differ in how important they say God or spirituality is to them? No. With the appropriate characteristics accounted for, black and white Christians are indistinguishable in the centrality of God or spirituality to them.

We also asked people how important *religion or religious faith* is in their personal life. Again, we find no differences between black and white Protestants. In fact, the findings (displayed in descriptive table B.3I) show that for about three-quarters of them (mostly the church-goers), religion or religious faith is at least "very important" to them. For slightly more than 1 out of 5 of them, they report that religion or religious faith is "by far the most important part" of their lives.

The General Social Survey (GSS) also includes two questions about the centrality of religious faith: (1) "To what extent do you consider yourself a religious person?" and (2) "To what extent do you consider yourself a spiritual person?" Two findings stand out at first glance: a much greater percentage of African Americans than whites say that they are "very" religious and spiritual, and a greater percentage of whites than blacks say that they are "moderately" religious and spiritual (see descriptive tables B.3J and B.3K). Once again, however, these differences are due to other characteristics, such as age, income, and educational levels. After we account for these differences and apply the appropriate statistical test, we find that black and white Protestants are identical in their reporting of how religious and how spiritual they consider themselves to be.

All of our questions about the centrality of faith provide the same answer: black and white Protestants do not meaningfully differ from each other, overwhelmingly defining God or spirituality, and religion or religious faith, as at least "very important" to them. Most black and white Protestants consider themselves to be "moderately" or "very religious" and "moderately" or "very spiritual."

Conclusion

So what does it all mean? In short, those questions, murmurs, and rumors that sometimes float within all-white or all-black gatherings—the ones that question the lack of orthodox Christianity of the other group —receive essentially no support from two major, nationally representative surveys. On measures largely drawn from the orthodox Apostles' Creed and on the centrality of faith, black and white Protestants look like identical twins. While we did not have measures for all aspects of the Apostle's Creed—such as belief in the Holy Spirit—we have little reason to expect any differences, given the findings of this chapter.

Though black and white Protestants typically gather for worship separately from one another—and have very different histories and very different present daily realities—the two groups are of the same mind on the core tenets of Christianity and the importance of religion and spirituality in their personal lives. In many ways, this similarity is remarkable. Although there are many other aspects of the Christian faith and its practice that we have not yet examined, we have seen that black and white Christians are essentially twins when it comes to their commitment to fundamental Christian beliefs.

This conclusion is important because our remaining chapters are dedicated to documenting and detailing the often vastly dissimilar ways in which black and white Protestants think about and practice their religious faith. In sum: our quantitative and qualitative findings from this point on challenge Christianity's status as a "universal religion" because black and white believers often radically differ in their faith-based thoughts and practices. In fact, it will soon become evident that the Apostles' Creed is the strongest tie that binds blacks and whites together as followers of Christ. Nevertheless, we must not forget that despite all the differences we will examine in the remainder of this book, on the core tenets of their faith, black and white Christian Protestants are in near unanimous agreement.

4

Learning and Burning

*Racial Differences in "Academic" versus
"Experiential" Models of Christianity*

The preceding chapter showed that black and white Protestants are similarly steadfastly committed to core Christian theological tenets—those specifically referenced in the Apostles' Creed. However, that does not mean that there are not profound differences between blacks and whites in their identification with and understanding of Christianity. Although black and white Protestants worship the same God and similarly subscribe to the faith's bedrock beliefs, it will soon become clear that *worldly* forces impede Christianity's ability to inspire an unyielding camaraderie among blacks and whites.

In this chapter, we establish a framework for understanding how racial group membership color-codes one's experience as a Christian. More specifically, we begin developing the *Experiential building block*: (1) *black Protestant faith is active and experiential; it is less concerned with precise doctrinal contours than is white mainline or evangelical Christianity.* We accomplish this goal by focusing on findings from our in-depth interviews with high-ranking clergy. These data are critical. Survey research is an invaluable tool for determining whether different variables impact attitudes and actions among a large group of people. However, it tells us very little about why individuals or smaller groups see the world in the way that they do—their deeper thoughts, emotions, rationales, and so on. Our qualitative interviews allow us to do exactly that, which explains why they are so important.

Our theoretical framework for understanding racial differences in religious sensibilities derives in part from the remarks and analyses communicated by members of the pastorate. We chose this approach for two reasons. First, high-ranking clergy, rather than the laity, were specifically asked to comment on race relations among Christians and racial differences across our survey results because of their widely respected level of religious knowledge and awareness. Second, people in the pews typically consult with clergy because of their esteemed position within the church and society in general. Clergy are often viewed not only as local (and sometimes even national) spiritual and moral leaders but also as political and social leaders. Pastors deal with everyday Christians' thoughts, emotions, and rationales on a daily basis. Their job requires that they be Biblical scholars and church leaders as well as explain how religious faith impacts everyday people's personal, political, and social lives.

Our in-depth interviews with high-ranking clergy began with the following open-ended, straightforward questions that could have been answered in any number of ways: "Do you think that there are any differences between black and white Christians in how they go about their religious faith? If so, are these differences important?"

Each of the 14 pastors that we interviewed discussed some meaningful difference between blacks and whites with respect to how they go about (i.e., think about and practice) their religious faith. It is worth reiterating that *all* of our interviewees said there are significant differences. In other words, they *all* referenced some distinction regarding how racial group membership color-codes one's experience as a Christian. Their interesting—and no doubt controversial—answers to this initial set of questions are the focal point of this chapter. While our interviewees addressed differences between blacks and whites across numerous spheres of religious life, the impressive consistency with which black Baptist, Methodist, and Pentecostal clergy explained such differences suggests that among the high-ranking clergy members that we interviewed, racial group membership trumps one's individual denominational affiliation. This is not to say that differences across historically black denominations with respect to rituals, liturgies, and governance issues are not heated topics for discussion (we will soon see that they are). However, such differences pale in comparison to the similarity with which our interviewees' believe that the legacy of racial discrimination and inequality in the United States has shaped religious identity among African Americans.

Cultural Imperatives versus Epistemological Explanations

Both scholars[1] and everyday Americans across all backgrounds have long since recognized culturally based distinctions between black and white Protestants, such as preaching styles, praise and worship methods, music ministries, and artistic forms of religious expression. In fact, most Americans believe that individualistic and cultural differences primarily explain why majority and minority groups often vary in their attitudes, behaviors, and circumstances in society.[2] They view culture as being *imperative* in the sense that it takes precedence over all other relevant social factors. While the primacy of culture remains open for debate, scholars generally agree that culture provides meaning for people's lives by supplying the lenses that individuals use for interpreting the social world and for forming an awareness of their place within it. Moreover, for members of racial, ethnic, and religious minority groups, culture also provides a framework for understanding one's *social heritage*—a constellation of group-specific outlooks, attributes, artifacts, traditions, and shared history that provides a framework for interpreting the meaning of one's group membership, as well as its social boundaries.[3] Indeed, one clergy member whom we interviewed described the impact of cultural factors best when he said, "There are distinguishing characteristics that define any particular culture, and that's how you're able to become a part of that culture —if you participate in the traits and the habits and in the conduct that defines that culture."

Most of the responses to the initial interview questions that we posed to high-ranking clergy can be easily classified into one of two emergent categories: cultural imperatives and epistemological explanations. Those pastors who described cultural imperatives between blacks and whites were not in agreement about whether such distinctions were "important." While there was an optimistic sense that

cultural differences are largely surface distinctions that should be recognized and even celebrated, there was also another stream of thought
positing that cultural differences are so deeply rooted that they cannot
be bridged.

As we hinted earlier, cultural imperatives have become extremely
popular for explaining why there are differences between majority
and minority racial, ethnic, and religious groups in the United States.
Interestingly, although the wider American public subscribes to such
sentiments, cultural imperatives were initially referenced by only three
of the pastors whom we interviewed. Rev. Henderson's remark is probably most consistent with the popular cultural imperative that most
Americans employ when explaining perceived differences between
black and white Christians. This female United Methodist senior pastor in Los Angeles described African American modes of praise and
worship in the following commonly recognized way:

> Black people are more expressive in their worship—demonstrative
> and in raising their hands and shouting or dancing. And that's not
> just in a Pentecostal church. You find it in a Methodist, a Baptist, of
> course the Pentecostal. You find it in the Presbyterians and the Lu-
> therans and etc. . . . I also think that many times you have a lot of
> black people who don't mind sharing their faith—in conversation or
> just say, "Child, you know, Jesus will work everything out, all right."
> And many times, blacks express this in a vociferous way.

Deacon Harris, the director of Christian counseling at a mega-
church in New York City, also advanced a cultural imperative when
explaining why he believes that blacks and whites experience Christianity differently. His comments substantively and comprehensively
explain how deeply embedded cultural factors strongly influence how
black and white Protestants in general—and Pentecostals in particular
—go about their religious faith:

> Culture in my opinion is kind of like the water, like a goldfish is in an
> aquarium swimming in the water but doesn't see it. Culture is just so
> much around us, a part of everything we do. Just even worship styles,

by the fact that African American Christians tend to be expressive in their worship style, so-called "ecstatic" in their worship style. Where white Christians tend not to be that way, tend to be less expressive, less ecstatic, more inner-focused. Where we [blacks] tend to be more outer-communal-focused.

How it really came clear to me—this is one of my favorite topics —but how it really came clear to me is when I went to the World Pentecostal meeting, and it was primarily white people and people from other international backgrounds, although they were Pentecostals. The worship experience there was not much different than the white American Baptists!

These were Pentecostals? So I had to ask myself the question, "Well, what is this?" They weren't just all "oh, hallelujah!" I mean they did it a little bit, but it wasn't like when we [black Pentecostals] get together.

Okay, that's when I said to myself, "Well, this is a cultural thing." It's just that—and it's hard for us to admit it—but from our African culture, we were just more open to communal expressions of worship. For example, if you go to one of our services, the praise leaders will say, "Come on now, make a joyful noise unto the Lord! Come on and bless the Lord!" and then they'll say, "You think you're too cute to come in here and not give God the praise! God is worthy of your praise! God is worthy of your noise. God is worthy of you doing something."

Where in many white settings, that's not the focus. We [blacks] worship *together*. And we don't feel the worship has happened until somebody hollers! [*laughs*]. That's not their [whites'] focus. Now what's the difference? It's culture. We believe that expressing joy and praise about God is what is absolutely needed. And when you do, then the Holy Spirit comes. The Spirit comes and He moves, and now things are happening and everything is alright. Where in other settings, if that happens, it's disruptive. It's scary. People say things like, "Somebody's hollering over there! Take them out or something!" [*laughs*].

How do you explain it? I think on a deep basis it is part of the culture that has grown in our [black] Christian spirituality, and it's a different cultural approach from European spirituality—which tends to be a more contemporary inner (or even sometimes a group) experience. Whites feel that if you have a worship outburst, then it's against the group. In that way, it's a group thing but not an individual thing.

We believe that the individual has an influence on the group and helps to move it forward. They see that same individual as being a disruption to the group. For example, if they [whites] say that we're going to be quiet now, then everybody's going to be quiet. You see?

Deacon Harris's comments touch on a host of relevant cultural factors influencing racial differences in religious sensibilities between black and white Protestants. For instance, his remarks address the ongoing historical impact that African and European forms of praise and worship have had in shaping present-day modes of religious expression. According to him, these distinct approaches have fostered racial differences in individual (or "inner-focused") versus communal (or "outer-focused") forms of praise and worship. While Deacon Harris recognizes that whites do, in fact, embrace some group-based forms of worship, in his estimation they expect individuals within these groups to follow along with the religious program and not to rock the "outer-focused" boat—even if one is personally touched by the Spirit.

Only one of the pastors whom we interviewed emphatically declared that cultural differences between black and white Protestants are not meaningfully "important." Rev. Johnson of Texas—who at the time of our interview was in the process of writing a book on blacks in the Bible—believes that differences in the manner in which blacks and whites go about their faith are "important" only as a "matter of fact, as an observation." His comments are especially relevant considering that he is often invited to guest preach at predominantly white churches. Two points stand out about Rev. Johnson's statement: (1) his thought process changes slightly over the duration of his point, and (2) he clarifies that blacks are not better Christians because they are more ecstatic than whites are.

Fundamentally, I don't think there are substantive or major differences between black and white Christians as to how they pursue or develop their faith. I think a blueprint for developing your faith comes from the Bible. And so if people use the Bible as the guide for how to develop or practice your faith, then they're pretty much going to follow the same pursuit of pattern.

If there is a difference, generally speaking, as to how black and white Christians might go about pursuing their faith, it relates to a corporate worship experience. In the black tradition, I think it's not only a matter of learning. They want to be informed. That's what Sunday school's about—discipleship; and people want preaching with content. It's not just about learning; it's also about *burning*. They want to feel, *experience* God and the Holy Spirit. You don't always find the burning aspect, but you'll definitely find the learning aspect in white churches. In white Christianity, the burning feeling or experiential aspect is not always as pronounced or expected as it is in many or most African American churches (even among the evangelicals).

Now, it's not important, as to suggest there is something deficient or lacking or missing in the Anglo Christians experience if they don't have the burning. And with the African American Christian, I think there's a real good balance in the pursuit of the burning and the learning. I don't think that to have the burning or to desire the burning or experience the burning means you sacrifice learning. You can have both! [*smiles*].

Most of the pastors whom we interviewed did not find fault with or disparagingly disapprove of what they considered to be a less expressive and more individualistic manner in which whites tend to go about their religious faith. Our interviewees merely pointed out what they considered to be objective differences between the races, regardless of their "importance." In fact, several clergy members (like Rev. Johnson) went out of their way to state specifically that African Americans' approach to Christianity makes them neither "more religious" nor "greater followers of Jesus" than whites are. Only one of our interviewees was overtly judgmental of whites in substance and tone.

Reverend Shannon asserted the least favorable view of what she described as white Protestant modes of praise and worship. Although she said that her visits to predominantly white churches have been "friendly," she was also quite critical of the manner in which white Protestants go about their religious faith:

Differences? Yeah, I think we worship a lot differently. In the black church, the music is different. The preaching is different. The message, often, is different. I could go on and on about how we are different. One of the keys, though, is that in black churches we're more centered toward our social and economic status, and our theology is based on that. So it sounds different than in a white church.

White church services are shorter. I've visited white churches, and the pastors have been told, "After 15 minutes, they [the parishioners] don't want to hear it" and "Don't get your voice up. Just give them the message, just like you're talking to them." Black churches kind of want the emotion in the preaching. We give them an additional feeling.

That doesn't mean it's the rule of thumb; it's just that I find I don't get spiritually moved. Sometimes you say, "I can't get my praise on" in a white church.

They [whites] just say, "Give me the word. Give me the message. Don't give me no ups and downs in your voice. Just tell me that scripture says this and preach that word, give me 10 minutes on it, and then I got my spiritual food for the day and I'm gone."

I've gone to white churches and experienced that, and I leave unfulfilled.

Cultural differences are often a noticeable product of other more elusive and consequential lines of demarcation. A critical limitation of cultural imperatives is that they fail to adequately account for important macro-level social institutions, forces, and arrangements in society that can create, nurture, or amplify preexisting cultural differences between groups. In other words, cultural imperatives minimize the role played by large-scale *structural* determinants that lie beyond a person's control—such as racism, childhood poverty, political conditions, and our nation's economic system—in erecting or preserving social boundaries.[4] Cultural imperatives are *individualistic* in orientation since they focus on the decisions that people make, their values, and the distinguishing characteristics and values of different groups. This is important because the aforementioned structural determinants can shape and constrain the decisions, values, and distinguishing characteristics of different individuals and groups in society.

Moreover, while structural explanations acknowledge that members of racial, ethnic, and religious minority groups enjoy participating in their particular group's culture, they also recognize that enduring commitments to one's social heritage are influenced by factors beyond personal loyalty and dedication. For instance, in addition to autonomous cultural factors (such as the basic idea that most racial, ethnic, and religious minorities brought their culture with them in coming to America), the rank ordering of individuals and groups, dynamics of oppression and privilege, disparities in life-chance opportunities, and wide distinctions in social status are all relevant to explaining why cultural differences persist between majority and minority groups in the United States.

In contrast to cultural imperatives, 9 of the 14 pastors with whom we spoke responded to our initial interview questions ("Do you think that there are any differences between black and white Christians in how they go about their religious faith? If so, are these differences important?") by asserting an epistemological explanation for racial differences in religious sensibilities. Most of these interviewees either (1) specifically used words such as "racism," "discrimination," "slavery," "segregation," and "oppression" or (2) told a story, gave a parable, or issued a declarative statement consistent with these terms when telling us about the differences between black and white Christians. Moreover, 8 of these 9 pastors went on to describe in detail what they deemed to be fundamental cleavages between blacks and whites with respect to their sense of identification with and understanding of Christianity. Our interviewees linked historical and contemporary forms of racial discrimination and inequality with differences between blacks and whites with respect to their views of God, God's power, and their personal expectations of their relationship with God.

Epistemology is widely known as a philosophical area of study that addresses the origins, nature, methods, and limits of human knowledge. We use the word "epistemological" to describe our interviewees' responses because their comments generally addressed the unique origins, nature, methods, and knowledge bases that have helped to solidify racial differences in religious sensibilities. In this study, epistemological explanations are *structural* in orientation since they posit that macro-level factors (such as racism, slavery, and discrimination) beyond the cultural realm strongly influence how black and white Protestants go about their religious faith. All of the pastors who asserted an epistemological explanation were in agreement that faith-based distinctions between blacks and whites are not only "important" but also inextricably linked to darker (pun intended) structural periods in American history when blacks were subjugated by whites. In different ways, they all discussed how the legacy of past and present racial discrimination and inequality in the United States has color-coded one's experience as a Christian. These interviewees also agreed that epistemological explanations for racial differences in faith-based thoughts and practices are a more significant and troublesome distinction than are cultural imperatives.

This is not to say that epistemologists ignore the importance of cultural factors. To the contrary, they strongly believe that cultural factors are critical to understanding the often distinct ways in which black and white Protestants go about their religious faith. However, what distinguishes their view from a purely cultural imperative is that the epistemologists in this study believe that culture plays a *secondary* role in shaping how racial group membership color-codes one's experience as a Christian. These pastors argued that the legacy of racial discrimination and inequality in the United States takes precedence over cultural differences between black and white Protestants and helps to explain why those cultural differences have become magnified. While they believe that black culture has a great degree of autonomy from black oppression (i.e., that the African American Protestant religious tradition is rooted in *African* religious sensibilities and that most black Protestants enjoy the African American Protestant religious tradition irrespective of its ignominious roots), they also believe that racial stratification in the United States has nurtured and exacerbated cultural differences between blacks and whites.

These pastors' position on this issue is not without merit. Researchers in race and ethnic relations have long maintained that most cultural imperatives—especially those aiming to explain issues pertinent to minority groups—are *astructural* in orientation. This means that they ignore or at least underestimate the often deleterious effects that stratification-based systemic forces have in shaping intergroup relations. In addition to the forces already mentioned, studies have shown that these determinants include concentrated poverty, prejudice, residential segregation, social isolation, joblessness, unequal access to a quality education, party politics, and social injustice.[5] These are the *worldly* forces that hinder black and white Christians' ability to all just get along. They are also the same elusive and consequential variables that help to shape the form and content of group-level cultural factors such as the meaning of one's social heritage.

Academic versus Experiential

More than half of the high-ranking clergy members whom we interviewed drew a racial distinction between what we are generally describing as *academic and experiential* models of Christianity. These divergent typologies are opposite sides of the same epistemological coin; they both begin from the assumption that elusive and consequential factors beyond the cultural realm are at least partly responsible for racial differences in religious sensibilities. Nine of our interviewees believe that the broader *structural* dynamics of race-based oppression and privilege are a major reason why faith-based *cultural* differences between black and white Protestants are so pronounced. All of these pastors (and even some of those who initially advanced a cultural imperative) discussed how conditions in society overall—most notably hostility and prejudice toward blacks—are the reason why African Americans pray and go to church more often than whites do.

Although many of the high-ranking clergy members whom we interviewed did not use the specific terms academic and experiential, they nonetheless advanced their own race-based dichotomous typology when describing the divergent manner in which blacks and whites go about their religious faith. Some of these classifications included the following: "formal versus informal," "doctrine versus practice," and "cognitive versus need-based." Terminology aside, we are confident that these nine pastors would agree that whites tend to think about and practice their faith in an "academic" manner, while blacks tend to think about and practice their faith in an "experiential" manner.[6] The following general guidelines enhance our awareness of racial differences in religious sensibilities.

With regard to the academic classification, the pastors with whom we talked explained that whites tend to go about their faith in a formal, precise, and less emotionally intense way that leaves little room for spontaneous and enthusiastic praise and worship. Many of them drew the analogy of a classroom setting in which a teacher teaches a nondescript lesson that is structured, ceremonial, and emotionally reserved (this conceptualization is squarely in line with Rev. Shannon's previous comment). Some of the more common words that these interviewees used to describe how they believe that whites think about and practice Christianity include "academic," "formal," "learning," "beliefs," "doctrine," "intellectual," and "propositional."

In contrast, with regard to the experiential classification, these same pastors explained that blacks tend to go about their faith in an informal, less theologically defined, but practical way that leaves much room for spontaneous and emotional praise and worship. Some of them drew the analogy of a music concert (or church service) in which the musicians (or preachers) get the crowd (or parishioners) involved through call and response and playing songs that people in the audience request, and the audience members themselves stand up, sing, dance, and shout along with the musicians (or preachers) as a sign of their involvement and appreciation. The audience members also grant the musicians or preachers a great deal of latitude with respect to playing impromptu songs or engaging in different modes of praise and worship. Some of the more common words that these interviewees used to describe how they believe that African Americans think about and practice Christianity include "experience," "feeling," "emotion," "intense," "survival," "practice," "actions," "expressive," and "suffering."[7]

Before proceeding, we must emphasize that neither the academic nor experiential model is superior or inferior to the other. Neither of these distinct approaches to Christianity is more valuable or correct. If anything, they are equal in that they both include accompanying advantages and disadvantages (which we will address shortly). That blacks tend to lead with their hearts while whites tend to lead with their heads does not mean that either group is deficient or operates at a faith-based deficit. Moreover, not all blacks subscribe to the experiential model, and not all whites subscribe to the academic model. The authors of this book both know white Protestants who like to get their "praise on" in the aisle, and we both know black Protestants who look at people with contempt for doing so (in all likelihood, you probably do too). Similarly, there are black Protestants who are brainiacs about the Bible, and there are white Protestants who are emotionally intense about their faith. Furthermore, we are aware that there are major similarities in religious identities and worldviews across different groups.[8] However, our goal in this book is to grasp the "different degrees of emphasis and valences"[9] (as Lincoln and Mamiya put it) across black and white Protestants' religious identities and worldviews. The *academic-versus-experiential dichotomy* provides only a general set of guidelines for understanding racial differences in religious sensibilities at the group level. It does not apply to all individuals and must be applied with caution and attention to detail. That being said, the fact that most of our interviewees advanced structurally based epistemological explanations rather than cultural imperatives suggests that African Americans do not undertake an experiential understanding of Christianity merely because they choose to do so. More poignantly, the dynamics surrounding their involuntary arrival as slaves and persistent experience as second-class citizens in the United States ensured that blacks would not have the privilege of developing an academic understanding of Christianity.

For instance, Rev. Davis, a Baptist preacher who has led several multiracial congregations on the West Coast, answered our initial interview question by evoking structural determinants such as slavery and racial inequality within the social "system" and describing how whites' higher status position on the social ladder cultivates an academic understanding of Christianity. Notice how Rev. Davis concludes his remarks by hinting that in today's world, a growing number of African Americans are coming to embrace an "intellectual" understanding of Christianity:

I do think that African Americans and Anglos tend to think differently about faith, and I think part of it has to do with a historical understanding of life and the role that God plays or played in the
survival and the life of people. For example, with African Americans,
Christ was central to everything in life. If you had any hope at all, it
was hope because of Him, and in times when we [blacks] didn't have
any idea that there could be hope in anything else, there was hope
in Him. Slaves, for example, were given basically a couple of things.
They were given work, and they were given Jesus. The Jesus that was
given to them was designed to have them be in line with the master's wishes, but what happened was the slaves began to understand
that they had a bigger master than the one that was on the plantation.
They had a better master in Christ, in God.

So with that understanding of Christ—of religion and the way it
paves into every aspect of life—their only liberty was found through
Christ, through the institutions of Christ, for example, the church.
Their only hope was there; and so they could endure the most vile
situations because they had hope in God. They had almost an escha-
tological hope in God, and a lot of the songs that were sung had to do
with the sweet by-and-by [i.e., Heaven] and not lamenting about the
nasty here-and-now.

So with that as a backdrop to the way in which many of us [Afri-
can Americans] have been raised over the years and the way in which
that has been passed down from generation to generation, it does
make us think Biblically, if not Christocentrically, about most things
that happen.

The unfortunate thing is, as we've gone over time, we're [blacks]
beginning to lose some of that because we are getting to the point
now where we are thinking more like the majority culture than we
might need to. For example, in the majority culture, among Anglos,
I'll say, it seems to me that they had a great number of their physical
needs met, and when you're not hungry and all those kinds of things,
then faith becomes a decision that you make in Him.

Whites had hope that there was justice. If you were white, you had
hope that even when you did wrong, somehow the system was going
to pay off in your favor. And so with that as a way of life, a number

of Anglos had options other than God to appeal to for assistance, to appeal to for support and help. And when you have other options, you can begin to philosophize about God, as opposed to really being driven to know Him. So with that understanding, a number of white people began to think about faith as just an intellectual thing.

Rev. Washington advanced a similar argument. In chapter 1, we foreshadowed his answer to our opening interview question by relaying part of his statement about the difference between "doctrine versus practice" (he feels that blacks are more practice oriented while whites are more doctrine oriented). By "doctrine," he means that whites tend to embrace "a hard and fast holding to a specific understanding of certain Christian doctrines based on certain Biblical interpretations." Rev. Washington believes that historically, whites have not religiously practiced what they have preached. He feels that beginning with slavery, many whites have remained committed to a particular set of evangelical beliefs that they often violate in practice. For instance, he cited an example of how after selling a slave's spouse away to another owner, many masters expected the spouse who remained on his plantation to honor Sunday worship-service lessons about resisting adultery and copulation. This contradiction led Rev. Washington to ask rhetorically (and quite powerfully), "How could the slave master require me to follow these rules when he's the one who sold my wife away? How is any of that Christlike?"

A seasoned Pentecostal preacher in the Dallas–Fort Worth area described the racial dichotomy between blacks and whites as a gap between "cognitive" versus "need-based" understandings of Christianity. Rev. Boyd, who credits his reserved yet discerning demeanor to his upbringing in a small Louisiana town, specified the links between racial inequality and *academic versus experiential* models of Christianity. His comments also address whites' emphasis on religious formality, precision, and intellectualism:

Caucasians have the tendency and propensity to have a *cognitive* approach to Christianity, and I believe African Americans have a *need* approach—an emotional need. They are coming to God to get that need met. We're [blacks] coming to God to get our physical needs met. God is for us a kind of last link. He is our survival; Caucasians see Him as being a complement. Life for whites is really okay without God having to be their center because many of the things that we would go to God for—like asking God for breakfast, lunch, and dinner—they probably have enough supply for a week, so it causes you not to be so intense. So when they pray, they pray cognitively to make sure certain doctrinal elements are included in the prayer, make sure that certain ritual is there, form is there. They're doing it in honor of the Lord, but they don't have the same intensity.

But for us, we're talking about food, a place to stay, a little money. That's very intense. We're always at the desperate level.

In a Caucasian church, they have a hymnal, and it's important to them that they sing all four stanzas. We don't have a hymnal. We don't like that kind of singing. We want to sing in our soul, and we want to sing it until we feel it. We *feel* deliverance. They *process* deliverance. So that would be a difference: that we go to God through our emotion, but they go to God through their cognitive thoughts. If you are preaching in a Caucasian church, you want to make sure you have three points because they can't hardly survive or make it without those three points and a conclusion! [*laughs*]. You will really mess it up! Here they got their pad taking notes, and they only got two points down. You know, that's almost an emergency because, see, they are waiting for point number three [*laughs*].

Rev. Boyd mentioned during his interview that he graduated from an influential, Biblically centered, predominantly white college in Tennessee. He said that while attending classes there, he was taught how to preach and teach in a "cognitive" manner. This presented a dilemma when the time came for him to preach, teach, and take on a more active role as a pastor at his predominantly African American church home:

When I would visit my church home on the weekend, my pastor wanted you to have a sense of the presence of God. Now, I don't believe either cognitive or need-based approaches to Christianity are wrong. They're just different. First of all, there's no need for me to be trying to be too cognitive if I can't spell and I can't read and write. If whites' process was cognitive and procedural and ours was speaking, moving from the heart, that doesn't mean that I can't get in touch with God.

But, remember, as a people, our Bible is what we [blacks] experience and feel, and you're going to have to teach a long time to get us to change. And so that's the reason why, when for years—what will happen? If you get up and you preach your sermon and you use a principled cognitive approach, our people at the door will say, "Reverend, that was a good talk." But if you get into it and pull their emotions, like Aretha Franklin can, they say, "Oh, you *preached!*" [*laughs*].

Yeah, see, my grandmother would come home sometimes, and I would say, "Big momma, how was church?" She would respond by saying something like, "Oh, my soul is blessed." Then I would ask, "Big momma, what did he [the preacher] say?" And she would reply, "Don't you start, boy!" Yeah, yeah [*laughs*]. It wasn't about—it's not about—what the preacher says, and it's not about what we're going to do. It's about us having to get in touch with Him. I want to feel Him. You know, *show up!* Because I've got a need. I've got a broken heart. Comfort my heart.

And so that's a great difference I see between blacks and whites.

Finally, it was Rev. Robinson—a young Pentecostal minister who is also a rocket scientist with degrees from Harvard University and the University of California at Berkeley—who most cogently articulated the difference between academic and experiential models for identifying with and understanding Christianity. His insightful comments address two important issues: (1) the trials and tribulations that African Americans face on a daily basis and (2) that racial differences in *academic versus experiential* understandings of Christianity are closely related to racial differences in "access" to theological training:

I think there has been a more vital experience of faith through the years for the black individual. It's one thing to have the propositional faith and the catechistic-type faith. It's another thing to actually be walking through the Valley of the Shadow of Death and have to call on the Power of God. I think that's really what we're seeing. If I can generalize, for whites the faith is more academic, and for blacks it's more experiential.

Interviewer: Can you to elaborate on what you mean by "academic"?

Sure. In general, the white Christians are going to know more church history; they might know a little bit more Greek and Hebrew and that type of thing. They've had the Trinity explained to them. God is three persons: Father, Son, and Spirit. They can sort of regurgitate the theology because they've had more training in formal theology. Maybe I'll say it that way: academic and formal versus being informal and experiential. When I say "informal," I guess I mean not as much formality. Collectively whites have had more theological training than blacks. They've had *access* to more academic material than blacks.

Interviewer: When you say "experiential," can you elaborate on that? What do you mean?

What I mean is, they read what's in the text and they try to live that. If they read that somebody was healed in the text, then they're going to ask God to heal them. That's experiential. If they see God provide for someone in the text, then that's what they expect to see in their life or experience. They've been taught this, they've seen it in the Bible, and they want to see that experience in their own life.

If you've been just overintellectualized, then you're going to have the 10 reasons why miracles don't occur today, and the 5 reasons why it's not intellectual to believe in healing, and the 3 reasons, and so on. You get all this other baggage to deal with, whereas if you don't have that baggage, you just sort of accept what's in the text and apply it to your life. Granted you have to have a foundation of something solid to base your belief on, but I'm just saying that there's not enough time to read a commentary on the New Testament when you're in the midst of a battle.

As with Rev. Washington, Rev. Robinson also described what he sees as a deeply embedded historical contradiction among white evangelicals: their steadfast commitment to certain Christian beliefs has been continually contradicted by their lack of goodwill toward nonwhites. Rev. Robinson emphatically responded in the affirmative to our follow-up question about the "importance" of perceived racial differences in *academic versus experiential* models of Christianity. He, along with several other preachers whom we interviewed, argued that a key distinction between black and white Protestants is their differing views on the relationship between "faith" and "works."

I think for many blacks, they've seen certain aspects of—especially evangelical Christianity in the United States—they've seen certain things proclaimed, but they haven't necessarily seen a consistency of behavior with that belief. For example, in the book of James, he says that "faith without works is dead." Okay and so what he's really stressing is that there has to be a consistency of action with belief. So you can proclaim to believe something, but if your action doesn't conform to that belief, that portrays the fact that you really don't believe whatever it is that you say you believe in.

Interviewer: Do you think that there might be an inconsistency among some Christians in terms of their actions and beliefs, particularly among evangelicals?

I think so. It's easy to subscribe to a set of propositions. It's harder to actually put those propositions into practice. It's easier to think that you're "okay with God" if you believe all of these things, but then you have to really go through the soul searching to say, "Am I really conforming to what it is that I say that I believe?"

So the Apostle James basically says if a brother comes in and he's hungry and naked or whatever, well it's easy to say to him, "Be warmed and filled" or "I wish you well." That's easy to say. It takes a little bit more effort to actually meet that need of hunger or whatever it is that he needs.

Back in the 19th century, many white Christians were quoting the slavery passages in the Bible, telling the slaves that they needed to submit to their masters. But many of the slaves were actually experiencing a relationship with God. That made them [the slaves] stop and say, "Wait a minute. The God that we've come to know in the Bible is different than the God that is being pushed on us by the slave masters." And so they're like, "Okay, well, you [whites] can say you're

Christian, and you can say you believe certain things, but what really matters is action."

I think that might be one thing that affects it. So as African Americans have experienced collectively great suffering, there comes this sort of experiential dimension to their faith.

At this point you might be wondering: does our argument regarding racial differences in commitments to *academic versus experiential* models of Christianity have any scholarly merit? What does Dr. James Cone think about a supposed racial dichotomy that systemically patterns distinct outcomes with respect to how black and white Protestants identify with and understand Christianity? How did he answer our initial questions about possible differences in the manner in which black and white Protestants go about their religious faith?

Dr. Cone's sentiments mirror those conveyed by the high-ranking clergy members who advanced an epistemological explanation for racial differences in religious sensibilities. While he distinguished between an "ethics versus creed" dichotomy, his broader argument is consistent with the idea that past and present racial discrimination and inequality in the United States plays a meaningful role in shaping one's experience as a Christian. Dr. Cone's reference to "creed" is closely related to core Christian tenets such as the Apostles' Creed. Here is his answer to our questions about possible differences in the manner in which black and white Christians go about their religious faith:

> I think the defining core of black Christians as they express their faith —go about living it—is in their *ethics*. Blacks may not live up to that ethical standard, but they never separate the faith from it, and they know that failure to live up to it is critical because God stands in judgment on them. Their faith is a self-criticism that comes from their faith and not from the society. They get enough criticism from the society. Everybody is a sinner, and black Christians see that sin in the failure of the ethics.
>
> Now, with white Christians, the center of their faith is their *creed*: what they say, not what they do. And with what they do, they've got

theologians to explain that away. They have a kind of cheap grace when it comes to ethics because they've got "justification by faith" that's going to get them in Heaven no matter what they do. See, with blacks, they're not sophisticated in no "justification by faith." With blacks, you are justified by what you *do*. And therefore they are like the Apostle James. Without your works, faith is dead, and blacks believe that. So they believe faith and how you live it is inseparable from the ethics, how you treat others. Whites don't look at it that way. They look at it by what they *believe*. Their faith is defined by their beliefs —believe in the Trinity, believe in this, believe in God the Father, God the Son, believe in that.

See, blacks haven't done much theology. Their heart is in ethics, how you treat others. That's true in their own community, and it's true in their relation to others. Ethic is the key, when they talk about the meaning of the faith. Now, they know they fall short. That's why they pray! [*laughs*].

See, when you've had 400 years of all kinds of suffering—from slavery, segregation, lynching, and all kinds of tricky discourse to make you think that you're not who you are—when you have to fight against a highly sophisticated, the most dominant oppressor in the world, when you have to fight against that, you need a religion that's going to take you through this. You don't have much power. You don't have much economic power. You don't have much intellectual power. You don't have much political power. You don't have much of anything. . . . So, what blacks do have, still—and the only thing they have that's not controlled by whites—is their faith.

But you see, you cannot act wrong and think right about God. If your ethics are flawed, your understanding of the faith is flawed too because your understanding of the faith flows from your ethics and your ethics flows from your understanding of the faith. See, again, blacks were not theologians. They didn't have an intellectual wall reflection on the gospel. What they had was common sense. That is, a commonsense understanding that you cannot treat your neighbor wrong and enslave your neighbor and at the same time claim that you are doing the will of God.

Clearly, Dr. Cone's comments closely correspond with the epistemo-logical arguments advanced by the African American pastors whom we talked with. This logical consistency suggests that among high-ranking black clergy, the *academic-versus-experiential dichotomy* is a widely accepted and deeply rooted explanation for racial differences in black and white Protestants' religious sensibilities. Our interviewees who advanced epistemological explanations staked similar claims re-gardless of the specific labels they used, such as "learning versus burn-ing," "doctrine versus practice," "cognitive versus need-based," and "ethics versus creed."

Folk Theology

We would be remiss if we failed to mention that several pastors we interviewed explicitly stated that African Americans' experiential approach to Christianity includes an accompanying flaw: generally speaking, these pastors believe that blacks are not as knowledgeable about Christianity as they should be. Most of them—and many oth-ers whom we interviewed—would agree with Dr. Cone's statement that in general "blacks are not theologians" and that "blacks haven't done much theology" (Rev. Johnson was the only high-ranking clergy member to commend blacks' balance between learning and burning). With this as their backdrop, they posited that if white Protestants have historically failed to practice what they have preached with re-spect to how they have subjugated blacks, then African Americans have failed to do their due diligence, especially in recent decades, to intellectually enhance their broader comprehension and awareness of the faith.

All of the ministers who asserted this claim of blacks' overall lack of a critical Christian education also advanced an epistemological expla-nation for how racial group membership color-codes one's experience as a Christian. These pastors believe that blacks' less scholarly and in-tellectually informed understanding of their religious faith is primarily due to the legacy of racial discrimination and inequality in the United States. Our interviewees' concerns are consistent with a combination of new and old structural, cultural, and individualistic barriers associated with minorities' level of access to and ability to achieve a high-quality education. In their defense, a number of recent studies have shown that despite significant gains, meaningful gaps persist between blacks and whites across various levels of educational attainment (see appendix A, table A.2, for example).[10]

Nevertheless, these high-ranking clergy members considered blacks' lack of an academic understanding of Christianity as a problem for both individual believers and their pastors. For instance, before being called to the ministry, Pastor Thomas was a full-time practicing lawyer who had earned several collegiate degrees. He responded to "the Lord's call" by enrolling at Turner Theological Seminary, a highly respected A.M.E. institution of higher learning. Pastor Thomas expressed unease (in both words and body language) with what he perceives as a "theological training" gap between those African American ministers who have studied in seminary and those who have not:

> Traditionally, in mainline white denominations, theological training was required. And so, much of that teaching that you would get in theological training you had in white mainline denominations. In black churches—you take the A.M.E. Church, for instance, which probably has by far the most stringent requirements in terms of theological training—it wasn't until 2000 that we required a master of divinity degree. But at the General Conference in 1844, when there were few formal educational opportunities for people of African descent, the Reverend Daniel Payne introduced legislation requiring ministers to complete a course of study in order to be ordained in the A.M.E. Church. This developed into a five-year training course that all A.M.E. ministers must complete as part of the process for ordination.
>
> And so you have many pastors in many churches, many African American pastors, who have never had *any* type of formal theological training. That doesn't mean that everybody who goes through theological training looks at things the same way, but I think someone who has had formal theological training is more likely to see the Bible at least slightly differently than the way many black people who have not had formal theological training see it.

Pastor Thomas's remark has implications for a longstanding hot-button issue among black Protestants: what role should education play (if any at all) in determining whether a person is "fit" to pastor? While we do not attempt to answer that question here, the ongoing debate among African Americans over education's place within Christianity cannot be ignored. For instance, Deacon Harris—a seminary-trained director of Christian counseling—agrees that African American Protestants stand to religiously benefit from a more rigorous academic understanding of Christianity. Consider this assertion:

I think part of my life and my job in Christian education is we [blacks] also tend to have a suspicion against intellectualism. There is this suspicion against science; there is a suspicion against critical thinking. Rightly and wrongly, it's been a tool of the people that oppressed us and tried to take away our faith.

At the same time, I think we have to learn how to embrace critical thinking in a way that works for us. I think that there is a strong suspicion against intellectuality and critical thinking that all those arguments . . . [*His thought trails off.*] There are a lot of evangelicals that have all kinds of arguments about the creation of the world, for instance. There are some that say, "Well, God created the world in six days," and some that say, "Well, those are just six periods, and you know, it could be a million years long" and things like that. For most of the African Americans that I know, it's not important. They think that that kind of speculation is not helpful.

Both Deacon Harris's and Pastor Thomas's statements suggest that African Americans must come to embrace a more intellectually demanding view of Christianity in order to enhance their personal knowledge and comprehension of the faith. These high-ranking clergy members do not stand alone on this issue; most of the pastors whom we interviewed are uncertain about the role that education should play within the African American Protestant religious tradition. In fact, academic concerns involving support for science, intellectualism, and relying on sources of knowledge beyond the religious realm are troublesome areas of tension for our interviewees, regardless of denomination. They feel this way for several reasons, one of which was eloquently captured by Deacon Harris's statement that science and critical thinking have historically been used as "tools" by whites in order to oppress blacks.[11]

Pastor Smith—a young A.M.E. minister who recently took over a troubled congregation in a the Dallas–Fort Worth area—is gravely concerned that the combined influence of a lack of formal educational and religious training, family traditions, and cultural factors have fostered the onset of deeply misguided and idiosyncratic understandings of Christianity that are at times out of step with conventional church teachings. He describes this personally nuanced form of Christianity as *folk theology*.

Before proceeding, we should mention that Pastor Smith sees the connection between "faith" and "works" differently from Rev. Robinson and Dr. Cone. This is important because many of our interviewees feel that faith-based actions—not just beliefs—are critical to improving race relations among black and white Christians. For them, a close connection between "faith" and "works" (which is a topic that we will revisit throughout this book) is central to their understanding of how to achieve racial reconciliation. However, Pastor Smith does not feel this way:

It's important to be taught theologically what it means to be a Christian, and believers should want to learn from a theological perspective all of the inherent components that help us to be better at what we do. I deal with this a lot since I deal with black people in the context of a learning environment. For some reason we shy away from that. I don't know, maybe it reminds us of being in school again [*chuckles*].

I think that limits our ability to really understand what the principles are about because scripture clearly teaches us that it's not what we do [i.e., actions] that makes us Christians. We are not saved by our works. There are certain things that we have to believe in order to be saved. We have to believe those things, or else you're not a Christian. So take the time to really seek and learn. I like this passage of scripture that Paul tells Timothy: he says to study and to show thyself approved.

And so it is with the Christian tenet that many of us . . . [*His thought trails off.*] I don't think we have a sound understanding of what it means to be a Christian, because if I am a Christian, there ought to be some identifiable characteristics about me. I'm following some sort of command. I'm following some sort of tenet. I'd like to deal with this, and I don't want to say too much about this, but it opened up an area for me that I've always been concerned with. I think that the gap that we're dealing with has to do with the fact that we deal in—and when I say "we," I mean black Christians—what I like to call *folk theology.*

Interviewer: What do you mean by that?

A folk tale or folklore are stories that have been handed down from generation to generation, and they're not necessarily right and they're not necessarily wrong. What ends up happening is that we can take something that we see or that somebody's told us and we make it scripture without ever really understanding the truth behind it. To understand what it really means then, we would have to pursue further study. We would have to look at our Bibles in concordance with other historical texts that give us the picture of why the author was writing what he wrote, what were his intentions, if he was writing about the conditions that were going on around him, and how do we transcribe that into how we are living today.

The problem that we face is that if we don't get that deep in study, then we're always still superficial with what the scripture tells us, and that gives us the ability to manipulate it to our own liking to help us to feel good with ourselves but at the same time have a foot in the church and a foot in the world.

I think white Christians have the opportunity and the ability, and the teachings that they get are from pastors who have been similarly trained, who have their doctorates, and they are teaching at that level to their members—as opposed to particularly, even today you have black Christians who go to church, and they're dealing with preachers who most of them have not been trained at a high level, even some of them at a collegiate level. Yet they're preaching to move the crowd and to make people feel good instead of getting them to change the behavior of their lives. So when you misconstrue and you don't search for yourself what it means to be a Christian, then you have that gap. So, yes, theology I think is the culprit. . . .

A primary example is if you ask somebody, "What does the devil look like?" Many believers respond with, "He's red, with horns and a long tail, and he's living in a fire pit." Well, we do not we encounter that description of Satan in the scriptures anywhere. But we believe that because that's what you know, and the folklore comes from all different types of avenues. It comes from my parents, my grandparents, TV, from my community, my immediate environment, my culture that I deal with on a daily basis. . . .

What ends up happening is that I build my foundation on what was told to me as opposed to what actually *is*. The struggle then—and I think this has to do with a lot of decline in black churches—is that, well, if my religious foundation is built on what was passed down to me and I can't prove it to be so, and you come along and counterattack what I believe in and I can't defend it, then I'm going to get angry. If I get angry, then I will leave, and I go somewhere else to another church. People say things like, "Well my momma believes this, and this is right. Yep. And momma can't be wrong."

Revisiting the Building Blocks

The findings presented in this chapter provide strong support for the *Experiential building block of black Protestant faith.* Most of the high-ranking clergy whom we spoke with advanced an epistemological explanation rather than a cultural imperative for perceived differences in how black and white Protestants go about their religious faith. Moreover, all of the epistemologists—and even some of the pastors who asserted the primacy of cultural imperatives—theorized that African Americans identify with and understand Christianity in a manner that is far more "experiential" than "academic." These pastors agree for both better and worse that blacks are less concerned with religious formality, less interested in propositional and intellectual approaches to Christianity, and less likely to prescribe to faith-based absolutist doctrines apart from the faith's core tenets than are whites. These findings

reinforce our claim that as compared to white mainline or evangelical Protestants, African American Protestants are less concerned with
Christianity's precise theological and doctrinal contours.

Our interviewees agree that African American Protestants are far
more interested in developing a down-to-earth and heartfelt understanding of God that is profoundly subjective and emotionally intense.
They strongly believe that cultural factors play a significant role in explaining why blacks are more expressive and informal than whites are
with respect to how they think about and practice Christianity. However, most of the pastors whom we sat down with do not believe that
cultural differences chiefly explain why blacks choose to "make a joyful noise unto the Lord" while whites choose to sit quietly. More point-
edly, they believe that (a) faith-based cultural differences between
blacks and whites have been prevalent since blacks arrived in America
as slaves (we develop this point in great detail in chapter 7; it is consistent with the *Mystery* building block) and (b) past and present structural forces such as racial discrimination and poverty have ossified racial differences in religious sensibilities, making them more apparent.

Cultural differences between blacks and whites are important but
not imperative. While culture does have independent effects apart from
structure, the primary reason why blacks undertake an experiential
approach to Christianity is because they have historically been denied
the opportunities necessary for achieving an academic understanding
of the faith. Historians have long documented how black slaves were
barred from attending churches where whites worshiped.[12] They were
also forbidden to read. If for no other reason, it was difficult for blacks
to develop an intellectual awareness of God because whites purpose-
fully erected barriers to impede their educational development.

These are just some of the race-based structural dynamics of oppression and privilege that have enhanced racial differences in religious
sensibilities among black and white Protestants. Although cultural
factors are in many ways autonomous, slavery provided the historical basis for securing color-coded understandings of Christianity in
America. With time, other macro-level determinants such as segregation, poverty, and political arrangements in our society at least preserved the racial gap in religious sensibilities. These structural factors

go a long way toward explaining why many of our study participants agree that blacks and whites differ in their "options other than God to appeal to for assistance," why "life for whites is really okay without God having to be their center," and why blacks and whites view their religious faith through different "economic, political, and social eyes."

One Final Note

We hope that scholars who are interested in studying race relations among Christians will have better luck than we did in convincing high-ranking white clergy members to participate in their interviews. Future studies will have to take up the task of assessing the extent to which white pastors believe black and white Christians differ in how they go about their religious faith. Nevertheless, our scholarly intuition leads us to believe that like most Americans, white pastors—if they feel comfortable enough to speak their mind—would probably acknowledge that there are meaningful faith-based distinctions between blacks and whites. However, in all likelihood, most high-ranking white clergy members will probably advance an astructural cultural imperative rather than an epistemological explanation for the perceived difference. We feel this way for various reasons, including this: in the moments immediately after the white male Methodist pastor mentioned in chapter 1 declined to be interviewed, we asked him why he thought that we were having such a difficult time getting whites to participate in our study. At first he said that he had "no idea." Then he mentioned that his church occasionally "swaps pastors" with other local congregations, some of which are predominantly African American. As he escorted us from his office he said, "Sometimes when I preach at my own church, I have to wonder if they're hearing me. I don't have to wonder that in a black congregation. There's more emotion; it's like they're talking back to you."

5

Religious Convictions
Everyday Faith-Based Actions and Beliefs

People are different, and whites and blacks have different traditions. So when it comes to religion, I think the differences are
all based around the intensity of people's faith when it comes
to what you believe in. Blacks have been through a lot, so we
may be more likely to reach and grab something to hold on to.
. . . Religion is one of the only things that gives us somewhat of
a true sense of history. I don't think all races have had to deal
with that. —Rev. Edwards

In this chapter, we build on our theoretical framework for
understanding racial differences in religious sensibilities. Our goals
are twofold. First, we continue our analysis of the *Experiential building
block of black Protestant faith* by explaining how the African American
Protestant religious tradition is active and experiential. By "active," we
mean that African American Protestants place a stronger emphasis on
subscribing to and engaging in certain widely recognized faith-related
thoughts and practices than white Protestants do. However, we cannot accomplish this objective without beginning to clarify the *Survival building block: (2) black Protestant faith is critical to survival and
helps individuals cope with suffering associated with everyday trials and
tribulations.* As we will soon see, our interviewees are in agreement:
African Americans view certain faith-based thoughts and practices as
a supernatural call for help to protect against the consequences of racial stratification.

Second, we test the *academic-versus-experiential dichotomy* across a wide range of everyday faith-based actions and beliefs. More specifically, we seek to determine whether black and white Protestants differ in their attitudes about whether the Bible should be interpreted literally or figuratively, how often they read and study the Bible, and the extent of racial differences in prayer (as a result, we continue our discussion on the contested role that education plays in the African American Protestant religious tradition). This portion of our analysis is by no means exhaustive. We selectively examine only a few of the potentially endless number of faith-based thoughts and practices (albeit some of the more important ones). Time and space prevent us from being comprehensive.

In a nutshell, the quantitative and qualitative findings presented in this chapter are best foreshadowed by comments conveyed by a 50-something-year-old, highly educated focus group participant in Cleveland. In responding to a general question—one that did not specifically mention blacks and whites—about a statistical connection between (a) beliefs about the "importance" of one's race and (b) one's everyday religious activities, she emphatically but comically stated,

Well, for those of us who are of African descent in this country, we've had to pray more and worship more and read the Bible more to *survive* in an oppressive situation. So I'm going to ask you: is there a correlation between the black people who say their race is "important"? Because if you're white, it doesn't matter! They don't even have the same construct about race!

Since I spend a little time in a college/university environment, I know that researchers are just beginning to understand that there is something called "white privilege." Duh! [*The room erupts in laughter.*]

And so if you [i.e., Christians in general] just thought that as a believer you are *supposed* to worship God and go to church, you might think that those things just come along with the package. But if you have had to *overcome*, if you've had to make a way out of no way, if you didn't have any food for your children and God provided food on your table, then you're gonna go to church and praise and worship Him because He's worthy.

Biblical Perspectives

Biblical perspectives are critical to understanding why the African American Protestant religious tradition is active and experiential. African Americans are active in their religious faith because they want to experience God moving in their personal lives in the same way that He does in the Bible. Thus, blacks' interpretation of the Bible is religiously *definitive* because it defines the frequency with which they should pray, attend worship services, and emphasize certain religious convictions and activities. This process is mutually reinforcing in that blacks pray and go to church so often in the hope that God will move in their lives, and when He does, they pray and go to church in order to give thanks.

One of Rev. Robinson's statements from the previous chapter sets the tone for this discussion. He attributed blacks' belief in divine "healing" to their literal interpretation of the Bible: "If they read that somebody was healed in the text, then they're going to ask God to heal them. That's experiential. If they see God provide for someone in the text, then that's what they expect to see in their life or experience. They've been taught this, they've seen it in the Bible, and they want to see that experience in their own life." Most—if not all—of the pastors whom we interviewed for this study would probably agree with this statement. In fact, 11 of the 14 high-ranking clergy members whom we spoke with specifically stated or drew a parallel to illustrate their belief that blacks' tend to take the Bible at face value; they argued that African Americans are less interested in investigating or uncovering hidden lessons that lie beneath the Biblical surface.

Our survey findings support this contention. For instance, 71% of black Protestants in the General Social Survey (GSS) believe that the Bible is the "actual word of God and is to be taken literally, word for word." However, only 41% of whites feel this way (see descriptive table B.5A). Moreover, only 25% of black Protestants say that the Bible is the "inspired word of God but not everything should be taken literally, word for word," but half of all white Protestants feel this way. Our multivariate results reveal that these very wide percentage gaps hold constant after accounting for relevant background factors: black

Protestants are significantly more likely than white Protestants to say that the Bible should be interpreted literally, word for word, and significantly less likely to say that not everything should be taken literally. These results—which partially hold when we restrict our analysis to black Protestants and white evangelicals—indicate that racial group membership color-codes beliefs about the Bible.

Why would this be so? How is it that a person's racial group membership patterns her or his understanding of religious text? Although the vast majority of the pastors whom we interviewed agree that blacks interpret the Bible verbatim, they nonetheless advanced contrasting explanations for blacks' strict adherence to the Biblical letter. Some of our interviewees argued that blacks' literal interpretation is a cultural imperative that has been handed down over generations. However, others described it as a product of blacks' commitment to an experiential model of Christianity. Despite these differences in rationale, most of the pastors whom we interviewed agreed that there are times—more often than not—when the Bible should be interpreted literally. Nevertheless, many of our interviewees stated that they would like African American Protestants to achieve a more complex understanding of when, where, and how to interpret the Bible literally or figuratively.

Before going any further, we should mention that much of the interview data presented in this chapter is associated with one of our preliminary findings: that African American Protestants are significantly more likely than whites to believe that God created the world in six 24-hour days. We asked high-ranking clergy to comment on this finding, only to discover later that it became statistically insignificant after controlling for the respondent's region of residence. This is important for two reasons: (1) In the discussion that follows, many of our interviewees specifically comment on this early finding regarding racial differences in whether one believes that God created the world in six 24-hour days. However, (2) they use it to illustrate the broader point of blacks' commitment to Biblical literalism. Although our rigorous set of predictors wiped away the racial difference in beliefs about creation, our statistical finding for blacks' verbatim reading of the Bible holds true to form (as shown here).

Rev. Boyd, a Pentecostal preacher in the Dallas–Fort Worth area, described blacks' devotion to the Biblical letter as a family-based cultural "tradition" within the black community:

Well, here again, that's tradition. It's what they've heard. They have never researched it. Caucasians came up with that "six 24-hour days" explanation because of evolution. Was it 24-hour days? Was it 24-hour periods? And because, when you go to school and you begin to develop your cognitive ability, then you become more reflective in your thinking.

In the black community, whatever Big Momma said pretty much dictated how things were going to be. We were getting our teachings and lessons in life from our mothers and from the women that were around. And when they spoke, that was it. You notice I don't refer to Big Daddy too much, because he was out trying to get some grits and ham on the table. So we think, "Oh, you know what? I don't even have time to reflect upon that. If that's what the Auntie or Big Momma says —that it's six days—then it's just as she says."

Rev. Johnson also described blacks' commitment to Biblical literalism as a family-based cultural tradition. However, he took this point a step further: he believes that the Bible takes precedence over all other sources of knowledge in shaping how African Americans develop an understanding of the social world and their place within it.

The vast majority of black Christians do not label themselves as "evangelical," because that is a white term used by white people. However, the way that term is defined would most certainly describe the average black church, because we tend to take the Bible literally.

We take the most simplistic interpretation of the Bible at face value. We've been taught to respect the Bible as the inherited, infallible word of God. And the Bible is a very special book in our home. Even if we didn't read it, it was sitting on the coffee table. You knew something about that book that was different from every other book. A huge respect has been taught to us from our parents and grandparents about the Bible. So when we read in the Bible that God created the world in six days—as my preacher would say, "God said it, that settles it, whether I believe it or not."

That's been the majority of black folks' mind-set, and that's basically how [white] evangelical Christians look at it. What the Bible says, it trumps or prioritizes any other opinion out there, any other viewpoint.

This idea—that for African Americans, Biblical wisdom trumps or predominates over nearly all other available sources of knowledge, even those that have scientific or intellectual merit—was a common sentiment expressed by our interviewees. Pastor Jenkins, a boisterous comedian and assistant pastor at a small Pentecostal congregation in Southern California, provided an example of how commitments to Biblical literalism shape African American viewpoints. He used the debate over evolution to illustrate the point that while blacks have been "exposed" to scientific knowledge, they nonetheless still subscribe to a Biblically based view of creation. Smiling widely, looking toward the sky, and waving his hands as if performing a magic trick, he stated,

And the Bible says, "Behold . . . and He breathed over it and waved His hand and created the waters." And then when we [blacks] get to the part where it says that He created the Earth in six days and He rested on the seventh, that's where we get it from. We assumed that He was at it 24/6! [*laughs*]. And on the seventh day, He kicked back and said, "Look what I've created. And it is *good*" [*laughs*].

But see, white people, in some cases, they want to deal more with the scientific aspect of it and start talking about the Big Bang Theory and all that kind of stuff. The universe is evolving with stars and volcanic eruptions and all that kind of good stuff. But our [blacks'] whole thing is while we've been exposed to the research and arguments about evolution, the holy scripture is inspired by God Himself and written down for us as a blueprint on how to live our lives so that it would be pleasing unto the Lord.

Our survey findings support Rev. Johnson's and Pastor Jenkins's declaration that Biblically based convictions are widespread among

African Americans. For instance, no more than 15% of both black and white Protestants in the Portraits of American Life Study (PALS) at least "agree" that the Bible contains "moral or religious" and "scientific or historical" errors (see descriptive tables B.5B and B.5C). Our multivariate results indicate that black and white Protestants do not meaningfully differ on these survey items. Nevertheless, these results —when coupled with our previous results for blacks' "word for word" reading of the Bible—suggest that African Americans are justified in interpreting the Bible literally precisely because they believe it does *not* contain errors.

Take, for example, the comments expressed by a 30-something-year-old, black, male focus group member from Cleveland. He not only subscribes to a definitive interpretation of the Bible but also takes issue with those believers whom he feels "pick and choose" what to take at face value:

> See, there's a conflict between the secular worldview and what God's word says. And that's been in conflict for as long as I know. Science and religion are in conflict; I was taught one thing in church and another thing when I was sitting in my classroom.
>
> It's like people cannot come to terms with the word of God being the *real* word, the *real* thing. So they say, "Well, I know they said that in church, but in science class, I was taught this. So I'm sticking with this particular part of the science, but I believe the religious parts of everything else."

Concerns over Reflective Thinking

More than half of the pastors whom we interviewed mentioned pitfalls associated with strictly adhering to a literal interpretation of the Bible. This opinion was expressed by Baptist, Methodist, and Pentecostal clergy at big and small churches across the regions where we conducted interviews. In some way, shape, or form, most of our interviewees conveyed concerns that a verbatim reading of the Bible impedes one's ability to gain greater knowledge of Christianity in general and the Bible in particular.

Many of our interviewees linked their concern for blacks' commitment to a strict interpretation of the Bible with longstanding tensions between education and religiosity: they believe that a lack of adequate education or religious training can hinder one's ability to achieve a greater understanding of Christianity, while too much education or training can lead to overintellectualizing. Take, for example, Rev. Boyd's previous commentary on links between going to school and becoming "reflective" in one's thinking. By "reflective," he means a tendency toward speculative or contemplative reasoning that can challenge conventional wisdom. As a college graduate, he—like most of the pastors whom we sat down with—believes that reflective thinking should have a place within the African American Protestant religious tradition. However, he—like most of the pastors whom we sat down with—is not quite sure how much space should be preserved for reflective thinking.

Why are our interviewees so mindful yet indecisive about the role that reflective thinking should play within the African American Protestant religious tradition? It is because, in general, advances in education weaken one's religious sensibilities. Consider our multivariate results presented in appendix D, tables D.5A-1 through D.5C). As education increases, survey participants (regardless of race) are less likely to take the Bible literally and more likely to say that the Bible is the "inspired word of God but not every word should be taken literally." Furthermore, better-educated survey participants are more likely to say that the Bible contains moral, religious, scientific, and historical errors.

On the other hand, these same tables show that church attendance (a proxy for religiosity) strengthens one's religious sensibilities: survey participants who attend church more frequently are more likely to take the Bible literally and less likely to say that not every word of the Bible should be taken literally or that it contains errors of any sort. This pattern of findings—which we should reiterate is based on data for Protestants *only*—can be found across most of our multivariate tables, regardless of the topic under analysis.

These statistical findings precisely explain why our interviewees have concerns over reflective thinking. Most of the high-ranking clergy members whom we interviewed are college graduates, so they are keenly aware of higher education's diminishing effect on religiosity. Nevertheless, many of them believe that African Americans must take steps toward embracing a more "academic" understanding of the Bible. (This is precisely what Deacon Harris meant in the previous chapter when he said about blacks, "We have to learn how to embrace critical thinking in a way that works for us.") They believe that reflective thinking is critical to one's awareness of Christianity in general and the Bible specifically because, according Rev. Edwards, "Jesus used parables. He would say something that meant something else. So you have to look at it [a particular Bible verse] as a parable. You have to understand that He had a different meaning. In the Old Testament, they meant what they said, but we just don't really know exactly what they meant [*laughs*]. So we have to have extensive study and then even after that extensive study; you still don't know for a fact if that's what it was."

Ironically, the tension between Biblical literalism and reflective thinking was best explained by Rev. Robinson, the rocket scientist. His comprehensive comment underscores what he believes to be a need for Christians to develop a more "nuanced" and "critical" understanding of the Bible. However, he also believes that academic understandings of the Bible include their own set of unique theological problems, which he describes as "*tortured exegesis*":

> I believe that blacks for the most part take the Bible literally. They read the Bible, and they believe what they see. They may not be aware of all of the nuanced explanations for a "day" and how a "day" may be "an age" and that type of thing. They don't know all of that. They just read the text, and it says in six days. He created the world, and on the seventh day He rested. I'm not taking a view for or against that interpretation. I'm just saying that's what the text says, and so that's what they believe.
>
> The Bible is written in different genres. There are historical books, there are prophetic books, there's poetry, and there are gospels. These

genres must be taken into account. But the average person would probably never think about the need for accounting for some of these genres; they may not have been introduced to the type of language that poetry uses. So when they read through their Bible, everything is pretty much taken literally.

It's just like in regular human speech, there are things that a person says that are to be taken literally, and you understand that from the context or some type of medium. Like if I say, "Throw the baby out with the bathwater," that's understood to be an *idiom*. If somebody heard me say that—and let's say that person understands English but doesn't know that idiom—he or she might actually take me literally.

All I'm saying is that to a person who is just reading the Bible un-critically—and I mean "critical" in an interpretive rather than negative way—there may be certain things that might have a nuanced interpre-tation that they may not be aware of. It's a matter of maybe disparity in education or disparity in Biblical experience or that type of thing.

Now greater education can have a negative effect as well, because if you're trying to make symbolic or figurative that which is to be taken literally, you can sort around all kinds of things that the Bible tells you to do or not to do. I see that happening as well. I call it a *tortured exegesis* or creative exegesis—a person finds a reason to get around or not follow a simple commandment that God gave to do something. It's like saying, "Well, I'm not going to be obedient because the Bible wasn't written in my time. It doesn't apply to me."

Not surprisingly, although we conducted interviews with high-ranking clergy across each of the three leading African American Protestant denominations—Baptists, Pentecostals, and Methodists (as well as followers of subdenominations within these traditions)—it was the A.M.E. pastors who most forcefully argued for the need for blacks to develop a more reflective line of theological thinking. This is plausi-bly due to the fact that the A.M.E. Church—the first of the historically black denominations—has long placed an emphasis on educational at-tainment among its pastorate. (The highest-ranking ordained clergy must possess a master's degree in divinity; see Pastor Thomas's com-ment in chapter 4.) Each of the A.M.E. pastors whom we interviewed discussed (a) blacks' strict commitment to Biblical literalism and/or (b) the need for African Americans to be more reflective in their Biblical views. For instance, Pastor Thomas of New York City emphatically stated,

> Here's the very simple answer: I think in many black churches a literal reading of all scriptures is emphasized, and so the notion of the creation story being allegorical is taken as a sign of a lack of faith. Most of us [African Americans] believe that you have to embrace the Bible as a literal truth as opposed to an allegorical truth. Otherwise it shows that you don't have the right type of faith.
>
> And in white churches—since long ago—many of the stories in the Bible were looked at as being allegorical as opposed to literal, and so they had no problem reading that and interpreting it not as something that literally happened but something that explains a theological truth.
>
> But in many black churches, that is not true. And part of that goes to theological training. . . . It's a little bit different now, with a lot of these independent churches sprouting up and people just start a church. You know, one day you're working for the post office, and the next day you're a senior pastor.

Pastor Thomas's point gets directly to the heart of the matter: according to him, many African Americans believe that a reflective view of the Bible is a "sign of a lack of faith." If blacks generally believe that the Bible trumps all other sources of knowledge and that it should be interpreted literally because it does not contain errors, then does that mean that reflective thinkers are lesser Christians? What does it mean if, in borrowing from our young, black, male focus group member, some Christians do not see some information within the Bible as "the real thing," or they sift through the Bible and believe some things verbatim but not others? Clearly, this is a major point of contention among African American Protestants.

Pastor Smith, a young A.M.E. minister in the Dallas–Fort Worth area, believes that reflective thinking is critical to one's understanding of how the Bible is relevant to today's world. However, his comment stands out because he uses a hot-button issue among Protestants—the role of women in society—to explain why African Americans should not always interpret the Bible literally:

> I think a deeper area exists in our limitations of the understanding of scripture: we [Christians in general] are not able to understand the original language that the Bible was written in. What I mean is that we read the Bible as has been translated. But African Americans take it literally; you run into an error when you do that because translations lose meaning at some reference or some point in time. For instance, you said "a day," so that's a 24-hour day to me. To the original Hebrew, "a day" means something totally different. So a lot of scripture is not meant to be taken literally.
>
> There are several avenues by which we interpret scripture and interpret the Bible. One of those has to be revelation from God—God revealing Himself to us through His word. The second thing is that we have to deal with the historical: What was happening at the time when the author wrote what he wrote? What was the scene or what was the setting or what was the cultural system like in that time? And then we also have to recognize *when* scriptures are meant to be taken literally and when they are given to us as signs and symbols or when they are given to us as allegories or parables. We have to be able to distinguish between all of those things.
>
> If we don't understand all of those things, then we are more apt to take things literal in the scripture. One of the arguments is—and I will probably get into some arguments with my Baptist brothers on this—that there is a lot of the division among Christians in terms of women not wearing pants in the church. Well, if you look at the cultural setting of that time in which the Bible was written, Paul was dealing with a culture where it was believed that women were not necessarily "sane." But that was *their* societal culture; that was what they were taught for whatever reason, and they had to do that.
>
> But what else did he mean? Well, those *particular* women, *they* were talking too much, they were causing problems within the church. But if we take the scripture as it is written, all women are supposed to be seen and not heard. So we must deal with the cultural context.

Today in America that's not our culture. Women are embedded so much into our culture that they run organizations and they have leadership positions. Our culture is totally different from the culture that Paul lived in. We've had movements—women's liberation and all of that. Our culture is *not* the same.

Pastor Smith's comprehensive comment addresses what he believes to be a need for understanding cultural history and the prevailing social arrangements in society during the days when the Bible was written. He believes that this information is critical for making the Bible's lessons and teachings relevant to today's world. At the end of his comment, Pastor Smith revisited his previous point about *folk theology*: Pastor Smith believes that many blacks' *definitive* view of the Bible is often inaccurate, and so this further complicates the problem of idiosyncratic understandings of Christianity.

The angst surrounding the tensions between reflective thinking versus a literal interpretation of the Bible was best captured by Rev. Shannon, a female A.M.E. pastor from Cleveland. She passionately described the need for both interpreting the Bible literally and also knowing when and why Christians should be reflective in their Biblical thinking. Her words are especially powerful considering that she is a volunteer counselor at a shelter for battered women. Notice how she continually restates her belief that the Bible is God's "infallible word" yet also asks Him to "breathe life into His words" specifically for her:

Why would I, as a black person, believe that [God created the world in six 24-hour days]? Because it's scripture, and I believe in the scripture. I believe that the Bible is God's infallible word. It was written by man but inspired by God. So I believe in it. I believe in everything in the Old and New Testament. But I am informed by how the word inspires my heart to exegete it, to understand it.

There are some things I'm going to interpret differently in the Bible, like when Paul said women should be seen and not heard. In the Bible, you can't be a preacher and be a woman. It's right there, in black and white. But the Bible is God's *infallible word*.

So I ask the Lord to breathe life into the Bible for me. He [God] says, "That's my word, but here's how I want you to understand it, and here's how I want you to preach it." And He ain't saying that I can't be a woman preacher. So that's how I can take God's infallible word. He whispers in my ear how He wants it done.

I have women who come to me for religious counseling, who say, "My husband beat me up, and he pointed to a passage in the Old Testament where a man beat up his wife, and he says that's okay. He stripped her naked. He killed her, and that's okay because man controls his wives? My husband beat me. Why is that all right?"

So I say to Him: "Okay, Lord. I'm putting my hand on your word. Now what am I supposed to tell these women who are abused? I need for you to breathe some life into this." And He does. It is still His infallible word . . . and I'm sold.

Reading and Studying the Bible

African Americans' strict interpretation of the Bible and accompanying application to their everyday lives helps to explain why Black Protestant faith is "active." For instance, Rev. Shannon connected blacks' understanding of the Bible with their commitment to faith-based activity: "Ever since slavery, our faith has had everything to do with who we are, how we think about and perceive our tomorrows. So we read the Bible because it is *our* dictionary. It's *our* encyclopedia on how to live our lives. The Bible *helps* us that's why we go to church." It's worth noting that this statement is also consistent with the idea that for African American Protestants, the Bible is the most important source of knowledge used to organize one's perception of the social world.

In chapter 1, we discussed findings from the Pew Research Center's widely respected "U.S. Religious Landscape Survey" of over 36,000 Americans. One of the many interesting results from that study showed that followers of historically African American denominations tend to read the Bible more often than do followers of evangelical and mainline Protestant denominations.[1] Our survey findings corroborate this claim. Nearly 90% of black Protestants in the PALS say that they have read the Bible outside of religious services during the past year.

However, just 74% of white Protestants say that they have done so (see descriptive table B.5D). We asked a follow-up question to those study participants who responded "yes" to whether they had read the Bible. We found that 54% of black Protestants say that they have read their Bible at least "once a week" outside of worship services during the past year. In contrast, 44% of white Protestants say that they have read their Bible as frequently (see descriptive table B.5E).

Our multivariate results do, in fact, show that racial group membership color-codes the frequency with which believers read the Bible: black Protestants are *twice* as likely as whites to have picked up and read their Bible away from worship services at all over the past year. This finding remains when we restrict our analysis to black Protestants and white evangelicals. However, there is no meaningful difference between those blacks and whites who have read the Bible at least *once* over the past year. The percentage gap between these groups is explained away by intervening factors, namely, age and church attendance. Those blacks and whites who read the Bible similarly do so on a regular basis.

By now you might be wondering: does the finding that black Protestants actively read the Bible (or their "dictionary/encyclopedia," as Rev. Shannon put it) challenge our argument that blacks are less committed to an academic model of Christianity? Could it be that blacks are more academic in orientation than we are giving them credit for? It is quite possible that we (and some of our interviewees) have underestimated the black laity's efforts to read and study the Bible. In fact, additional survey findings support this conclusion. About 35% of black Protestants in the PALS report participating in a Bible study group, while 25% of white Protestants say that they have done so (see descriptive table B.5F). Although our multivariate results show that controlling for church attendance nullifies this difference, the finding that blacks are no less likely than whites to participate in a Bible study group suggests that Biblical knowledge is important to both black and white Protestants. It seems that black Protestants should be given more credit for learning (not just burning) with respect to their devotion for reading the Bible and participating in Bible study groups.

But neither of these results meaningfully undermines our theoretical framework. Devotees to both academic and experiential models of Christianity rightfully concern themselves with reading and studying the Bible (yet as predicted, blacks are more actively engaged in the former than whites are). However, with respect to these particular findings, what is most important is how devotees *think about* what they are reading and studying. This is where our second building block —*Survival*—comes in: the average African American Protestant subscribes to a literal interpretation of the Bible and engages in certain faith-based thoughts and practices so that God might move to resolve their everyday trials and tribulations. Remember, blacks want to *experience* God moving in their personal lives in the same way that He does in the Bible. Thus, racial differences in Biblical literalism—which are shaped by deeply rooted cultural, structural, and interpersonal/ familial factors—ensure that when black and white Protestants read and study the Bible, they not only often reach different interpretations about what they read and study, but their understandings of the Bible profoundly vary with respect to the role that its lessons play in their personal lives.

Racial Differences in Prayer

Racial differences in reading, interpreting, and studying the Bible are just the tip of the proverbial iceberg. Back in chapter 1, results from both our descriptive and multivariate analyses showed that black Protestants more frequently attend worship services than white Protestants do and that black Protestants are more likely to be official members of a religious congregation. These findings also support our contention that the African American Protestant religious tradition is active and experiential. But it does not end there. The previously mentioned Pew Research Center poll found that 80% of African American Protestants reported praying at least once daily, while 69% of all other Protestants (regardless of race) reported praying at least once daily. Findings from both the PALS and the GSS are consistent with this result. For instance, we found that 62% of black Protestants in the PALS pray at least "once a day," not including meals and worship services, while only 40% of white Protestants do so. Similarly, 84% of African Americans in the GSS pray at least "once a day," while 68% of whites say that they do so (see descriptive tables B.5G and B.5H). (The percentage differences between these two surveys are most likely due to the PALS's attention to the frequency of prayer apart from worship services and praying over meals, as well as its expanded answer possibilities.) Lastly, 61% of black Protestants say grace over their meals at home at least "once a day," while only 29% of white Protestants say that they do so (see descriptive table B.5I). Taken together, across all three of these nationally representative surveys, it appears that African Americans pray more frequently than whites do. It is worth noting that in each of these highly respected national surveys, a much greater percentage of blacks than of nonblacks report praying more than once a day.

Our multivariate findings reveal that these wide racial gaps in the frequency of prayer hold constant after accounting for the relevant background factors. In fact, the results for racial group membership are highly statistically significant and strong in magnitude. What is more, findings for our corresponding "special" models reveal that black Protestants pray up to nearly *three times* more often than white evangelicals do. These findings are indeed astonishing. By themselves, our findings for racial differences in the frequency of certain religious activities means very little. But collectively, they powerfully reinforce our argument that racial group membership color-codes how black and white Protestants go about their religious faith.

But for the Grace of God

But what role does racial discrimination play in all of this? *All* of our interviewees agree that the legacy of racial discrimination and inequality go a very long way toward explaining why African American Protestants pray, attend worship services, read the Bible, and find a church home more frequently than white Protestants do. Take Rev.

Robinson's point, for instance. He attributed blacks' emphasis on certain religious activities as a deeply embedded cultural tradition within the black community: "I think it's become a part of our culture. Christianity it is truly what brought us through. People have had a relationship with God for a long time, and it's been passed on from generation to generation." At first glance, this explanation seems to be a cultural imperative. However, it would be improper to view it in that way. The thrust of his epistemological perspective became clear when we asked him to clarify what he meant by the phrase "brought us through":

Once again, I think this is a great testament to the power of Christianity, even though Christianity was being used to oppress blacks. Select passages of the Bible were used, like "slaves obey your masters," and there's this erroneous "Curse of Ham" idea that was promulgated at the time. It basically stated that the black race was cursed because of Noah's son, Ham. But that's an erroneous kind of thinking. Even though that kind of stuff was happening, you still saw blacks embracing Christianity and the gospel.

So they were discovering something deeper than what was being pushed on them. The essence of Christianity was really coming through. The love and the deliverance aspect as they read the Exodus story and that type of thing. It was really something to be held on to. And so Christianity has been a powerful part of our lives since slave times. It's been passed on from generation to generation.

Most of our interviewees advanced a decidedly epistemological explanation for why black Protestants partake in certain faith-based activities more often than white Protestants do. They not only argued that that African Americans lean on their faith to protect against the consequences of past and present racial discrimination and inequality in the United States, but they also agree that Christianity has "brought blacks through" slavery, segregation, and even the contemporary period of black/white race relations. However, this point was expressed in different ways. While some high-ranking clergy members were straightforward, others stated a parable in making the point that African Americans use their religious faith to cope with and defend against racism. Still other interviewees discussed how the dynamics of race-based oppression and privilege fostered the institutional centrality of the black church. Rev. Boyd, a seasoned pastor who is originally from a small town in Louisiana, best articulated this latter position:

> Prayer, going to church, that was our life. The church was the one place, after you chopped cotton—remember now, all the black people in the North have all of a sudden been touched by where we came from. We didn't come from the North. We came from the South—chopping cotton and picking cotton. I chopped cotton from seven o'clock in the morning, which means you have to get up at about five because you've got to walk to the fields and you carry your dinner with you. You get off at 5:30 or 6:00 p.m. That gave you just a little bit of time to wash off and get to church. After a long day, you still went to church, because your only solace was in church. That's where we socialize. On Sunday, you have a big nice pan full of cake and fried chicken. And so you get to the church, you have Sunday school, morning service, you take a break and eat, and you church some more 'til that night. It was your strength for the week. We collaborated with one another; it was our everything.
>
> When the boys and girls from the South decided to migrate to the North, one of the things—probably the last words that Big Momma said were, "When you get there, you go get in a church, and go to church. Go get a job, work—do whatever you do—but don't forget church." Why? *Because that's what brought you thus far.* So that was our spiritual and social life.

Aside from a handful of comments spotlighting the centrality of the black church, most of our interviewees posited that the dynamics of racial stratification help to explain why black Protestants pray and attend worship services more often than white Protestants do. For instance, Rev. Johnson argued that "problems in society" (such as racial and gender disparities) have helped to nurture differences in black and white Protestants' religious sensibilities. He believes that these dissimilarities were prophesized in the Bible:

That question [regarding racial differences in church attendance, prayer, etc.] seems consistent with what I recently read, a report from a Pew poll, and what I've been hearing the last 5 or 10 years. I've picked up glimpses of information in other places where the substance of that question seems to be right in line or on target with that kind of information.

So why do I believe that? I could theorize on that question all day long, but I guess, uh, oh boy—this is probably gonna be the most interesting answer you get from anybody on this question! [*smiles, laughs*]. I think it was predicted in the Bible and a fulfillment of prophecy—in Psalms 68:31 and then in Zephaniah 3:10. The Bible is very clear that descendants of Africa at some point in the future—and I believe we're now at that point—would stretch out their hands to God, which means they would be pressing in God, they would be pursuing God, reading their Bible, praying, going to church. "The Ethiopians shall stretch out his hands to God"—"shall" is futuristic. And the day is coming. . . . Zephaniah 3:10: Ethiopians would be bringing gifts. I've also been told that black Christians, as a whole, give more of their money to the church than Anglo Christians. And so I think that your survey findings are a fulfillment of at least those two scriptures. Another passage in Isaiah—I don't remember the exact place—talks about Africans experiencing a Renaissance, a revival.

That's number one. Then number two, I think, is also driven by major improvements in race relations today as compared to 25 years ago, certainly 100, 200 years ago. But having said that, does the glass ceiling still exist? Racism is still in the marketplace and the corporate world, academic world, the church world, on and on and on. I think we're still basically the last hired and the first fired. A woman still gets paid less than a man for equal work, so equal pay is not a reality. That's what Martin Luther King marched and died for, getting garbage workers equal pay. These kinds of inequalities in promotions and pay in race and gender spawn other problems in our society.

Everyone needs God, but I think that because of problems that black people face—and these problems do not necessarily affect white Christians—they force us to pray, to go to church, and seek God in ways for peace to make sense of it. . . . Members of other races may not be driven to God for those reasons.

I told ya I'd say something ain't nobody else said [*laughs, smiles*].

Rev. Johnson is most certainly correct that none of our other interviewees explained racial differences in certain everyday religious activities within the context of Biblical prophecy. (It is worth noting that this part of his analysis supports our contention of Biblical literalism among blacks.) However, his assertion that the "problems" that black people face strongly influence the manner in which they go about their religious faith was very common. As a matter of fact, high-ranking clergy across each of the three predominant African American denominations consistently espoused this viewpoint. Take, for instance, this powerful comment from Rev. Washington. His statement addresses the fundamental epistemological role that religious identity plays in the lives of many African Americans:

The church is that place that gives them [blacks] dignity and recognizes them, even though they may not be doing everything that they should do to be more religious or a better Christian in that sense of what it means to be a follower of Jesus. They love Jesus, and this restores their dignity. It restores their identity when they are stripped of it day-in and day-out through all of these other factors I mentioned —sociological, socioeconomic, and right on down the line.

Their humanity, their personhood, their identity, almost even their own sense of destiny is stripped away from them, and they come to this place [the church], and it gives them dignity, even if just for those few hours on Sunday. That music is their music. Those prayers are their prayers. They aren't told that you can't pray this way. You can't sing this away. You can't preach this way. You can't shout and scream, because sometimes folks are shouting and screaming about some other else.

Deacon Harris made this exact point in a less impassioned way. Over the course of his interview, he calmly and pragmatically detailed how he believes that many white Christians "wrap themselves" around the cross and the American flag yet also still support "confining black people to a certain realm in society, whether it is like apartheid or segregation." Consequently, he situated our finding for racial differences in everyday faith-based activities within the context of the "difficulties" that African Americans face. His rationale fits squarely in line with our argument that blacks lean on their faith as a supernatural call for help to protect against the consequences of racial stratification:

> That's a very interesting question [about why blacks engage in certain religious activities more often than whites do]. Again, I think I might go back to what I said in terms of black people. We realize that God is a *helper to us* and can *help us*. So because most of us have had to deal with so many difficulties in life, we've learned to turn to God and let Him be our source of strength. So we pray and read the Bible more because we're trying to get help, trying to get answers, trying to find strength.

The moments when our interviewees explained why they believe that blacks engage in certain religious activities more frequently than whites do could also be peaceful and serene. Sister Anderson, a 50-something-year-old assistant evangelist at a Pentecostal church in Cleveland, made the same epistemological point that Rev. Johnson, Deacon Harris, Rev. Washington, Rev. Shannon, Rev. Boyd, Pastor Thomas, and many other black preachers and black people in the pews did. However, she did so in a very different way. Her reasoning for why black Protestants go to church and pray more often than white Protestants do is subtle and allegorical yet no less powerful:

> Well, you know what? I read a story not too long ago about three women who often went to church to pray—same type of women, same community, almost the same age, and principally part of the same community since they were very young. And this is just a story.
> They all kneeled before the Lord and sought Him. When Jesus showed up, He went to see the first lady, but He never touched her or engaged in conversation. He didn't stay very long, either. He left her and went to see the second woman. He touched her and labored with

her for just a few moments and spoke a few words. And then He left and went to see the third woman. There, the story goes that He stayed for hours, had conversation, gave her instruction, direction, and had a lengthy involvement there. The story ends when another woman who had been observing the situation ran to Jesus and said, "Jesus, what's with this inequality here?"

And He says, "And what, may I ask, is that?"

She said, "Well, that first lady, you just didn't say a word to her. The second lady, you stayed there and talked for only a little while. But with the third lady, you were there just all day it appeared."

And He said, "My dear, I'm always there for the one who needs me the most."

And so one day, as I thought about that, I kind of reversed the story, and I thought about people who seek the Lord more than others. I believe, in the black community, because of our experience in life, we seek Him more. We've had the experience of being poverty stricken in some areas and being academically and economically disadvantaged almost on every level. We have been labeled not only as inferior but as characters of lack—so it has been written all the way from the beginning of time. So we sought Him more because we needed Him more.

Revisiting the Building Blocks

The quantitative and qualitative results presented in this chapter provide strong support for *the Experiential* and *Survival building blocks of black Protestant faith*. The African American Protestant religious tradition is active and experiential. This is partly because the average black Protestant subscribes to a literal interpretation of the Bible that defines the frequency and intensity with which she or he prays, attends worship services, and engages in other widely recognized religious activities.

The findings presented here also support our claim that African Americans use their religious faith to protect against the consequences of racial discrimination and inequality in society. Thus, a second reason why the African American Protestant religious tradition is active and experiential is because blacks collectively believe that the conservative manner in which they go about their religious faith has "brought them through thus far." In other words, African Americans pray, attend worship services, and engage in other widely recognized religious activities because their faith has helped them survive racially oppressive conditions in society.

We strongly believe that blacks' emphasis on subscribing to and engaging in certain widely recognized faith-based thoughts and practices holds constant across outcomes not examined here. For instance, the average African American Protestant has no doubt about the meaningful role that God has played in his or her life. A whopping 93% of black Protestants in the GSS declare, "I know God really exists and I have no doubts about it," while 71% of whites report having such confidence. Furthermore, only 5% of black Protestants say, "While I have doubts, I feel that I do believe in God," but nearly 18% of whites feel this way (see descriptive table B.5J). Our multivariate results show that after controlling for relevant background factors, black Protestants are at least *twice* as likely as white Protestants in general and evangelicals[2] in particular to report having no doubt that "God really exists." Blacks are confident in their faith because they strongly believe that they as individuals and African Americans as a collective group would not have made it in this country *but for the grace of God.*

Lastly, during the course of our interviews, several interviewees either speculated or directly asked us whether African American Protestants give more money to their church homes than white Protestants do. We went back into our PALS data and examined respondents' financial contributions to their religious congregations (see descriptive table B.5K). In 2005, the average African American Protestant donated $1,647.19 to her or his church, while the average white Protestant donated $2,509.15.[3] (This latter figure should be interpreted with caution since eight of our white Protestant study participants reported giving at least $15,000. These exceptional amounts—some as high as $50,000 —pull whites' average donation amount much higher.)

Our multivariate results for financial contributions testify to the importance of controlling for relevant background factors: black and white Protestants do not meaningfully differ in the amount of money that they gave to their church. Adjusting for income, education, church attendance, age, gender, and region of residence reduces the racial gap in giving to less than $40. This finding is especially meaningful considering that scholars have long since established that more than 80% of African Americans report an income in the lowest 60% of the total U.S. income distribution.[4] That there is no significant difference in the dollar amounts that black and white Protestants give to their respective churches is telling because blacks have significantly less wealth in the first place.[5] African Americans devote so much of their time and limited resources to the church, interpret the Bible literally, pray, and read their Bibles in order to thank God for helping them to "overcome" and "make a way out of no way."

6

Shaded Morality
Not So Black and White

Black religion, then, is . . . a creative and bold wrestling with
history in order to place black bodies in healthier spaces, with
a greater range of possibilities.
        —Anthony B. Pinn, *Terror and Triumph* (2003)

Sherita Wilson, a 37-year-old African American woman,
has been working as a mail clerk at her local south-Atlanta-based post
office for 12 years. The mother of three children aged 13 to 17, she has
been divorced officially for 10 years, but her husband disappeared
13 years ago, when she was four months pregnant with her youngest
child. Unable to hold down a solid-paying, full-time job and faced
with another mouth to feed, her husband simply did not come home
one day. While she occasionally received child-support payments, she
had to find full-time work to keep her family going. Using connections
through her Baptist church, she found her current job at the local
post office.

Life has never been easy for Sherita and her family, but being a
single parent has only intensified her difficulties. The constant struggles to make rent, to get her children to and from school safely, to get
medical care, to be both mother and father, to afford transportation
—all are nearly daily realities. Despite these many ongoing challenges,
Sherita is generally positive and upbeat, often humming gospel songs
to herself throughout the day. She is certain that God is with her, that
God knows and loves her and is watching out for her and her family.
In fact, she says that if *not for the grace of God*, she would not still be

here. God has provided her a church family, a caring and wise pastor, and an extended network of people who, though facing issues of their own, are there for her. She prays "without ceasing" to God, looks to the Bible not only for inspiration but also for answers, and receives counseling from her pastor. Far from being angry with God for her situation, God is, she says, her source of hope and direction.

Sherita (who did not officially enroll in our study but granted us the privilege of an in-depth conversation one day) let us know that when there is a family crisis requiring money that she does not have, she sometimes turns to what she describes as "below the table" dealings. By "below the table," Sherita means getting paid for styling a woman's hair but not reporting the income, or purchasing lottery tickets and then reselling them to people who lack transportation to the local market. In the strict sense, she sees these crisis-alleviating opportunities as wrong—at least in a worldly, socially defined way. She does them on occasion, however, because she believes God wants her and her family to survive and thrive. Thus, Sherita views these occasional activities as morally right in the larger narrative of God's purpose for her. Still, she is quite convinced that when she does something against God's will, He directly punishes her. "If I get out of line, He lets me know real quick: 'Don't be messin' with that.'" Thus, God guides her, providing as needed and at the same time correcting her when she has gone outside of His moral law.

Sherita's story foreshadows the findings presented in this chapter. More specifically, results from our survey and in-depth interview data show that racial group membership color-codes beliefs about morality. The legacy of racial discrimination and equality in America has strongly influenced black and white Protestants' beliefs about right and wrong. We demonstrate this by completing our analysis of the *Survival building block* of black Protestant faith: (2) *black Protestant faith is critical to survival and helps individuals cope with suffering associated with everyday trials and tribulations.*

In this chapter, we examine whether racial group membership influences black and white Protestants' beliefs about whether people's lives have a purpose, what is considered to be right and wrong, whether God punishes people for their sins, and the extent to which people lean on their faith when facing major problems in life. By chapter's end, it will become evident that the past and present consequences of racial stratification have fostered profound faith-based nuances and complexities within the African American Protestant religious tradition. This is because beliefs about morality are often not black and white (pun intended) but rather can be color-coded shades of gray.

Convinced of Purpose but Not What Is Right

In 1967, the German-born sociologist of religion Peter Berger made an important argument in his influential book *The Sacred Canopy*. Religion's ultimate purpose is not to provide happiness and comfort, he wrote, but to push back chaos and meaninglessness. Religion is then, he argued, a sacred canopy of purpose, order, and meaning. Why do humans toil? Why do we exist in the first place? Various religions answer such questions differently, but what religions have in common is that they provide answers to such questions.

We asked black and white Protestants in the PALS how much they agreed with the following fundamental statement: "I believe there is some real purpose for my life." When people agree with such a question, they likely feel that their own individually lived life means something beyond merely fate or chance. Such people believe they exist for a clear reason: to do something, to be something, that they were created for someone. From a Christian perspective, God created humans with a purpose (perhaps to love God, to do good works for God, to improve the lives of others, or more generally, to glorify God). Indeed, our survey findings show that 72% of white Protestants "strongly agree" that there is some real purpose for their life. However, more than 90% of black Protestants do so (see descriptive table B.6A). After accounting for relevant background factors between black and white Protestants (such as where they live, educational and income levels, age, how often they attend church), our multivariate results show that the odds that black Protestants believe that there is a real purpose to their lives are up to three times that of white Protestants in general and evangelicals in particular.

Why are African American Protestants in such agreement that their lives have a purpose? And why are they so much more likely to agree their lives have a purpose than are white Protestants? In our interview with Dr. James Cone, he emphasized that in a racially stratified society such as the United States, the personhood and value of black Americans has long been questioned—directly and indirectly. Thus, he believes that black religion works to counteract the dynamics of race-based oppression and privilege in society: "Whites don't need religion to give them a purpose in quite the same way that blacks do. African Americans have so much to work against them in a society that says they don't have a purpose. So they really reach down to that deep spiritual source to give them purpose, in spite of what they have to cope with."

Indeed, theologians and scholars of black religion have identified as fundamental to black religion its provisions for identity and purpose. For instance, scholars Nicholas Cooper-Lewter and Henry Mitchell discuss in their book *Soul Theology* the ten core "soul affirmations" of African Americans. These affirmations include that each person is wholly unique and fully worthy of respect. Life has meaning because God has individually breathed into each person purpose, uniqueness, and worth. They trace this affirmation to its African religious roots (which, incidentally, is consistent with our *Mystery building block of black Protestant faith*): "In African traditional belief, souls appear before God and receive their unique character. The Yoruba call it one's 'ori'; the Ashanti call it 'kra.' In both cases it means an unchangeable destiny as well as a character of personality."[1]

Scholar of black religion Anthony Pinn, in his influential book *Terror and Triumph: The Nature of Black Religion*, goes even further. He argues that black religion is in its essence a quest for *complex subjectivity*. Let us explain what he means by this. The history of blacks in the United States has been characterized by continual reduction to singular caricatures: from being viewed by whites as mere property during slavery to the more general view as infantile bodies controlled by oppression, discrimination, and prejudice—inferior in every way to whites. Given these contexts, Pinn argues that the essence of black religion is to counter such reductionist, simplistic views and instead to "imply *more*—more possibilities, more complexity, more vitality."[2] The quest for complex subjectivity, then, "means the desired move from being corporeal objects controlled by oppressive and essentializing forces to becoming a complex conveyor of cultural meaning, with a complex and creative identity."[3] According to Pinn, black religion instills meaning, purpose, and identity by making whole those persons constantly viewed as something less than.

For African Americans, then, religion helps to build individual and group-based self-esteem by counteracting the historical and contemporary barrage of race-based negative images, thoughts, and practices. African American Protestants may be in such strong agreement that their lives have a purpose because—given the foundational function of black religion—identity, meaning, purpose, wholeness (i.e., complex subjectivity) are stressed in churches and among black Christians. It is no surprise, then, that our survey findings also reveal the following: those African Americans who attend church more frequently are *even more likely* to be in agreement that their lives have a purpose than are African Americans who attend less frequently.

We personally have witnessed an emphasis on lives having meaning and purpose in black churches to a degree, frequency, and intensity that we have not observed in white churches (this, of course, is not to say that white churches do not emphasize meaning and purpose). That black lives have a purpose is taught in religious educational classes, in choir rehearsal, and in youth groups and events; it is proclaimed powerfully from the pulpit; and it is communicated in events, bulletins, websites, and much more. ("I Am Somebody," the widely popular call-and-response poem often recited by the Rev. Jesse Jackson, is a classic example of blacks' attention to meaning and purpose.) The central message? "Don't you let anyone question your worth. You stand tall. You are created by God and have been designed for a purpose. You matter, we matter." The cultural context in which African Americans live, as Dr. Cone noted, demands a faith that says humans do indeed have a purpose. And as Pinn writes, the very essence of black religious conversion and black religion is that "blacks no longer simply wonder if they are more than objects of history. A recognition that they are much more than this becomes the 'real self,' the center of consciousness."[4]

Given the high agreement among African Americans Protestants that their lives have a purpose and given that, compared to white Protestants, they pray more, attend religious services more, and engage in many other high expressions of religiosity, the following finding may strike some readers as counterintuitive: black Protestants are significantly more likely than white Protestants to agree with the statement "It is sometimes okay to break moral rules if it works to your advantage and you can get away with it." Our findings indicate that the vast majority of Protestants, regardless of their race, at least "disagree" with the statement (see descriptive table B.6B). However, our multivariate results show that compared to white Protestants, black Protestants are more than one and half times as likely to agree with this statement. Thus, even when we account for differences in other factors (income, education, church attendance, age, gender, and region of residence), black Protestants—whether we compare them to white Protestants generally or white evangelicals specifically—are significantly more likely to agree that it is at times okay to break moral rules.

This finding did not, however, come as a surprise to the high-ranking clergy whom we interviewed. Nearly all were careful to say they were offering an explanation of—not a justification for—the finding's meaning. Their responses were clearly based on the current racial order and the racialized past. They specifically or indirectly referred to racial inequality, segregation, slavery, a lack of political inclusion, oppression, or social power in their explanations for why African American Protestants' view of morality can at times dramatically differ from white Protestants' view of morality.

Before we fully delve into our interviewees' main themes, we should point out that Rev. Johnson, the senior pastor at a large Baptist church in the Dallas–Fort Worth area, strongly opposed a belief that some blacks hold: "[It] justifies breaking the rules and letting it work to my advantage because I'm just simply doing to 'the man' (i.e., white America) what has always been done to me and my family. That mentality, unfortunately, exists." Although he believes that "historically, America and her government and all her institutions have been so incredibly unfair and unjust in every conceivable way toward African Americans," he does not believe that racism should have any bearing on blacks' understanding of morality: "By the way, I totally, 100 percent disagree with that mind-set. It is absolutely wrong because our mommas taught us that two wrongs don't make a right. You cannot ultimately have the peace of God and God on your side if you knowingly are engaging in an action that you see is wrong but you justify it based on racism [from whites]. That's unscriptural and un-Christlike thinking."

Rev. Johnson was the only interviewee to assert this opinion so candidly. By contrast, most of our interviewees argued that black Protestants sometimes willingly break the rules because many of our nation's laws have been purposely designed to hold African Americans back. Regardless of whether our remaining interviewees are Baptist, Methodist, or Pentecostal, the region of the United States in which they reside, and whether they preside over big or small congregations, they linked racial differences in beliefs about morality with the legacy of racial discrimination and inequality in America.[5]

For instance, Pastor Jenkins, an assistant pastor at a small Pentecostal congregation in Los Angeles, stated, "White people tend to play by the rules because they created the rules." Similarly, Rev. Shannon, an A.M.E. assistant pastor from Cleveland, declared that many of our nation's laws and rules—such as those that provided the legal framework for Jim Crow segregation—specifically aimed to "keep blacks down":

Sometimes as black folks, we think the rules were not made for us. They were made for white America, and if you don't break the rules, then you are going to always be behind the eight ball. So sometimes you've got to break the rules because the rule was not created to benefit you. That's what Dr. Martin Luther King did. For example, the rule that blacks could not sit and eat at lunch counters in the South—that was a rule, and it needed to be broken.

Significantly, 8 of the 14 high-ranking clergy members whom we interviewed specifically stated or implied that racial differences in morality were fostered by slavery, not segregation. Take Pastor Thomas's point, for instance. His rationale clearly supports our *Survival building block of black Protestant faith*:

My response almost sounds like an excuse, but I think it's part of our survival technique. We know the odds are against us, even going back to slavery. The notion of "tricking the master," trying to "outwit" the oppressor, and [proclaiming] falsehoods were part of our survival strategy. Even after slavery, we still don't receive justice, and if we need to break the rules in order to get our fair due, then that's what we'll do. Again, that's an explanation, not a justification.

Interviewer: What do you mean "survival"?

[I mean] trying to make ends meet, trying to have enough food on the table, being able to pay your bills so you don't get evicted and so the lights don't get cut off.

Rev. Washington, of Ohio, fully agrees. His point speaks to the moral consequences of white Christians' historic failure to practice what they have preached with respect to how they have subjugated blacks:

Well, this reminds me of a number of the slave narratives. We're back to the difference between *doctrine versus practice.*

A slave narrative goes something like this: The master's preacher came and said to the slaves, "Don't steal your master's hogs. Don't steal your master's chickens. Don't steal whatsoever belongs to your master." After he finished talking, amongst themselves, the slaves decided that they weren't "stealing." They were just getting an honest day's pay for an honest day's work.

Pastor Jenkins, Rev. Shannon, Pastor Thomas, Rev. Washington, and nearly all of our remaining interviewees argued that many of our nation's past and present laws and rules have been racially biased, made to advance the interests of whites while penalizing blacks. Thus, they believe that African Americans must survive by often violating the "man-made" rules that whites have put in place. This rationale was best explained by Rev. Robinson. He connected the dots between slavery, Christ's messages, and everyday survival:

Let me go back to the point about slaves obeying their masters. Let's say the slave master whipped me. Jesus's commandment to love your neighbor and that in Christ there is neither male nor female, slave or free, is being ignored. Why must I obey my master when I look around me and there is a lot of rule bending going on?

It's not that a black person is less committed to morality than a white person, but you've got to take the *spirit* of the law into account. Sometimes that causes the rules to be bent a little bit. We see Jesus doing that kind of thing, when they accused Him of not obeying the law by healing on the Sabbath day. Well, then He comes in and says, "The Sabbath day was made for man, not man for the Sabbath."

When David was hungry, he went into the temple and took the bread and ate. That's breaking the rules. You've got to look at the *larger issues*; you've got to look at whether a human is being violated, or you've got to take into account these other factors.

Also, from a survival mentality, people will say, "I've got to forget about the rules to survive. My baby is hungry, so rules be damned."

Nearly all our interviewees who advanced an epistemological explanation for our survey finding told us that the real question boils down to this: what is more important, *man's rules* or *God's rules*? As one might imagine, our interviewees argued that African Americans place a much stronger emphasis on God's rules—and so accordingly they might appear to violate man's rules. Deacon Harris, the director of Christian counseling at a New York City megachurch, explained this tension within the context of *liberation theology*:

Well, it depends on what they [our survey participants] mean by "the rules." In general, I think that your survey finding represents us blacks being typically on the outside and that most of the so-called rules of the society don't work for us, they work against us. Also that we have a different view about the rules, and so whatever those rules are, any kind of societal rules, I think that we've not equated those rules necessarily with the word of God. Societal laws are the word of the people that are *in control*. It's not the word of God no matter what they say about it.

So it's just like being a runaway slave. The master told us, "Don't run away." But if God says "run away," then in our minds that's real freedom. That's what *liberation theology* is all about. Martin Luther King said, "I've got a higher law than the laws of segregation." So I think that's a part of what is in our [black] culture and why we would justify that. We can see that there's a [social] system that is not necessarily fair and not necessarily helpful. The system confines who we are and doesn't take into account who we are.

A focus group member from Cleveland advanced a similar point. He said, "There's a whole lot of things people call 'rules,' but they're really not *God's rules*." A few moments later, another parishioner added,

Christ came to liberate the oppressed, break the bonds and yokes of bondage to set the captives free. So, if you're talking about a person like Martin Luther King who broke the rules, in terms of segregation, that was illegal, immoral, or whatever. He broke the rules, but he didn't do it for his advantage. He did it for *liberation*. You can break the rules if the rules are unjust, if the system is oppressive, if it's working to the detriment of the people of God.

All of these religious leaders and lay people essentially said that same thing: that the legacy of racial discrimination and inequality has profoundly influenced black Protestants' understanding of morality. Additional survey findings corroborate their opinion. For example, we found racial differences in beliefs about the role that religion plays in shaping attitudes about the basis of right and wrong. More specifically, 72% of black Protestants believe that "God's law" provides the basis of right and wrong, while only 59% of white Protestants feel this way (see descriptive table B.6C). Furthermore, a more substantial minority of white Protestants (35%) than of black Protestants (24%) believe that the basis of right and wrong is "a matter of personal conscience." Our multivariate results show that these wide differences withstand more rigorous tests of scientific scrutiny: black Protestants are significantly more likely than white Protestants to say that right and wrong are "based on God's law." They are also less likely to assert that right and wrong are a matter of "personal conscience." Thus, reminiscent of the words of Rev. Dr. Martin Luther King, Jr., and other African American religious leaders, God's rules are *higher*, universal, and more humanitarian than man's rules. As result, sometimes laws—even when they are labeled "moral rules"—must be broken in order to bring about more equitable and just circumstances for individuals and groups. Sherita, whom we met at the beginning of this chapter, seemed to echo this perspective.

Still additional findings support our contention that racial group membership color-codes beliefs about morality. For instance, black and white Protestants in the GSS were asked the following question: "Right and wrong are not usually a simple matter of black and white; there are many shades of gray." Based on our previous findings, we would expect that African American Protestants would be more likely to agree with this statement. That is exactly what we found. Although 80% of both black and white Protestants at least "agree" with this statement, nearly half of black Protestants "strongly agree" that when it comes to right and wrong, there are many shades of gray, as compared to 39% of white Protestants (see descriptive table B.6D). Our multivariate findings uncover yet another *suppressor effect*: the difference between blacks and whites becomes magnified once we account for differences across relevant background factors such as age, income, education, church attendance, and region of residence. In fact, the gap grows wider when we restrict the analysis to black Protestants and white evangelicals.

Perhaps the greater willingness to sometimes break earthly rules in favor of God's rules is also related to other survey findings. We found that a greater percentage of African American Protestants than white Protestants believe that "those who violate God's rules must be punished," and that blacks more often feel that God has personally punished them for their sins or lack of spirituality (see descriptive tables B.6E and B.6F). The former black/white Protestant difference—"those who violate God's rules must be punished"—is wiped away by controlling for relevant background factors. However, the latter black/white Protestant difference—"how often have you felt that God is punishing you for your sins or lack of spirituality?"—holds steady. A majority of white Protestants say that God has "never" punished them for their sins or lack of spirituality, while the majority of black Protestants say that God has at least "rarely" punished them. This is a profound difference in worldview (not to mention that the survey item is time specific in that it concerns the "last three years"). At the very least, this finding expresses a significant racial difference in understandings of who God is—what God is like, what God does. In this case, the majority of black Protestants seem to view God as punisher or judge; the majority of white Protestants do not view God in this way.

We wondered about this finding, so we consulted a battery of GSS items from the early 1980s that assessed people's views of God. (These early survey items dramatically differ in content from the more recent ones that we discussed in chapter 3.)[6] Specifically, people were asked how likely it is that their image of God is a "judge," a "redeemer," a "lover," a "master," a "mother," a "father," a "creator," a "spouse," a "friend," a "king," a "liberator," or a "healer." We tested for differences between black and white Protestants and found interesting patterns— ones that are consistent with our results thus far. First, when the characteristic of God was a benevolent characteristic—redeemer, lover, creator, friend, healer—we found either no difference or little difference between white and black Protestants. However, when the characteristic of God was either as an authority (judge, master, king), familial (father, mother, spouse), or linked to the black theology of God as liberator, the differences were substantial. Slightly less than half of white Protestants were extremely likely to view God as a judge, but two-thirds of black Protestants were extremely likely to do so. Only 21% of white Protestants were extremely likely to view a characteristic of God as mother, whereas 57% of black Protestants held such a view. Less than half of white Protestants were extremely likely to view God as a liberator, while two-thirds of black Protestants were extremely likely to view God in this way.

Sociologists Paul Froese and Christopher Bader classify American believers into four main groups in their well-received work on views of God: those who view God as primarily *authoritarian* (that is, involved and judging), those who view God as primarily *benevolent* (that is, involved and loving), those who view God as *critical* (uninvolved but judging), and those who view God as *distant* (uninvolved, uncaring). They found that even if the comparisons are limited to white evangelicals, black Protestants are more likely to view God as authoritarian. If the comparison group is white Protestants more broadly, the gap grows even larger. Again, then, we see evidence of racial differences in what characteristics of God are emphasized.[7]

The evidence is consistent—black and white Protestants emphasize different aspects of God (in chapter 7, we address this finding in even greater detail). Black Protestants see God as a greater authority figure, more familial, and more often a liberator of humanity. They view God as a central family figure who punishes people for their sins but also understands when breaking rules is not sin but rather is necessary. Although the discussion in chapter 3 suggests that black and white Protestants do not worship different Gods, the differences in what *attributes* of God are emphasized are large enough that at least to some people it seems as if these believers are worshiping different Gods. This is precisely what Derek Hicks meant when he argued in chapter 2 that black and white Protestants have "dueling evocations of the same God."

Dealing with Major Problems

In the early 1980s, on a skit for the television show *Saturday Night Live*, the comedian Eddie Murphy, who is black, wonders what it might be like to be white. He decides to go "undercover," disguised as a white man. After his transformation by the makeup artists is complete, he sets out in New York City. What he discovers in this spoof is that life as a white man is amazingly trouble-free. He first goes into a convenience store, where he is the only customer, and attempts to buy a newspaper. After selecting a newspaper, he walks up and places the money for the paper on the counter. The white sales clerk asks the white Murphy, "What are you doing?" "I'm buying this newspaper," responds Murphy in his "white" voice. The sales clerk replies, "That's all right, there's nobody around. Go ahead, take it." As he is saying this, he also hands Murphy his money back. Seemingly shell-shocked, Murphy slowly takes the paper and the money, looking confused the entire time.

In Murphy's narration to explain what the viewer has just witnessed, he says, "Slowly I began to realize that when white people are alone, they give things to each other, for free." While the narration is occurring, Murphy is shown waiting at a city bus stop. Entering the bus, we see several white people and one black man (other than Murphy, who of course is disguised as white). All seems normal, until the black man pulls the stop string and exits at Forty-Fifth Street. With only white people on the bus, the white bus driver then switches on some refined "white" music, and one of the passengers removes her coat, revealing that she is in fact an attractive cocktail waitress who is now passing out free glasses of Champaign. She is even flirting with the white male passengers. Over this scene of happy white people, lightly dancing to the refined music and drinking Champaign, Murphy's narration says, "The problem was much more serious than I had ever imagined."

In the final scene, Murphy is sitting in a bank, requesting a loan from an African American loan officer. The black loan officer, noting that Murphy would like to borrow $50,000 from the bank (keep in mind that this is in early 1980s dollars), points out that he has no collateral, no credit, not even any identification. He tells Murphy that he is sorry, but the bank is not a "charity, it is a business." At that point, a white loan officer, overhearing the conversation, steps in and tells the black loan officer to take his break now and that he will go ahead and take care of Murphy (who we learn is named Mr. White). The white loan officer—named Bob—and Murphy, now alone, begin to chuckle. Bob says to Murphy, "That was a close one, wasn't it?" And as Bob tears up the loan application, he says, "We don't have to bother with these formalities, do we Mr. White?" Murphy, by this time a seasoned white person, leans toward Bob and says of the black loan officer, "What a silly Negro." And to that, both Bob and "Mr. White" have a hearty laugh. While still laughing, Bob pulls out a metal box full of cash, telling Murphy, "Just take what you want." And he says, "Pay us back any time, or don't. We don't care." Another hearty chuckle is shared by the two of them. Clearly, life as a white person is one of surprising ease, in which society's rules do not seem to apply or at least a different set of rules exist.

Of course, this was a skit, meant to be humorous, ridiculous, and make-believe. But humor, to work well, must be rooted within at least a seed of truth. As we saw in the previous section, many (indeed most) of the high-ranking clergy members whom we interviewed said that the rules of society simply do not apply in the same way to whites, that the rules are set up to serve the interests of whites or, in some cases, that a very different set of rules applies to whites and blacks. As a consequence, as in the skit, it seems that whites—armed with a different set of rules, or rules made to serve their interests, and armed with a much greater array of resources—have fewer problems. Not only do they seem to have fewer problems, but the problems they have seem less severe; and they have many more places to turn to address whatever problems they might have. Conversely, African Americans have more problems, more severe problems, and far less access to the power structure of the nation and to material resources. The vast literature on racial inequalities bears this out repeatedly, from poverty to unemployment to incarceration rates to health issues to the chances of a family member or friend being murdered. As the scholar Elizabeth Anderson writes after her extensive review of black/white life differences, "African Americans are worse off . . . than whites on virtually all major objective measures of well-being. These inequalities are large and enduring and have grown in some cases."[8]

Here, to give concreteness to this issue, we name just a few of these objective measures. Nearly one-third of black children will experience poverty for 10 or more years while growing up in the United States; less than 1 percent of white children will experience the same.[9] Black men are imprisoned at *six and half times* the rate of white men. In fact, incredibly, there is about a one-third chance that a black man will be imprisoned at some point in his life. If he was born after 1975 and did not finish high school, the lifetime chance of imprisonment is an astronomical sixty nine percent.[10] Black men are *11 times* as likely as white men to die of homicide, so the experiences of losing two close friends to murder described by author Derek Hicks in chapter 2 is vastly more common for African Americans.[11] Middle-class blacks, as compared to middle-class whites, are three times *less* likely to be able to pass on their middle-class status to their children. That is, their children are three times as likely as the children of middle-class whites to end up poor.[12] African Americans live shorter lives than do whites, and they suffer from many more physical ailments. In health terms, then, on average African Americans have a lower quality of life. They also have a substantially more difficult time being approved for loans, and when they are, they pay on average higher fees and higher interest rates. They are much more likely than whites, when approved for a loan, to receive subprime and predatory loans. Under such unfavorable conditions, not surprisingly, blacks are more likely to experience foreclosure on their homes than are whites.[13] Black neighborhoods, even if we account for income differences between blacks and whites, have fewer supermarkets, banks, non-fast-food restaurants, retail outlets, movie theaters, parks, and other consumer services than do white neighborhoods.[14] We could go on—from lower salaries and substantially less wealth to greater unemployment to the likelihood of being burglarized to the likelihood of being discriminated against —but the point is clear: African Americans experience more measurable problems.

Given the greater religiosity and role of God and faith in the lives of black Protestants—coupled with the social, political, and economic realities that lead to trials and tribulations in daily life—we would expect that African Americans would turn to several spiritual resources in search of solutions. Deacon Harris stated it this way: "Being that most African Americans are dealing with so many problems [compared to whites], . . . they're trying to find answers and using as many resources as they can to find the answers." Similarly, Pastor Thomas told us that given the great difficulties that blacks face, African American Protestants often think, "If I do my part, then God's going to do His part. So I have to pray more. I've got to see what the pastor has to say. I've got to see what my prayer partner says about this. I've got to read my scripture. That's just been engrained in us."

Has it? When faced with major problems in life, are black Protestants more likely to use faith-based tools and outlets than white Protestants are? In other words, are black Protestants more likely to turn to their faith when facing major problems in life? To find out, we asked our PALS respondents a series of questions that all began with this statement: "Think about how you have tried to understand

and deal with major problems in your life over the last three years. To what extent did you [1] try to make sense of the situation and decide what to do on your own? [2] consider passages in the Bible? [3] consider church teachings or talk to a religious leader? [4] talk with people in your church? [5] look to God or a larger spiritual force for strength, support, and guidance?" Our respondents could select from the following answer categories: "not at all," "a little," "quite a bit," or "a great deal."

Our survey results are telling (see descriptive tables B.6G through B.6K). The first finding to note is that, though always the minority of our sample, for each of the five questions, more whites than blacks simply said the question did not apply to them, meaning they did not face any major problems over the last three years. But when they do face major problems, how do they deal with them? Interestingly, for each of our five questions African Americans Protestants were more likely to say "a great deal." They were more likely to try to make sense of the situation and decide what to do on their own (61% versus 45% for white Protestants), to consider passages in the Bible a great deal (59%, versus 28%), to consider church teachings or talk to religious leaders (41% versus 19%), to talk with people in their church (28% versus 18%), and to look to God or a larger spiritual force for strength, support, and guidance (72% versus 46%).

That African American Protestants turn to the five ways we listed to deal with major problems more than whites do is no surprise, given that they are faced with more problems. The more interesting comparison given our focus is to examine the *black/white Protestant gap* in the likelihood of using each of these means, relative to using other means. Let us examine these comparisons. In dealing with major problems, black Protestants are 1.36 times more likely (61% divided by 45% for white Protestants) to try making sense of the situation and deciding on one's own a great deal. This is the smallest gap of any of the ways of dealing with major problems. In all the remaining ways—all of which are religiously based ways—the gap between black and white Protestants is larger: black Protestants are one and a half times more likely than white Protestants to talk with people in their church a great deal, one and a half times more likely to look to God a great deal, more than *twice* as likely to consider church teachings or talk to religious leaders a great deal, and more than *twice* as likely to consider passages in the Bible a great deal. Our multivariate results show that for all of these questions (except for talking to people in one's church), these significant gaps remain after accounting for the relevant background factors. They remain too if we narrow the comparison to just black Protestants and white evangelicals. Thus, although in times of trouble black Protestants turn a great deal to all the means of addressing these problems more than white Protestants do, *it is the religiously based means where the black/white Protestant differences are greatest.*

We also can learn about differences in who or what black and white Protestants turn to in times of trouble by examining *the ordering within each group.* For white Protestants, when they face problems, they are equally likely to look to God a great deal and to decide what to do on their own (46% and 45%, respectively). They turn to the Bible a great deal (28%), church teachings or religious leaders a great deal (19%), and people in their church a great deal (18%) much less often. However, for black Protestants, they are most likely to look to God a great deal (72%). They are about equally likely to turn to their own understanding and consider Bible passages a great deal (61% and 59%, respectively), and sizable minorities of blacks turn to church teachings or religious leaders a great deal (41%) and talk with people in their church a great deal (28%).

Even after adjusting for differences in socioeconomic status, region of residence, religious attendance, and other factors, black Protestants clearly turn to religious sources more often than white Protestants do when confronting major problems. The high-ranking clergy members whom we interviewed had much to say about these patterns. For instance, Rev. Johnson linked blacks' reliance on multiple faith-based outlets to their African cultural sensibility and the institutional centrality of the contemporary black church:

> I think it may go back to African tribal traditions, as well as slavery
> and the development of Christianity in America. The African tribal

tradition had a chief, and if you had an issue or problem, you went to the chief, and it was his job to help you solve your problem. That tradition was carried over to the African American church. And in many ways, the pastor became the tribal chief, and the church became the place that was expected to address your major problems and issues. Additionally, the black church was the only black institution that was economically independent from the white power structure. So black preachers and the laity could say and do what they wanted without fear.

For the most part, you could go to the black church and seek help, counseling, encouragement, or whatever. They often had answers to someone's situation that you couldn't get anywhere else. This is why the Civil Rights Movement was really more of a church movement than a secular social movement.

Rev. Washington also emphasized the historical importance of the black church. He says that blacks have historically had few resources to rely on in the larger society, so they look to the church in order find solutions to their problems in life:

Blacks don't have the options that whites have. See, now we're back to the sociopolitical, socioeconomic, and dynamics of power. If a white man has a financial problem, before he starts to lean on God or go to the church or to his pastor, he's got a relative or friend that's got the economics to help him. If he's having emotional and psychological problems, he's got the money to pay a psychiatrist, sociologist, or psychologist. So many more options are available to whites because of the sociopolitical and socioeconomic dynamics and differences between blacks and whites.

Historically, the black church has been more central for those things. Lincoln and Mamiya talk about the role of the black church in the black community. There were different halls in the same church: the social hall, the political hall, the economic hall. The church was all of these things because it was our only option. They [blacks] went to the church because they were mistreated in society.

Pastor Thomas told us during his interview that many members of his A.M.E. church espouse the following views: "I can't do this myself; I need God" and "I need to try as many different ways to reach God and to make sure that God is hearing me, to make sure that I'm in line with God's will." A focus group member who attends a small Pentecostal church in Los Angeles advanced a similar assertion. He said, "We believe that Jesus intercedes with God on our behalf, so the more people that you ask to pray for you, the more you're asking for intercession. . . . You're pleading your case before God just as Jesus does for us." In short, for various reasons and in various ways, black Protestants are more likely to turn to religion for answers and more likely, given their communal emphasis, to look to multiple religious sources.

It has already become apparent that many of the high-ranking clergy members whom we interviewed believe that white Protestants have far more societal "options" or outlets for seeking assistance than black Protestants do. (By now, it should be clear that this recurring theme was mentioned by most of our interviewees irrespective of the particular questions that we asked them.) This belief is also rooted in sociohistorical realities. Many of our interviewees would agree with Rev. Shannon's assertion that "white Christians have other resources to get answers. They've never had the Bible pulled away. They've never had a slave master bar them from reading." Thus, they believe that the dynamics of racial oppression and privilege have allowed whites to take many things—including their faith in many ways—for granted. As a result, they feel that white Protestants (a) may not appreciate as deeply the value of their religious resources because they have been able to control their production and availability, (b) have a long tradition of looking elsewhere—themselves, family, or friends—for answers and assistance, and (c) are more individualistic than communal. (Such assertions are consistent with Deacon Harris's assertion from chapter 4 that whites are more "inner-focused," while blacks are more "outer-focused.") So what are the implications of a, b, and c? In short, our interviewees believe that white Protestants are more secular in their beliefs and practices when it comes to addressing major problems in their personal lives. And as has been the leitmotiv of this book, black Protestants are not just at times differently religious; religion fundamentally is more thoroughly infused as a way of life.

Revisiting the Building Blocks

The results of this chapter provide further support for our *Survival building block of black Protestant faith*. African American Protestants believe in an involved God who is concerned with each person in each community and helps to instill an ultimate sense of meaning and purpose. We also learned that black Protestants are more likely to say it is acceptable to sometimes violate "man-made" moral rules and that right and wrong are more adequately described by the color gray than black and white. This is because many African American Protestants believe that some of our nation's laws were intentionally designed to protect whites' political, social, and economic interests. As a result, black Protestants place a premium on following *God's rules* over and above *man's rules*.

The empirical evidence presented here closely corresponds with what scholars of black religion have written about the nature of religion and God for African Americans. Given the social context of the United States, African American Protestants' belief in a God who is involved with meaning, purpose, and wholeness—yet also punishes people for their sins—attests to the importance of complex subjectivity, liberation, and the role that religion plays in overcoming suffering.[15]

As a final note and illustration of the depth of racial differences in relying on religious resources, two additional survey findings stand out. Despite the fact that African Americans face substantially more measurable worldly challenges than whites do, black Protestants are no more likely than white Protestants to say that God has "abandoned" them (see descriptive table B.6L). Moreover, a higher percentage of blacks report having "never" been "angry" with God (69% compared to 54%; see descriptive table B.6M). This latter gap remains even after holding constant background differences between black and white Protestants, such as age, income, and church attendance. Thus, it underscores our argument that black Protestant faith aids in coping with trials and tribulations and is critical to surviving and thriving in the United States. Despite all of the big and small problems average African American Protestants have faced, they have not been angry with God or felt that He has left their side. This is because blacks use their faith as a supernatural call for help to protect against the historical and contemporary consequences of racial stratification.

7

Far-Reaching Faith
Evidence of an Inclusive Religious Doctrine

Beginning with this chapter, we expand our investigation beyond widely recognized domains of Christianity. While some of the topics that we examine are closely associated with Christianity (such as beliefs about angels and miracles), others are typically not associated with Christianity (such as beliefs about astrology and reincarnation). Our analysis of these religiously related though not distinctly "Christian" topics helps us to specify the extent to which religious identities among black and white Protestants are shaped by thoughts and practices beyond the boundaries of conventional (i.e., mainline or evangelical) Christianity.

As will soon become clear, most of the high-ranking clergy members whom we interviewed expressed at least some form of dismay or bewilderment with the findings presented in this chapter. Some even conveyed great consternation. It is safe to say that the results discussed here are the most controversial and contentious thus far. For instance, several of our interviewees (most notably Rev. Robinson, Pastor Thomas, and Rev. Washington) declined to answer questions about our survey findings until *we* answered *their* questions about our research methodology. They were so taken aback by some of our results that they asked us to provide details on how we selected our study participants and analyzed the data.

Our goal in this chapter is to develop the *Mystery* and *Miraculous building blocks of black Protestant faith*: (3) *black Protestant faith is mystical and expresses an appreciation for the mystery in life; it includes folklore and cultural components deriving from the African Diaspora, the consequences of racial inequality in America, and non-Christian religions,* and (4) *black Protestant faith is confident and comprehensive; the miraculous is ordinary and the ordinary is miraculous.* We have already established that African American Protestants are more resolute in their faith that God exists than are white Protestants and that they subscribe to a "definitive" interpretation of the Bible that inspires them to pray, to attend worship services, and to engage in certain religious activities more often than white Protestants do. However, the results that we are about disclose reveal the complexity of the African American Protestant religious tradition: the *black sacred cosmos* is also theologically far-reaching. That is, it often embraces beliefs and actions associated with non-Christian religions and alternative supernatural beliefs that conflict with traditional church teachings.

Consequently, by the end of this chapter, it will become abundantly clear that the black sacred cosmos is simultaneously both theologically *broad and definitive.* It is *definitive* in that the African American Protestant religious tradition includes a conservative attentiveness to and focus on Christianity that, statistically speaking at least, largely surpasses that of white Protestants. Yet it is also *broad* in that the African American Protestant religious tradition includes a liberal welcoming space for faith-based beliefs and actions that many passionate believers (both black and white) do not consider to be "Christlike." Thus, while the African American Protestant religious tradition toes a very hard line with respect to its dedication and devotion to conventional Christianity, it also incorporates seemingly contradictory or atypical practices and convictions.

Is Being a "Good Person" Good Enough?

One especially revealing finding sets the tone for explaining the open-mindedness, tolerance, and recognition of diversity that is intrinsic to the African American Protestant religious tradition. The PALS contains a survey item that gauges the extent to which study participants "agree" with the following statement: "It doesn't much matter what I believe so long as I am a good person." This question sheds light on whether the Protestants in our study place greater emphasis on (a) their religious beliefs or (b) a favorable evaluation of their personal character irrespective of their religious beliefs. Before proceeding, it is necessary to provide context for interpreting the results for this item. We are confident that the vast majority of evangelical Christians would "disagree" with the aforementioned statement, and they indeed do.[1] They probably do so for two reasons. First, generally speaking, evangelicals believe that a person's religious beliefs and religious affiliations are critical to determining whether they themselves or some other person is worthy of being considered a "good person." And second, evangelicals tend to believe that *God* ultimately decides who is a "good person."

According to our findings, 44% of black Protestants at least "agree" with the statement "It doesn't much matter what I believe so long as I am a good person." In contrast, only 35% of white Protestants feel this way (see descriptive table B.7A). This initial finding suggests that a sizable minority of African American Protestants place a stronger emphasis on a positive evaluation of one's personal character than on his or her specific religious beliefs. Our multivariate results corroborate this finding. In fact, African American Protestants are *twice* as likely as white Protestants to emphasize the importance of having a favorable assessment of their own personal character. Furthermore, the racial gap widens significantly when we limit our analysis to black Protestants and white evangelicals: African Americans are nearly *three times* as likely as white evangelicals to "agree" with the statement. Thus, it appears that African American Protestants are more likely to be among the minority of Protestants who accentuate an assessment of one's personal character apart from their religious beliefs, while white evangelicals are more likely to be among the majority who emphasize the importance of one's particular religious beliefs and affiliations. Another way to describe this is that blacks tend to emphasize what people "do," while whites tend to emphasize what people "believe."

Why would this be so? That African American Protestants emphasize a positive evaluation of their personal character over and above their religious beliefs seemingly conflicts with their focused attentiveness to Christianity. If African Americans are such impassioned and literal believers, why would they minimize the importance of their religious faith? Depending on who is asked, the answer to this question is either incredibly complex or remarkably simple (at least that is what our interviewees seemed to say). According to at least five of the high-ranking clergy whom we interviewed, it is "simple" in the sense that for various epistemological reasons, African American Protestants lack a profound theological understanding of what it "means to be Christian." However, to at least six others, the answer to this question is "complex" because it forces us to consider how for blacks, the legacy of racial discrimination and inequality has fostered a deeply embedded respect and appreciation for faith-based thoughts and practices that differ from their own.

Still, a third yet much less popular sentiment emerged: our finding that African Americans place a stronger emphasis on a favorable assessment of one's personal character rather than on her or his religious beliefs evoked discomfort and confusion. These pastors—whose rationales fit in squarely with our previously discussed reasons for why evangelicals would "disagree" with the survey statement—were convinced that the average African American Protestant believes the same thing that they do: that being a "good person" is *not* good enough. Rev. Johnson's statement best captures this perplexity:

I would absolutely disagree with that understanding—*if* that's an accurate reflection of what many African American Christians believe. It doesn't matter what you believe, as long as you are a good person? Uh, uh, nope. [*He stares intently and shakes his head right and left as if saying "no."*] Belief matters, truth matters. As a matter of fact, eternity hinges specifically on what you believe. It's a part of your ultimate destiny.

Now, if what they [our African American study participants] mean is that a non-Christian can be a responsible, productive, good citizen, and a great neighbor, or co-worker, then the answer is "yes." Absolutely. But what a person believes about Jesus Christ is pivotal to ethics, personal responsibility, and witness of evangelism. So, no, I would have to disagree with the idea that as long as you're a good person, belief is somewhat inconsequential.

This comment typifies evangelicals' nearly exclusive focus on what an individual believes about Christ. But while only three interviewees discussed our survey results in this way, they are still in the majority because most of the high-ranking clergy we sat down with would agree that "belief matters, truth matters." Denomination, education, location, and congregation size aside, our interviewees similarly believe that (a) Christians in general should accentuate their religious beliefs over and above a positive assessment of their personal character and (b) in a profoundly deep and existential way, a person's religious affiliation *with Christianity* is critical in determining whether someone is a "good person." It is worth noting that there is little disagreement as to whether non-Christians in general are "good people." All of our interviewees would probably agree with Rev. Shannon's statement that there are "many wonderful people from many different walks of faith."

While the high-ranking clergy whom we interviewed go about their faith in a religiously conservative way, what distinguishes them from white evangelicals is not that "belief matters, truth matters," but rather that "race matters." This contention, which also logically applies to the average African American Protestant, is not directly stated but undergirds each of the *five building blocks of black Protestant faith.* At least part of the reason why the African American Protestant religious tradition is both theologically *broad* and *definitive* is because race matters. However, our interviewees emphasized different ways that race matters when explaining our survey finding for racial differences in beliefs about being a "good person." For instance, Rev. Boyd was one the pastors who attributed our result to an epistemological gap between blacks' and whites' theological understandings of Christian doctrine. His analysis is consistent with the *academic-versus-experiential dichotomy*:

> Here's what we [African Americans] know about Christianity historically: don't lie, don't cheat, don't steal, be obedient to your parents, and be good. If you're a bad boy, then you're going to get a whippin'. But if you're a good boy, then you're going to get a ho-cake [a popular Southern treat in which cornmeal is sweetened and cooked like a pancake].

See, we understand right and wrong, but we don't know the Bible. We haven't studied it because we haven't had time to. Now, as for the Caucasians, they have studied the cognitive principles of the Bible for more than several generations. They know it back and forth.

Deacon Harris, the director of Christian counseling at a mega-church in New York City, also believes that our survey finding can be attributed to an epistemologically based gap in blacks' and whites' knowledge of Christianity. However, his comment differs from Rev. Boyd's in its scope and content. More specifically, he gives a reasoned analysis for what he sees as a historical lack of theologizing within the black church, an explanation of the significance of religious diversity within the black community, and an assessment for the theological and doctrinal differences between black Protestants and white evangelicals:

> Two things help to explain your survey findings. Number one: I think that evangelical Christianity has been the rule of the day. The evangelicals have done a very good job of writing theology and writing doctrine. Their emphasis is on getting it right; it was a movement to establish—from their perspective at least—the fundamentals of the Christian faith.
>
> Number two: though it is a part of our [African American] history, there is not a lot of strong theologizing in our community. It's only now beginning to emerge. In general, most black Christians are looking at how a person lives their life, what are the results in their life; that's probably why your survey findings are what they are.
>
> For African Americans, it's not so much about what a person believes as a Christian because there's a lot of diversity in our community, and we're used to encountering that diversity. So for us, the proof is in "well, how does a person live?" Many of us are not so much aware of the theological subtleties that are in doctrine because we're not really presented with all of that.

At least half of our interviewees discussed our finding for racial differences in beliefs about being a "good person" within the context of "how a person lives his or her life." These interviewees feel that many blacks believe that the way a person "lives her or his life" is at least as important (if not more so) as the person's actual knowledge of Christianity. (This position is consistent with our argument regarding blacks' commitment to an *experiential* model of Christianity.) It is worth noting that the pastors who articulated this point typically did so within the context of the ongoing debate among Christians over the importance of "faith" (i.e., beliefs) versus "works" (i.e., actions). While Rev. Davis did not specifically mention this, his recognition of this lively debate is implicit in his explanation for our survey findings:

> With Anglos, it's all about precision, but with African Americans, it's all about living. And for us [African Americans], even when you have the right information, it doesn't necessarily mean that you live according to that information that you have.
>
> African Americans are reminded more about God when it comes to the way in which you live your life. On the other hand, whites get specific with respect to knowledge about God. Blacks say things all the time like, "Now you know God don't want you to act like that" or "I don't care how much you know. I want to know how much you care."
>
> If you say those things to Anglos, then you might run into problems.

Finally, our remaining interviewees argued that our finding for racial differences in beliefs about being a "good person" is attributable to a deeply entrenched cultural sensibility among African Americans that honors racial, ethnic, and religious diversity. These interviewees proclaimed that blacks emphasize a positive evaluation of one's personal character over and above one's religious beliefs because they, as a collective group, know what it is like to be treated as an outsider regardless of whether they are a "good person." These interviewees argued that the dynamics of race-based oppression and privilege—most especially slavery—have cultivated a profound sense of open-mindedness and tolerance for others (Christians and non-Christians, blacks and nonblacks alike).

Rev. Henderson, a senior United Methodist pastor in Los Angeles, described what she views as the roots of blacks' recognition of diversity. Her heartfelt contention that the hardships that African Americans have suffered have encouraged them to be accepting of others —even those who have trespassed against them—furthers our understanding for why the African American Protestant religious tradition is both theologically *broad and definitive*. Before articulating the following statement, Rev. Henderson admitted to being surprised by our survey finding. However, she also affirmed that it "makes sense" to her. This is important because while the high-ranking clergy members whom we interviewed do not subscribe to beliefs and practices that are typically not associated with Christianity, most of them understand why some blacks embrace a far-reaching faith that is sometimes at odds with conventional church teachings. Despite their evangelical sensibility, our interviewees never renounced or condemned our survey participants for engaging in beliefs and actions that they themselves deem outside the boundaries of conventional Christianity. This too is a testament to the inherent appreciation of diversity incorporated within the African American Protestant religious tradition. According to Rev. Henderson,

> I think that black people are generally more accepting, welcoming of people, and easier at forgiving than whites. We [African Americans] are just so warm with an unconditional love that we have for people.
> *Interviewer: Why do you think that is?*
> I would venture to say that it probably comes from when we were in slavery and from other hard times that we've had. How could black people learn to love their master after all the things that whites did to them? I think that there was a genuine love that they had for whites. And I think that when people have gone through tough times, when they've struggled, and when people have gone through depression and oppression, it softens their heart, and compassion is born through suffering.
> Christ went through a lot of suffering. And we as black people consider ourselves "Jesus people" because of our suffering.

Realm of the Supernatural

Supernatural phenomena such as angels, devils, and miracles occupy a special place in the minds of many Americans. Religious affiliation aside, a great number of Americans believe that paranormal entities (whether divinely ordained or not) or unexplained unearthly forces (again, whether divinely ordained or not) have a direct impact on our everyday lives. This is because while angels, devils, and miracles are closely associated with organized religion, for a growing number of Americans, these realms of the supernatural are not associated with organized religion at all.[2]

For instance, findings from the Pew Research Center's "U.S. Religious Landscape Survey" of over 36,000 Americans showed that nearly 70% of Americans believe that "angels and demons are active in the world." Not only do overwhelming majorities of Protestants, Catholics, Muslims, Mormons, and Jehovah's Witnesses feel this way, but so do a substantial minority of Buddhists, Hindus, and people who do not claim to be affiliated with a particular religion. Another compelling finding from this survey revealed that, save for Mormons, a majority of followers of each of the aforementioned faiths also believe that "miracles still occur today as in ancient times."[3]

These results show that Americans across a wide range of religious walks of life believe that paranormal entities or forces play an important role in shaping our day-to-day lives. However, a close inspection of the data suggests that racial group membership color-codes attitudes about supernatural phenomena. For instance, findings from the Pew "Landscape Survey" show that there are meaningful differences between black and white Protestants in their beliefs about angels, devils, and miracles.

Let us consider beliefs about angels and devils by racial group membership. Before going any further, we must acknowledge that there are major differences between the PALS and Pew "Landscape Survey" items. The former survey includes separate items for analyzing beliefs about angels and devils, while the latter addresses both topics within the same statement (as quoted earlier). The two surveys also dramatically differ with respect to question wording, substantive content, and response categories.

Nearly 75% of black Protestants at least "agree" with the statement "An angel has directly helped me in a time of need." However, just 47% of white Protestants feel this way (see descriptive table B.7B). In contrast, a similarly high percentage—at least 78%—of blacks and whites at least "agree" with the statement "The Devil, demons, or evil spirits exist" (see descriptive table B.7C). Taken together, these findings suggest that our strategy for developing separate survey questions about angels and devils was worthwhile: it appears that black and white Protestants espouse vastly dissimilar beliefs about angels but very similar beliefs about devils.

Our multivariate findings corroborate this conclusion: black Protestants are at least *twice* as likely as white Protestants in general and evangelical Protestants in particular to report having been helped by an angel. However, there is no statistically significant difference between blacks and whites with respect to their attitudes about devils. The prevailing belief among blacks that they have personally received assistance from an angel suggests that the miraculous is ordinary and the ordinary is miraculous.

As for miracles, the Pew "Landscape Survey" found that nearly 90% of Protestants in general (regardless of race) believe that miracles continue to occur in modern society. However, for the same reasons noted earlier, we are unable to compare findings from the PALS and the Pew poll. Even so, yet another distinction between these data sets deserves mentioning: our survey item gauges the extent to which our study participants believe that they *themselves* have experienced a supernatural miracle. This is an important distinction. When a *Christian* testifies to having experienced a miracle, it signals a profound belief that a divinely ordained (i.e., sanctioned by God) event has happened in that person's life.

A full 75% of black Protestants at least "agree" with the statement "I have experienced a supernatural miracle, an event that could not have happened without the intervention of God or a spiritual force." However, only 57% of white Protestants say that they have personally experienced a miracle (see descriptive table B.7D). Our multivariate results show that this very wide percentage gap holds constant after accounting for relevant background factors: African American Protestants are *twice* as likely as white Protestants in general and evangelicals in particular to proclaim having experienced a supernatural miracle.

Our interviewees agree that blacks' beliefs about angels and miracles are closely related to the consequences of racial stratification. Five of the high-ranking clergy members whom we spoke with at least intimated that the legacy of past and present racial discrimination and inequality in the United States has fostered differences in how blacks and whites view God's influence over their everyday lives. Deacon Harris best communicated this idea. He believes that racial differences in economics and culture have nurtured the development of "survival focused" themes within the African American Protestant religious tradition (this idea is consistent with our *Survival building block of black Protestant faith*): "African American spirituality tends to be very survival focused. God helps us through the problems of the vicissitudes of life. One of the themes in our theology is 'Hang in there. God's going to bring you through. You're going to make it. Don't give up. Don't throw in the towel. Believe in God. Help is on the way. Your miracle is coming.'"

Dr. Cone advanced a similar argument. Two things stand out about his comment. First, he believes that blacks and whites differ in what they consider to be a "miracle" in the first place. In his view, African Americans attribute everything from inexplicably escaping "situations of danger" to the enactment of major political and social policy as a "miracle." Second, Dr. Cone's statement addresses the underlying reason for why he believes that blacks and whites differ in their beliefs about angels and miracles: he says that *powerless* people (e.g., blacks) fundamentally have to believe in something to help "pull them through," while *powerful* people (e.g., whites) are less likely to subscribe to such beliefs due to their privileged position in society. It deserves mentioning that both Deacon Harris's and Dr. Cone's insightful critiques are consistent with our overall argument that most African American Protestants believe that they as individuals and blacks as a collective group would not have made it in this country *but for the grace of God*:

When you don't have much power to effect change in society, you tend to look for help outside of yourself. And when something does happen that you had nothing to do with, it's easy for you to think that if it's good, then it must be a miracle. I mean, blacks felt that it was a miracle to get liberated from slavery! [*laughs*]. Many slaves couldn't believe it when some white man named Abraham Lincoln liberated us from slavery. To them, that was a miracle! Or when the Supreme Court in 1954 ruled that segregation in public schooling is illegal—that's a miracle for us too. And in their personal lives, there is not a black person alive who has not been in a situation of danger and by some miracle got out of it.

And growing up in the South like I did, and also in the North, when you make it through that perceived danger, sometimes the only way you can explain it is that God was with us or that an angel pulled us through. So the miraculous is not unheard of from the point of view of those who are weak and powerless. But from the point of view of the powerful, they can do what they want to do. They don't need a miracle. They already have power. But when you are *powerless*, you need a miracle to get you through.

When you look at 246 years of slavery, another 100 years of segregation and lynching, that's nearly 350 years of unchecked white supremacy. White people could do anything to black people that they wanted—and *we're still here*. It's a miracle. The more I study black history, the more I believe in God 'cause ain't no way . . .

So the miraculous, a miracle, an angel, is not something unthinkable for those who are oppressed.

Alignment among the Stars

The realm of the supernatural also includes attitudes about astrology. Astrology is generally defined as the analysis of and subsequent belief that the intergalactic alignment of stars and planets influences people's everyday lives. While levels of support for astrology are not nearly as widespread as for angels or miracles, a Pew Research Center report titled "Many Americans Mix Multiple Faiths" revealed that 25%

of Americans in general and 21% of Protestants believe that the "position of the stars and planets can affect people's lives."[4] This finding runs counter to conventional church teachings. Contemporary church leaders instruct Christians to disregard astrology for three reasons. First, astrology is widely viewed as a form of *divination* since it attempts to foretell the future based on non-divinely-ordained knowledge or intuition. In this sense, astrology is thought to be buoyed by a false sense of prophecy that gives godlike powers to the alignment of stars and planets. (Church leaders are especially troubled by this since they steadfastly believe that God created the planets and the stars.) Second, most mainstream church leaders argue that even a passing interest in astrology requires a faith tantamount to the belief in God. Consequently, they view people's attention to the positioning of planets and stars as misguided because it puts non-divinely-ordained entities on a pedestal equal to God. Finally, when combined, these justifications represent a third overall reason why church leaders believe that Christians should not pay attention to astrology: they associate it with the occult. Contemporary church leaders more or less view astrology the same way that they do other realms of paranormal divination such as fortune telling, tarot card readings, magic, witchcraft, sorcery, séances, and psychics: as non-divinely-ordained bodies of meritless disinformation. These realms of the supernatural (as well as the individuals and groups associated with them here on Earth) are viewed as esoteric or secretive since they seemingly undermine the commonsense "good news" of Christianity that they believe is open to anyone.

Survey findings from the GSS show that racial group membership color-codes attitudes about astrology. For instance, nearly 63% of African American Protestants say that they read their horoscope or personal astrology report (note that the question says nothing about *how often* respondents read their horoscope, just whether they do at all). However, only 55% of white Protestants say that they have done so (see descriptive table B.7E). Similarly, 41% of black Protestants believe that astrology is "sort of scientific," and 11% say that it is "very scientific." In stark contrast, only 25% of white Protestants say that astrology is "sort of scientific," while 72% say that it is "not at all scientific" (see descriptive table B.7F). These percentage distributions suggest that black and white Protestants are deeply divided in their beliefs about astrology.

Our multivariate analyses confirm these initial findings. After controlling for relevant background factors such as income, education, attendance at worship services, age, gender, and region of residence, African American Protestants are nearly one and a half times more likely than white Protestants to say that they read their horoscope. Moreover, blacks are far more likely than whites to say that astrology has scientific merit.

There is strong reason to believe that astrology and other realms of supernatural belief have always garnered at least moderate levels of interest within the black community.[5] However, African Americans' openness to astrology may be attributable to growing support for *Afrocentrism*,[6] a cultural worldview that calls attention to the contributions and ways of life among people of African descent. It has long been established that astrology was a widely recognized feature of religious life among the ancient Egyptians (some Afrocentrists— both inside and outside of the academy—have argued this point as well).[7] While researchers across various fields of study continue to debate what is and is "not out of Africa,"[8] studies have shown that most blacks believe that the historical contributions of Africans in general and the Egyptians in particular have been minimized or even completely ignored.[9]

Afrocentrism is just one of the numerous ideological strains of Black Nationalism,[10] a multidimensional political and social ideology that emphasizes the importance of racial solidarity, black pride, and the preservation of black cultural distinctiveness. It posits that blacks must undertake group-based efforts of self-determination leading toward various forms of autonomy from whites.[11] Black Nationalism sets the tone for understanding why one of our interviewees believes that African Americans have only recently begun to push the boundaries of black religion and spirituality. Pastor Jenkins, who admitted to "dibbling and dabbling" with non-Christian faiths and alternative supernatural beliefs in his early adulthood, alluded to how the decline of the Civil Rights Movement and subsequent rise of the Black

Power Movement created a space for some African Americans to find "new religion." His interesting explanation includes subtle nationalist overtones:

> By the end of the 1960s—after all of the civil rights marches, singing "We Shall Overcome" and the nonviolent resistance—we [African Americans] realized that some of us were making progress while others were just getting our butts kicked, and we were tired of that. So by the 1970s, many of us could no longer see how the church was helping our situation. We came to realize that there were crooks in the church too! [*laughs*]. So many blacks started looking for a new religion. This is when black people got interested in transcendental meditation, Far Eastern religious stuff like yoga, numerology, and other stuff. White people were doing it, so you know that black people weren't too far behind! [*laughs*].
>
> Quiet as kept, astrology has always been a part of our [worldview] because we've always been a people who wanted to know as much as we can about our situation with whites. Yes, we love the Lord God Almighty. But a lot of us also believe that the 12 signs of the zodiac might tell us a little something to make our day that much easier.

A Far East Influence?

In some ways, our findings for racial differences in beliefs about astrology are not completely surprising. After all, horoscopes and astrology reports are published every day in newspapers, magazines, and on websites appealing to a wide swath of Americans. In fact, GSS survey data shows that the overwhelming majority of Protestants—regardless of their race or religious denomination—can name their particular zodiac sign (e.g., Taurus, Pisces, Libra).[12] The point we are trying to make here is that, while many Americans may not actually read their horoscope, they know at least something about astrology simply because it is an artifact of American popular culture.

However, this rationale does not explain why some Americans subscribe to other more controversial supernatural beliefs. For instance,

18% of Protestants believe that *yoga* is not merely "exercise" but should also be viewed as a "spiritual practice."[13] (Yoga is a physical, mental, and spiritual discipline found in Hinduism, Buddhism, Sikhism, and Jainism. There remains an ongoing debate among Christians as to whether this increasingly popular activity can be sufficiently separated from its Far East roots and practiced from a "Christian perspective.") Similarly, 20% of Protestants believe in *reincarnation*, the popular belief among Hindus that "people will be reborn in this world again and again."[14] These findings are difficult to explain because neither yoga nor reincarnation (a) has a historically deep-seated connection with American popular culture or (b) is even distantly connected to Christianity in the United States. Consequently, they suggest that a Far East influence is beginning to have a substantive impact on American Christianity.

Using the PALS survey, we assessed the extent to which our study participants "agree" with the following statement: "I believe in reincarnation, that people have lived previous lives." A minority of black Protestants—less than 4 in 10—believe that they have been reincarnated. However, less than 2 in 10 white Protestants feel this way (see descriptive table B.7G). Thus, it appears that blacks are more likely than whites to find themselves among the minority of Protestants who feel that they have "lived previous lives."

Our multivariate results buttress this preliminary assertion: African American Protestants are almost *three and half times* more likely than white Protestants to believe in reincarnation. This finding represents the largest statistical gap between black and white Protestants presented in this book thus far. Clearly, racial group membership color-codes beliefs about reincarnation. Or does it? Then again, maybe it does so in ways that are not immediately apparent.

Most of the 14 high-ranking clergy members whom we interviewed do not believe that this statistical finding should be interpreted at face value. However, we should point out that not all of our interviewees felt this way. Two of our interviewees did not seriously attempt to explain our result for racial differences in beliefs about reincarnation. They simply were not sure about what the finding means or how to explain it in real-world terms. Our 12 remaining pastors were in full agreement: they do not believe that even a minority of African American Protestants subscribe to the traditional Hindu belief in reincarnation. Nevertheless, their responses are distinguishable based on the extent to which they advanced one of two arguments: (1) those who explained African Americans' receptiveness to reincarnation within the context of longstanding black cultural traditions that honor one's deceased ancestors[15] and (2) those who described African Americans' receptiveness to reincarnation as an unfortunate consequence of their commitment to an *experiential* model of Christianity.

Eight of the high-ranking clergy members whom we interviewed believe that blacks' openness to reincarnation is rooted in an African cultural sensibility that recognizes the salience of "ghosts," "haints" (a popular southern slang term for describing spirits), and the possibility of interacting with one's ancestors long after they have passed away. As a result, they posited that blacks' understanding of reincarnation is an indelible *moment of spiritual clarity* whereby a person "sees an image" or "receives a message" from a deceased loved one in a way that is so timely and powerful that it only subjectively *feels* as if that person has "come back." This line of reasoning is by no means unfounded; scholars have long argued that several influential *Africanisms*[16]—or cultural customs of African origin such as the oral tradition, spirituality, significance of the drum, and salience of rhythm—survived the brutality of slavery and became part of the form, content, and structure of the contemporary *black sacred cosmos*. Consequently, these interviewees believe that our African American survey participants interpreted the statement about reincarnation from a black cultural perspective, not a Hindu perspective.

Take, for instance, Rev. Johnson's explanation for our survey results. At first, he admits to having a "difficult time" accounting for the finding. However, his reasoning becomes lucid as he links a profoundly personal story of death and dying to blacks' appreciation for the mystery in life:

That's new information to me [our findings for racial differences in beliefs about reincarnation]. My black history background has been so evangelical, literal, and fundamental that I was taught against reincarnation. I remember seeing it being talked about on the television one day when I was little boy, and my momma said, "Boy, that stuff ain't true."

I've never believed in reincarnation, and I personally don't know any black Christian who does, so I'll have a difficult time addressing this question. Reincarnation is not a main school of thought in the black community. It might just be a private belief that some people have.

Now having said that, I am aware that black folk talk about haints and ghosts. And I've heard old people say things like, "Oh, my [deceased] grandmamma came to see me last night." In fact, my mother died three years before my father, and I remember him saying to me, "Your mama came and talked to me last night." I don't think he was meaning that she physically or literally showed up. I don't believe that Dad would have said that was an example of "reincarnation."

I think if you asked [the people who participated in your survey], "Do you believe your grandmamma has come back [to Earth] in the form of a frog, a lion, tiger, or bear, or any other animal?," I think they would tell you no.

Statements of this sort were common among our interviewees. However, this point—that black Protestants' views have everything to do with black cultural sensibilities rather than Hinduism—was made in different ways. For instance, Pastor Jenkins (the Los Angeles comedian) explained our finding for racial differences in beliefs about reincarnation through humor. He began his response in a very scholarly and reasoned way but then dramatically shifted gears and went into "standup mode":

See, African American culture is interesting. Since slavery, and even going back to Egypt, the old folks would sometimes talk about haints and ghosts and spirits. Sometimes, they might see a child, and that little boy might have a certain look or do something in a certain way, and the old folks would say, "That child's been here before. He's an old soul."

So here's *your* reincarnation [*"your" meaning our survey finding; he smiles widely but then begins to look intently and point his finger at the fictitious child walking across the other side of the room*]:

"That's a 50-year-old man stuck in a 3-year-old's body [*chuckles*]. Ain't that Charlie's son? [*He directs this question to me, hoping that I'll play along.*] Look at how he walks—just like his daddy. I bet he talks like his daddy, too. But Charlie's been dead for most of that boy's life. Come here, little Charlie." [*He waves his hand as if asking the boy to "come here."*]

But check this out: it's only after he walks over to us that we find out that that boy's named Raymond! Charlie's been long gone, but he lives on in little Ray-Ray!

It is worth noting that most of our interviewees at least alluded to the idea that, generally speaking, African Americans believe that there is a strong possibility that you will "see" or "hear from" your deceased loved ones again sometime before you die. Even those interviewees who emphasized the limitations of blacks' *experiential* understanding of Christianity communicated this point. Furthermore, they believe that blacks' remembrance of and appreciation for the deceased can manifest itself in any number of ways, be it in a dream (à la Rev. Johnson) or through young children who are described as having an "old soul" (à la Pastor Jenkins). Indeed, findings from the Pew report on religious intermixture support our interviewees' claims of African Americans' culturally based recognition of the dead. For example, 37% of black Protestants say that they have "been in touch with someone who has already died," while only 25% of white Protestants say that they have done so.[17]

Our remaining four interviewees also referenced blacks' culturally based respect for the dead. According to them, however, our survey finding supports their claim that African Americans are not as knowledgeable about reincarnation or Christianity as they should be. These interviewees believe that black Protestants must devote greater time and effort to learning precisely what it means (and does not mean) "to be a Christian." For instance, Rev. Boyd, after explaining why he feels that African Americans do not subscribe to a Far East understanding of reincarnation, simply but sternly described our survey finding in this way: "We [African Americans] are not reflective enough." Similarly, Rev. Robinson stated, "That's why you need a solid theology because you need to understand *very well* the basis for your faith. The problem with being so experiential is that almost any kind of experience can creep in to what you believe. That may be what's going on with your survey finding."

Rev. Shannon communicated this point as well. However, she did so in a personally revealing way. She admitted that there was a time when, as a younger Christian, she once subscribed to a classical Far Eastern understanding of reincarnation. But her feelings about this dramatically changed as she became a more "knowledgeable Christian":

> I used to think that I was going to come back as something else: a butterfly, a dog, a cat, or something. I can remember as a young girl that something would happen, and I would say, "Gee, that seemed so familiar to me." And I thought that was because I had already experienced whatever it was in another life. As the years passed, though, those feelings just sort of faded away.
>
> It was mostly because, as a Christian, I came to realize that the only person that ever came back was *Jesus*. And the big thing about being a Christian is this: I don't want to come back. I want to live right so I can get to the Pearly Gates and be awarded with everlasting life. Why would anyone want come back to Earth?
>
> Your survey finding makes me think that just as I was not as informed about my faith as I should be, some of the Christians that were surveyed truly believe in Jesus, but they're not informed enough to understand what it means to be a knowledgeable Christian.

Deacon Harris would completely agree with the latter portion of Rev. Shannon's statement. His insightful comment touches on each of the relevant points that our interviewees advanced when explaining our findings for racial differences in beliefs about reincarnation. In an intellectual yet plainspoken way, he described how the cultural relevance of African spirituality, the significance of haints and ghosts, differences in theological emphases across black and white Protestants, and African Americans' supposed lack of awareness of Hinduism are all important for understanding blacks' beliefs about reincarnation:

> Okay, I can give a couple answers. First, I don't think there is a whole lot of theologizing from our [African American] pulpits in detailed ways. A theology that would correct something is more latent in our spirituality.
>
> I think the result has to do with our African cultural sensibility. We strongly believe in the world of spirits. For example, my grandparents were Christians, but it was common for them to say, "I saw Aunt So-and-So [even though she had long since passed away]," or they'd talk about haints and ghosts or say something like, "I had a dream that my grandmother came to me, and she said to do such and such, and I did it and everything worked out all right" [*laughs*]. This is typical in our culture, especially in years gone by.
>
> Though we would never admit it in a clear discursive way, we have this understanding of "Yeah, Big Momma will appear to you in your dream, so you will probably see her again."
>
> So your finding for reincarnation is very, very interesting. However, I don't know how deeply they [our survey participants] understand what "reincarnation" is, and if they really compare it to what Hindus believe about reincarnation, I don't think they believe in that kind of reincarnation.
>
> In our [African American] culture, we often say things like, "The spirit of the grandfather came in the grandchild." This is not to say that that's *really* the grandfather but rather that the child is *like* the grandfather. That's part of our view of the world, and so I think that's part of the explanation [for the survey results].
>
> Your survey finding has a lot to do with our cultural spirituality as it related to African culture. Our African cultural sensibility is so much more dominant than people really realize, and it's very dominant in our Christianity—although a lot of us may not want to admit it.

A Habit of Inclusion: How Far Does It Reach and Why?

So far, we have established that the African American Protestant religious tradition includes a welcome space for (a) religious convictions that are closely associated with Christianity and (b) religious convictions that are not closely associated with Christianity. We now turn our attention to addressing this habit of inclusion among black Protestants.

Turning back to our survey, 19% of black Protestants at least "agree" with the statement "The founder of Islam, Muhammad, was the Holy Prophet of God." However, only 9% of whites feel this way (see descriptive table B.7H). This finding suggests that blacks are more likely than whites to find themselves among the minority of Protestants who believe Muhammad is the "Holy Prophet of God."

Our multivariate results reveal that black Protestants are *twice* as likely as white Protestants to hold this highly favorable view of Muhammad. It is worth noting that we conducted further tests on this survey item to ensure the accuracy of our results: our findings do not meaningfully change after adjusting for the fact that black Protestants spend more time conversing with Muslims on a monthly basis than white Protestants do.[18]

This finding reinforces our claim of the open-mindedness, tolerance, and recognition of doctrinal diversity that is intrinsic to the African American Protestant religious tradition. While a passionate, wholehearted, and vigorous commitment to Christianity constitutes the nucleus of the *black sacred cosmos*, its dynamic outer margins are receptive to faith-related sensibilities that often lie well beyond the borders of conventional Christianity. Although blacks might collectively see themselves as "Jesus people" or subscribe to a "Jesusology" (as Dr. Cone says), that does not prohibit them from believing that haints, spirits, astrology, and even other deities cannot be part of God's plan.

Nevertheless, you still might be wondering, why would some African American Protestants—even if they are open-minded and respectful of non-Christian faiths—be more likely than whites to subscribe to the belief that Muhammad is the "Holy Prophet of God"? Isn't that a boundary that Christians shouldn't cross (pun intended)?

Maybe so. But then again, maybe not. At some point during the course of our interviews, more than half of the 14 high-ranking clergy members we sat down with addressed blacks' far-reaching appreciation for religious diversity. Their explanations help to further our understanding for why the African American Protestant religious tradition includes a welcome space for religious actions and convictions that some passionate believers (both black and white) may not consider to be "Christlike." For instance, Pastor Thomas described blacks' recognition of faith-based "inclusiveness" in this profoundly insightful way:

There are some explanations for your survey findings that could go back centuries. For example, the Africans who came to this country as slaves incorporated Christianity into their preexisting African religion. So black Christianity was never exclusive to begin with. In other words, they [African slaves] had their belief in Christianity, but it wasn't so exclusive that they could not see, appreciate, or even embrace other faith traditions. Remember, they were converted to Christianity as slaves. So part of the reason that we [African Americans] are able to adapt to Christianity so well was because of our inclusive background. And this has been passed on in our community. In many cases, we have been excluded from history, so we don't want to exclude others.

A number of African Americans—people in my church, in fact—were part of the black Muslim movement in the 20th century. Or they know black Muslims or have family members who are black Muslims. They don't want to view those loved ones as going to Hell [*chuckles*].

So this probably goes back to the earlier question you asked about "as long as you're a 'good person.'" We [African Americans] support the whole notion of inclusiveness, so there is a willingness to embrace other traditions.

Several things stand out about Pastor Thomas's comment. First, he makes it clear that he believes that the African American Protestant religious tradition was never "exclusive" in the first place. This is because black slaves incorporated Christianity into their already-established religious worldview. Second, he attributes blacks' openness to religious diversity to their longstanding history of being second-class citizens in America. Finally, he specifically links black Protestants' openness to Islam to faith-based political and social movements from the 1960s. By "black Muslims," he means the Nation of Islam (NOI), an influential yet controversial religious group with Black Nationalist leanings that aims to improve conditions for African Americans.

Dr. Cone also addressed the role that Black Nationalism has played in shaping black Protestants' commitment to a far-reaching faith. He begins his analysis by discussing racial differences in beliefs about the importance of "doctrines and creeds" (to reiterate, his argument is consistent with the *academic-versus-experiential dichotomy*). However, he concludes his statement by explaining why he believes that Malcolm X—the chief spokesman for the NOI for much of the 1950s and '60s —was and continues to be a beloved figure to many black Protestants:

> I think that [blacks' belief in a far-reaching faith] is largely because black Christianity is not primarily defined by doctrine and creeds. We didn't write those doctrines, and we didn't write those creeds, and we don't interpret them as important for us today. They are important only because we took them from the churches that made them important. But now, since they are not ours, we don't buy into it as deeply.
>
> See, when you have doctrines and creeds as centrally important for your definition of the faith—the way whites do—there is little left for mystery. But when you don't have doctrines and creeds as central, there is more room for mystery. When you have more room for mystery, then you have more room for astrology and voodoo.
>
> This applies to blacks' openness to other religions as well. Why do you think that Malcolm X was so popular among black Christians? He was a Muslim. But he was popular among black Christians because he spoke the truth. And black people respond to the truth.

Speaking of voodoo, Dr. Cone is correct that black Protestants report a stronger affinity for voodoo than do white Protestants (which makes sense considering voodoo's West African roots). For instance, the Pew report on religious intermixture showed that 32% of black Protestants believe in "the evil eye, or that certain people can cast curses or spells that cause harm," while only 11% of white Protestants do so.[19]

Finally, it was Pastor Jenkins, the part-time Pentecostal preacher and comedian from Los Angeles who best summarized the reason why blacks subscribe to a far-reaching faith (or what he described as a "habit of inclusion"). He attributed blacks' openness to other religions to the fact that "no one really knows what happens when we die." Thus, he believes that since no one really knows, then no one can legitimately finger-point or judge someone else:

> I think that we have this habit of inclusion because nobody's found the door, the path, or the stairway that leads to Heaven and then come back to tell everyone else exactly how to get to there. So what if a brother says that he believes in some other religion. That's okay because we're all reaching for the same thing. We all love God, and we all believe there is but one God in control of all of this, whether you believe in Buddha, Allah, Hare Krishna, Jehovah, Jesus, Yahweh, or whatever the case may be. Whatever you want to call Him, the bottom line is it's *God*.
>
> See, we [African Americans] cross these lines because we're looking for an answer. We all want to know where we're supposed to go after we make the transition and leave this fleshly world. Other Christians feel this way too; that's one reason why we switch denominations.
>
> So if you believe in God and you're not doing anything to hurt anybody while you're pursuing your beliefs and worshiping God, then we're cool—even if you and I don't see things the same way.

May "the Force" Be with You?

While it is true that the African American Protestant religious tradition welcomes diversity, it is equally true that there are limits to that diversity. Our interviewees believe that some faith-related convictions clearly lie beyond the accepted scope of the *black sacred cosmos*. For instance, the high-ranking clergy members whom we interviewed were in agreement that by far, the most troublesome and disagreeable survey finding we uncovered is that black and white Protestants differ in their broader conceptualization or view of God. No other survey result consistently elicited such animated and contested responses.

The PALS contains an item that gauges the extent to which study participants "agree" or "disagree" with the statement that "God is not a personal being, but more like an impersonal spiritual force." Most evangelical Christians at least "disagree" with this statement.[20] They probably do so because, as several of our interviewees have already mentioned, Protestants generally believe in the Trinity: that God (the Father), Jesus (His Son), and the Holy Spirit are One Being with anthropomorphic (or humanlike) attributes. And, second, evangelicals emphasize what they believe to be the fundamental necessity of developing a "personal relationship" with Christ.

However, we found that 58% of African American Protestants at least "agree" that "God is not a personal being, but more like an impersonal spiritual force." Only 38% of whites do so (see descriptive table B.7I). After accounting for differences across income, education, attendance at worship services, age, gender, and region of residence, our multivariate results show that black Protestants are at least *three times* as likely than white Protestants in general and evangelicals in particular to view God as an "impersonal force" rather than a "personal being."

Virtually every person whom we interviewed for this study—be they a high-ranking member of the clergy or an everyday person in the pews—expressed major reservations about this finding.[21] Many of our interviewees took umbrage with the fact that some Christians, regardless of their race, see God as an "impersonal force" rather than a "personal being." For instance, a 30-something-year-old, black, male focus group member from Cleveland said, "If a Christian is saying that God is an impersonal force, then the country and the world is in big trouble. Jesus walked and lived and died for our sins—that's real personal. That's a human being. He took on human form so that He could relate to our suffering. He interceded for us on a personal level. He's not an impersonal force like gravity. There's nothing holy about gravity." A moment later, a 50-something-year-old, black, female focus group participant elaborated on this point. Although she makes it abundantly clear that she believes that God is a "personal being," she also leaves the door open for understanding why some people might see God as an "impersonal force":

> In a Christian's life, often we speak of the power and the presence of God. Now, if you believe in the presence of God, and God is real in your life, you probably also believe that God is more like a being than a force. But He can manifest in *any way that he wants*. But in the lives of the believers, He's more like God the Father, God the provider. These are not forces; they are personal attributes.

The basic thrust of these sentiments—that God should be seen as a "personal being" and not an "impersonal force"—was widely agreed on among our focus group participants. Not surprisingly, the high-ranking clergy members whom we interviewed even more vehemently felt this way. In fact, it was almost as if the Baptist, Methodist, and Pentecostal preachers whom we spoke to operated on the assumption that God as a "personal being" was a foregone conclusion (some of the survey findings discussed in chapter 6 support their argument that blacks believe that God possesses humanlike attributes). This probably explains why nearly all of the high-ranking clergy members whom we spoke with expressed some form of uneasiness, confusion, or intellectual animus for this particular survey finding. What is most telling, though, is *not* that our interviewees were surprised that there is a statistical difference between blacks and whites with respect to how they conceptualize God. To the contrary, what is most telling is that nearly all of them figured that *whites*—not blacks—would be more likely to see God as an "impersonal force." This expectation is consistent with the *academic-versus-experiential dichotomy*: our interviewees felt that the ceremonially formal, intellectually precise, and less emotionally intense manner in which they believe that whites go about their faith would lead them to view God as an "impersonal force." Conversely, they felt that the informal, spontaneous, practical, and emotionally intense way in which they believe that blacks go about their faith would lead them to view God as a "personal being." Rev. Johnson's statement best captures the bewilderment over this survey finding:

I'm a little bit baffled and shocked as I listen to the question because I think it's just the opposite. Had you asked me, "Do whites see God more impersonally and blacks see Him more personally?," I would have answered that question "yes."

So now that you tell me that is not the result of the survey, I don't know how to respond. See by "personal," I mean intimate, accessible —a God who shows up when called upon, concerned, compassionate. He's more than just a theory, abstract or remote entity. We as African Americans believe God is transcendent. He's nearer to us than hands and feet. He's closer to us than breathing. We often describe Him in human, anthropomorphic terms. He's a mother to the motherless, a father to the fatherless. That is personal. He gives you bread when you're hungry. The language of the black church talks about an intimate, personal, and on-time God. A "right now" God, who shows up when needed.

In my African American experience, God has always been described as personal. So I can't even talk about Him being impersonal. I just don't know how to fathom that there is a generic understanding of how African Americans view God.

Rev. Washington stated a similar point. After expressing his apprehension about our survey finding, he explained why he believes that blacks do, in fact, embrace a personal understanding of God. His reply includes a critique of how Biblical literalism and contemporary racial stratification have influenced blacks' view of God:

> Blacks read the Bible, and the Bible speaks of God in personal ways: God in flesh, God Himself. He became human. That's very personal. God is characterized as getting angry, as having emotions. Those are anthropomorphisms, so it's personal. And sociologically, many black people identify with God in socioeconomic and sociopolitical ways. So that's personal as well.

Despite our interviewees' concerns, most of them advanced insightful explanations for our finding that black and white Protestants view God differently. These intriguing accounts included the following overlapping range of possibilities: (a) changing understandings of God among African Americans, (b) the cultural impact of mysticism within the black church, (c) blacks' reverence for the power of God, (d) a lack of reflective theological thinking among African Americans, and (e) epistemologically based arguments that Eurocentric renderings of Christ reinforce racial discrimination and inequality in the United States.

For example, Rev. Davis, the young and dynamic leader of a multiracial Baptist congregation in Southern California, attributed our finding for the difference between blacks and whites to what he sees as an emerging belief that God is "impartial." His explanation is consistent with the idea that there is a changing understanding of God among African Americans:

> I'm wondering whether the "impersonal" finding means that He is "impartial." It may be that we [African Americans] are coming from a broader understanding of God as opposed to a narrow understanding of Him. In recent years, I've heard Christians saying things that you would not have heard in past times, like "God is not a respecter of persons." So I'm hoping and thinking that maybe what they mean by "impersonal" is that He is "impartial" in judgment.

Deacon Harris was much more confident in his rationale for our survey finding. His reply, which focuses on the mysterious yet intense experience of "encountering" God, spotlights the significance of culturally based praise and worship methods within the black church:

> I would describe your survey result like this: in African American spirituality, we emphasize the role and activity of the Holy Spirit. Our worship style and spirituality is about encountering the Holy Spirit. That being said, we tend to encounter the Holy Spirit as a *force*.
>
> For example, in black Pentecostalism—which has influenced African American Christianity in general—we're praising the Lord because He's worthy but also so that the Lord can show up and we can

encounter God. This encountering of God is *very mysterious*. Something happens; it's the moving of the Holy Spirit. This is intense, so encountering God can be a forceful experience.

Nevertheless, I think that if you talked to black Christians, they would be quick to say that God is a "personal being" that they have a relationship with. But the experience is in encountering the mysterious force of the Holy Spirit. We believe that He is going to show up and do this and that. And then *wow . . . [He moves both hands as if stirring a pot, then there is an emotional pause.]* He's already done it.

Five of the 14 high-ranking clergy members whom we interviewed attributed our survey finding to blacks' recognition of the power of God (Deacon Harris's comment that "encountering God can be a forceful experience" loosely falls into this category as well). Rev. Robinson, the highly educated rocket scientist from Los Angeles, most eloquently described this line of reasoning. Two things stand out about his comment. First, he believes that an emphasis on God's power is an incorrect answer to our survey question (not because God is not powerful but because Rev. Robinson believes that Christians should emphasize that God is a "personal being"). Thus, he attributes blacks' response to our survey question to a lack of reflective theological thinking. Second, Rev. Robinson explains African American Protestants' understanding of "the anointing" in order to make the larger point that blacks do not believe in "magic" or "using the force" as much as they believe that the Holy Spirit has granted someone a special ability that can only be accessed through interfacing with Him:

> Typically, the sort of standard Christian belief is a Trinitarian model where we believe in the Father, the Son, and the Holy Spirit. It's hard to generalize like this, but many African Americans have experienced the Holy Spirit in a much more imminent way. They've felt His power, they've shouted in church and danced, and they may have seen Him do certain things. So maybe they [our African American study participants] are focusing on His power in general rather than the "personal being" who wields that power.

But I think that your survey finding is probably due to the fact that there hasn't been much theological reflection on the Being of the Holy Spirit.

Interviewer: What do you think it means if someone sees God as an impersonal force?

Well, that would mean sort of like a power to be manipulated or controlled. Like in Star Wars, there wasn't a personal relationship going on; they were just manipulating good and bad forces. In the black church—in Pentecostalism especially and various other expressions of Christianity—you hear people talk about the "anointing." When black folks talk about "the anointing," they're referring to God's power coming upon them and enabling them to do something. So an "anointing" means that the Holy Spirit manifests Himself in such a way that He gives you a special ability. So if a person has an anointing for healing, for example, that means that the Holy Spirit is present within that individual to heal others.

As human beings, we're operating and interacting with this person —the Holy Spirit—who is actually healing just like Christ did when He was a physical person. If I'm anointed, it's *not* that I just sort of received some magical power and now can conduct healing. No, I'm participating and interacting with a person [the Holy Spirit], and that's why I can heal someone else.

Pastor Thomas also theorized that blacks' response to our survey question is driven by an emphasis on God's power. Moreover, he—like Rev. Johnson, Rev. Washington, Rev. Davis, Deacon Harris, and Rev. Robinson—also believes that by and large, blacks view God as a "personal being" and not an "impersonal force." However, Pastor Thomas's comment stands out because he links our survey finding to a highly controversial topic that arouses deep-seated antagonisms for some African Americans: Eurocentric depictions of Christ as a "white man" with blond (or sandy brown) hair and blue (or light brown) eyes. For many African Americans, such renderings of Christ not only are historically inaccurate but also instill or reinforce feelings of racial inferiority within blacks while simultaneously elevating whites to a godlike status:[22]

That survey finding is a difficult one. One of the things that is emphasized in black churches is a personal relationship with God, and so the "impersonal force" and the "personal being" seem to be in conflict.

I'm not sure how your study participants interpreted that question. There could be a problem with the way the question was asked; it's somewhat difficult to understand. But to answer your question—and this is truly speculative—perhaps your study participants are placing an emphasis on the power of God and how God operates in our lives, and they're seeing God as the force in their lives that they need to get them through.

My guess is that even as they talk about Him as an "impersonal force," [their deeper sentiment] is more in the nature of the idea that "God is what supports me and keeps me going."

There could be another reason as well. I hesitated to say this before —and I'm not sure that this would be true for a whole lot of people— but some people have an issue with the way God has been presented. This idea that God is an old white man with a long beard that sits on a cloud—that does not resonate with some African Americans, especially young people. For some black people, seeing God as an "impersonal force" is a way to move away from a God that doesn't *look like me.*

Interviewer: It's funny that you're saying this because I noticed the paintings of Christ in your sanctuary. His skin color is quite a bit darker than some people might expect or even feel comfortable with. Why is that?

Actually, that was done about 15 years ago, before I became senior pastor. The artist's original depiction of Christ was much lighter than it is now; He was a white man. His skin color was darkened because some members of our church believed that the paintings did not reflect the people within our congregation. But it's not simply a matter of making the picture look more like the congregation but a serious concern as to whether or not they were historically accurate as they were originally painted.

There's a long tradition on this that began back in the 1800s; we've [the A.M.E. tradition] had bishops like Henry McNeal Turner, who wrote that "God is black" or "God is a Negro."[23] So we [African Americans] have a history of questioning traditional notions of who God is, who Jesus is, and what did Jesus look like, and those types of things. So, in my opinion, some of that probably has something to do with explaining your statistical finding.

Pastor Thomas's church was not the first and certainly will not be the last predominantly African American congregation to debate the racial implications of what Christ looks like. Nor was he our only interviewee to mention this issue in relation to our survey finding. In fact, Rev. Washington moved the debate over the implications of what God looks like beyond black/white relations and applied it to male-female relations:

Many people try to distance themselves from others who see God in ethnic and gender ways that are oppressive. For instance, some women believe that the fact of God in flesh, and God Himself in Jesus Christ—as *a man*—limits the roles of women in society. Similarly, many blacks believe that the Eurocentric casting of God—such as Michelangelo's image of Him in the Sistine Chapel—is the only image of God that whites can accept. For these people, this kind of imagery —that the Bible is all white or that it focuses too much on men—becomes oppressive.

We asked Dr. Cone to share his thoughts on our finding that blacks are more likely to view God as an "impersonal force," while whites are more likely to view God as a "personal being." As expected, Dr. Cone advanced a conceptually unique and methodologically insightful argument: he feels that our result can be explained by the fact that the survey question itself was specifically designed to gauge the study participants' beliefs about God, *not* Jesus. Consequently, Dr. Cone believes that our result would have turned out much differently had the survey question asked specifically about Jesus. He feels this way because, beliefs about the Trinity aside, Dr. Cone believes that Jesus occupies an inimitable place within the African American Protestant religious tradition:

That survey finding is a mystery. I would have thought it just the other way [i.e., that blacks would be more likely to view God as a "personal being," while whites would be more likely to view God as an "impersonal force].

Maybe what is not being captured there is that they see Jesus as the personal side of religion. We [African Americans] can call Jesus upon the telephone of prayer and talk to Him. "Jesus walked with me, talked with me."

But for some people, God can be viewed as removed, the omnipotent, omniscient, the all-powerful. Black folks don't say they can call God up and talk to Him in quite the same way that they say they can talk to Jesus.

See, we [African Americans] have a kind of "Jesusology." We focus on Jesus because He was the one that was crucified. God is far removed as a force, a creator. When you think about the term creator, it seems removed, not so close to people.

So your statistical finding is now clear to me. I would interpret it in terms of Jesus and God.

Revisiting the Building Blocks

The findings presented in this chapter provide strong support for the *Mystery* and *Miraculous building blocks of black Protestant faith*. Our quantitative and qualitative results for some African Americans' attention to astrology, openness to reincarnation, favorable beliefs about Muhammad, and conceptualization of God buttress our assertion that black Protestant faith is mystical and expresses an appreciation for the mystery in life. Black Protestants most certainly believe in life after death. However, as compared to white Protestants, their beliefs about life after death are complex and nuanced. This is because the African American Protestant religious tradition includes folklore and cultural components deriving from the African Diaspora, the consequences of racial inequality in America, and non-Christian religions. Furthermore, our finding that African American Protestants are far more likely than white Protestants to testify to having been helped by an angel and having experienced a supernatural miracle reinforces our claim that the average black Protestant believes that the miraculous is ordinary and the ordinary is miraculous.

In all, the results presented here show that the African American Protestant religious tradition is theologically far-reaching. This is not only because "belief matters, truth matters" but also because "race matters." The *black sacred cosmos* is dynamic, flexible, and theologically *broad* for the following correspondingly complex reasons: (a) the persistence of African cultural sensibilities, (b) past and present racial discrimination and inequality in the United States has cultivated a profound sense of openness and tolerance for others, (c) blacks are more likely to place a stronger emphasis on being a "good person" irrespective of their particular religious beliefs, (d) African Americans are less committed to an academic understanding of Christianity since they "didn't write those [religious] doctrines and didn't write those [religious] creeds," (d) various ideological strains of Black Nationalism have an influence on black religion, and (f) there are culturally imperative differences between blacks and whites in general. These postulates—which are all substantiated with quantitative or qualitative empirical findings—buttress our overall argument that racial group membership plays a critical role in shaping how black and white Protestants go about their religious faith. The findings presented here strongly support our contention that the legacy of race-based oppression and privilege in the United States has helped to fuel differences in black and white Protestants' religious sensibilities.

8

Reconciling the Race Problem

Identity Politics and the Gulf between
Black and White Protestants

In this final chapter, we turn our attention to beliefs among black and white Protestants that seemingly have little to do with religion at all. However, things are not always what they seem. In fact, it will soon become apparent that various dimensions of *identity politics* —that is, political beliefs and actions that are associated with a group of people that someone identifies with—are closely connected to *both* black *and* white Protestants' religious identities. This is important because many people inaccurately associate identity politics with *minorities* only. To the contrary, controversial racial issues as well as past and present injustices and inequalities are ideologically meaningful to both black and white Protestants. For instance, we show that beliefs about the causes of racial inequality and levels of support for government policies aimed at reducing racial inequality strongly influence the manner in which black and white Protestants go about their religious faith.

The results presented in this chapter suggest that we, as Americans, have yet to finally solve the "race problem" that has plagued our nation for centuries.[1] What is worse: the gulfs between black and white Protestants' beliefs about the roots of racial inequality and the role that the U.S. government should play in reducing racial inequality are typically wider and deeper than those between black and white *non-Protestants*. This is primarily due to disparate ideological commitments to *individualism* and *structuralism*. As a result, the possibilities for racial reconciliation among black and white Protestants seem severely limited.

Our goal in this final chapter is to develop the *Justice building block of black Protestant faith*: (5) *black Protestant faith is committed to social justice and equality for all individuals and groups in society*. This last building block focuses on the vital role that political and social attitudes play in shaping the African American Protestant religious tradition. The *black sacred cosmos* is neither apolitical nor disinterested in issues relevant to race relations. To the contrary, it contains a race-based ideological viewpoint that emphasizes structural explanations for and solutions to the problems of racial inequality. Thus, in addition to being both theologically *broad and definitive*, the black sacred cosmos also embraces people-oriented domains of Christianity that can help with solving problems in society.

Our Past and Present Race Problem: A Quick Review

The United States has a long and ignominious history of black/white race relations. Although the first slave ships arrived in North America during the early 1600s, the term "race problem" (or "Negro problem," as it was originally known) only emerged among whites in the aftermath of the Civil War. This popular phrase generally captured a range of issues relevant to the debate over whether blacks should have been granted full citizenship and participation rights following the South's fall from power. For instance, the Swedish economist Gunnar Myrdal argued in his groundbreaking text *An American Dilemma: The Negro Problem and Modern Democracy* (1944) that our nation's race problem primarily exists within the hearts and minds of the white population.[2] Although some blacks have always resisted slavery, segregation, and other forms of white racism, in general blacks have lacked the numbers, influence, and power to mount an adequate challenge to white supremacy. As a result, Myrdal (and many others in his wake) posited that the race problem largely boiled down to white people's answers to xenophobic questions such as "What should we do with our black population?" and "Now that slavery is over, should blacks be granted equal opportunity and protection under the law?"

Prior to 1865, few whites believed that America had a race problem (though obviously blacks and Native Americans saw this issue much differently). In their hearts and minds, most whites supported a system of chattel slavery in which blacks were forcefully controlled and exploited for the purpose of providing free labor. The end of the Civil War provided an opening for reassessing and restructuring the dynamics of black/white race relations. Unfortunately, most whites continued to believe that blacks were a biologically and culturally inferior people who were incapable of assimilating into the American mainstream.[3] As a result, a majority of whites had no problem with denying the four million newly freed ex-slaves inalienable rights such as "life, liberty, and the pursuit of happiness." Although slavery ended, it was soon replaced by other contemptuous forms of racial stratification, oppression, and inequality.

Shortly after the Civil War, city and state governments throughout the South (where the overwhelming majority of blacks continued to reside) established ordinances and laws that greatly restricted blacks' access to public accommodations and opportunities for improving their lives through education and employment. This set of formal and informal racial rules, which are commonly known as the "black codes," was designed to enhance whites' control over the black population. It received a federal stamp of approval in 1896 with the U.S. Supreme Court's ruling in *Plessy v. Ferguson*. Although a handful of blacks experienced limited socioeconomic gains during the Reconstruction era, the "separate but equal" doctrine of racial segregation prevented white America's potential Negro problem from becoming unmanageable.

In short, *de jure* segregation—or government-regulated segregation that was imposed by law—remained a deeply engrained feature of life in the American South long after the Civil War had ended. Moreover, during this time, thousands of blacks were physically dismembered, shot, burned at the stake, and lynched by angry white mobs. However, this does not mean that black/white race relations remained static. By the 1940s and '50s, the slow drip in the number of blacks who had decided to relocate to other regions of the United States had become a tidal wave. The outbreak of World War II granted African Americans unprecedented employment opportunities across manufacturing and industrial sectors throughout the Northeast and Midwest. As a result, more and more African Americans were beginning to transition from poverty to prosperity (despite the fact that various forms of residential and occupational segregation were developing in these regions as well). The growth of this new black middle class signaled that the dynamics of race relations were transforming.

These changes—as well as others including the desegregation of the U.S. military in 1948 and a gradual improvement in interpersonal relations among many individual blacks and whites—fostered the emergence of the Civil Rights Movement. A new generation of African Americans and their political sympathizers organized to challenge the system of white supremacy. It was during this time that black leaders such as Rev. Dr. Martin Luther King, Jr., Thurgood Marshall, and Rosa Parks became household names. The goal of the Civil Rights Movement was to ensure that blacks and whites have equal protection and opportunity under the law; its determined efforts led to watershed legal revisions such as the Supreme Court's 1954 decision in *Brown v. Board of Education* (which ruled the "separate but equal" doctrine unconstitutional), the passage of landmark legislation including the Civil Rights Acts of 1964 and 1968, the Voting Rights Act of 1965, and the development and implementation of equal opportunity policies such as affirmative action.

These successes considerably altered the dynamics of black/white race relations. Consequently, the contemporary "race problem" does not revolve around whites' dilemma over "what to do with" or "how to deal with" African Americans. As we will soon see, many hearts and minds within white America have dramatically changed for the better. Blacks have largely been granted equal protection and their inalienable rights. They are now free to pursue their American dreams. In fact, there are many positive signs that, as compared to previous periods of American history, blacks have made meaningful progress across a wide range of socioeconomic indicators.[4]

However, this does not mean that we have "solved" the race problem. In many ways, the contemporary African American experience personifies the classic Charles Dickens phrase "It was the best of times, it was the worst of times."[5] As we discussed in chapter 6, there are still very wide and deep gaps between blacks and whites across a host of quality-of-life indicators such as income, educational attainment, occupational prestige, unemployment, wealth, home ownership, life expectancy, health outcomes, family-related factors, drug usage, incarceration rates, and the list goes on and on.

The contemporary race problem, at its core, is fundamentally concerned with the problem of *inequality* between blacks and whites—and how to bridge socioeconomic gaps between the races. Regardless of whether a person sees blacks' recent progress as the glass being half full or half empty, there is no telling when blacks and whites will reach parity across even *a few* of the most important socioeconomic indicators. This precisely explains why in recent decades, scholars across various fields of study have devoted considerable time and effort to understanding Americans' beliefs about the modern origins of racial inequality and attitudes about the government's role in closing the socioeconomic gaps between blacks and whites. These studies aim to clarify why Americans believe that racial inequality persists—and how they believe we might overcome it—even though blacks and whites are now "equal" before the law.

There have been many important contributions to this line of research.[6] However, one major oversight is that social scientists know very little about how the combined effects of racial group membership and religious affiliations shape Protestants' commitments to identity politics. As we mentioned in chapter 1, knowledge in this area is critical to the political and social functioning of this nation. And to repeat, our analysis of these issues suggests that in this post–Civil Rights Era, black and white Protestants are by no means even close to reconciling the longstanding problem of racial inequality.

Beliefs about Racial Inequality

Researchers across various areas of study have established that most Americans subscribe to at least one of two sets of *stratification beliefs* (or explanations for why some people "make it" in America while others do not). These justifications for the realities of poverty and affluence can be either *individualistic* or *structural* in orientation.[7] Individualistic attributions focus on people's personal choices, their particular

talents, abilities, intelligence, work ethic, character, values, and motivation. Individualists emphasize not only the equality of opportunity
in America but that opportunities for achievement are plentiful and
accessible to all people, regardless of their particular walk of life. Consequently, they argue that personal merit is and rightfully should be
the most important determinant of a person's success. Classic phrases
such as "the early bird catches the worm" and "plan your work, work
your plan" reinforce the idea that those people who work harder,
make better choices, and carry themselves in the "right way" fundamentally deserve to live "the good life." The overwhelming majority
of Americans endorse individualism in some way, shape, or form; it
is so widely popular that scholars generally agree that it is our nation's
dominant ideology.[8]

On the other hand, structural attributions emphasize the role that
social factors beyond individual initiative play in shaping a person's
socioeconomic success. Structuralists argue that the American social "system"—or the way that our society's institutions, patterns of
relationships, and dynamics of status are organized—provides some
people with an advantage while placing others at a disadvantage. Consequently, they posit that determinants lying outside of individuals'
control—such as their race, gender, or age or the socioeconomic status
of the family they were born into—greatly influence whether they will
"make it" in life.

Structuralists do not believe that all Americans have an equal opportunity to succeed; to the contrary, they believe that most Americans neither begin their race to success from the same starting point
nor have the same number of hurdles to jump over before reaching
the finish line. Common adages such as "he was born with a silver
spoon in his mouth" or "she's a child of privilege" imply that hard work
is less central to some people's success. These sentiments help to explain why structuralists believe that individualists "blame the victim"
for their predicament rather than recognize that the deck is stacked
against some people and groups from the very beginning. Racism,
sexism, ageism, and macroeconomic forces (such as deindustrializa-
tion, suburbanization, globalization, and poverty) are often viewed as
insurmountable obstacles in people's path.

However, comparatively few Americans feel this way. Moreover, those Americans who subscribe to structural beliefs also tend to subscribe to individualistic beliefs.[9] For instance, studies have shown that structuralism typically operates in a "layered" or "compartmentalized" fashion whereby it complements one's commitment to individualism.[10] In the minds of many Americans, individualism and structuralism coexist, in that people must hurdle barriers beyond their control through hard work and merit.

One of the research questions that we aim to answer in this chapter is, what role does religious affiliation play in shaping attitudes about the causes of racial inequality? We are not the first scholars to ask this question. A number of studies[11] support sociologists Michael O. Emerson and Christian Smith's assertion that white evangelicals are more strongly committed to *motivational individualism*[12] (the idea that some people possess the "right" cultural values or internal drive to succeed) and *relationalism* (an emphasis on the importance of interpersonal relationships) than are other whites. White evangelicals are also decidedly "antistructural."[13] By contrast, these same studies have also shown that African American Protestants are less individualistic and more structural in their viewpoint than are both non-Protestant blacks and white evangelicals.[14] Taken together, these findings suggest that black Protestants and white evangelicals line up on opposing sides in the debate over individualism versus structuralism.

Using GSS data, we examined the extent to which black and white Protestants subscribe to the four most popular past and present explanations for racial inequality. Overall, the findings presented here are consistent with existing research: relatively few black or white Protestants believe that African Americans are biologically inferior to whites, and at least 40% of members of both groups believe that African Americans do not have equal access to quality education (not because of racism but rather because of the aforementioned macroeconomic factors). Moreover, as expected, it appears that white Protestants are more strongly committed to motivational individualism than are black Protestants and that black Protestants are far more likely than white Protestants to attribute racial inequality to racial discrimination (see descriptive table B.8A).

Our multivariate results are also consistent with prior research. Although black and white Protestants do not differ in their beliefs about blacks' supposed biological inferiority, whites are more likely than blacks to attribute contemporary racial inequality to motivational individualism. Furthermore, blacks are (a) one and half times more likely than whites to attribute racial inequality to macroeconomic disparities in access to a good education and (b) over *four times* more likely than whites to attribute racial inequality to racial discrimination. These findings clearly show that religious identities strongly influence black and white Protestants' beliefs about the roots of racial inequality. African Americans are more strongly committed to structural attributions than are whites.

But exactly how wide are these differences in opinion? As important as these findings are, they tell us nothing about how the differences between black and white Protestants compare with those of other Americans. Thus, our analysis of beliefs about racial inequality is far from complete. While we still have some important details to share on this topic, we must first address the role that religion plays in shaping levels of support for government policies designed to reduce racial inequality. This is important because, as we will soon see, black and white Protestants not only sharply differ in their beliefs about the role the U.S. government should (or should not) play in bridging the racial divide, but racial differences in identity politics often either gradually recede or intensify depending on one's degree of affiliation with Protestantism.

Support for Racial Policy

Existing studies have long since established the links between attitudes about inequality and support for redistributive policy.[15] More specifically, those Americans who espouse structural viewpoints largely support government policies aimed at reducing inequality, while those Americans who primarily espouse individualistic viewpoints largely do not. The belief that all Americans do not have an equal opportunity to succeed compels structuralists to favor government intervention;

they want the U.S. government to establish regulations and procedures that level the playing field by accounting for factors beyond a person's control such as one's race, gender, age, and that he or she grew up in poverty. For example, structuralists favor rewarding good students from disadvantaged backgrounds who excelled in otherwise bad public high schools with college admissions and scholarships.

In contrast, individualists oppose government intervention on grounds that it undermines personal merit. They believe that landmark legislation from the Civil Rights Era now permits members of minority and majority groups to run the race to success as fairly and squarely as legally possible. Moreover, many individualists contend that government policies that aim to assist members of lower-status groups penalize members of higher-status groups. As a result, they believe that such initiatives do not adjust for but rather parcel out educational and employment opportunities on the very basis that they were designed to overcome: race, gender, age, or that someone grew up in poverty. For example, individualists argue that many good students from disadvantaged backgrounds are not as "qualified" for admissions and scholarships (regardless of their grades and standardized test scores) as are those who attended better high schools.

There are two types of redistributive policies that aim to assist members of lower-status groups: *opportunity-enhancing policies* and *outcome-based policies*. Opportunity-enhancing policies help people "help themselves" by providing a chance for accomplished members of disadvantaged groups to further improve their academic or occupational skills. Job training programs, apprenticeships, and academic scholarships are well known examples of opportunity-enhancing policies. The American public tends to at least moderately support opportunity-enhancing policies. This is mainly because such initiatives maintain an emphasis on personal merit despite one's membership in a lower-status racial, ethnic, gender, or socioeconomic group.

Outcome-based policies, on the other hand, establish specific objectives for guaranteeing that members of disadvantaged groups are adequately integrated into mainstream organizations, institutions (such as colleges/universities), and corporations. These initiatives are group-oriented in that the most important consideration in evaluating a candidate is his or her group membership; performance-related factors such as employment qualifications, skill sets, work experiences, grade point averages, test scores, and letters of recommendation are considered less consequential. Outcome-based policies receive relatively low levels of support from the American public because they seemingly undermine personal merit by ensuring end results. In recent decades, the highly controversial debate over "quotas" has brought considerable attention to these initiatives.

What role does religious affiliation play in shaping beliefs about the U.S. government's role in ameliorating racial inequality? We are aware of only a handful of studies that have addressed this issue.[16] The following sets of results emerge from both the PALS and the GSS. For example, we found that 42% of black Protestants but only 10% of white Protestants at least "agree" that the U.S. government has a "special obligation to help improve living standards" among African Americans in order to make up for past discrimination (see descriptive table B.8B). Furthermore, a strong majority of black Protestants but only a minority of white Protestants at least "agree" that the U.S. government should "do more to help minorities increase their standards of living" (see descriptive table B.8C). These findings are consistent with prior research: blacks report much stronger levels of support for racially specific opportunity-enhancing policy than whites do.[17]

As for outcome-based policy, only 37% of black Protestants and 9% of white Protestants at least "favor" giving preferences to African Americans "in hiring and promotion" in order to make up for past racial discrimination (solid majorities of both groups at least "oppose" the initiative; see descriptive table B.8D). This finding reflects the American public's overall lack of support for policies that seemingly undermine personal merit.

Our multivariate results show that after controlling for relevant background factors, black Protestants are as much as *five times* more likely than white Protestants to support each of these government-based policies for reducing racial inequality. But as wide as these gaps are, they seem small when compared to an even more highly controversial outcome-based policy: reparations for slavery. Nearly 50% of black Protestants at least "agree" with the statement "The government

TABLE 8.1

Percentage Differences between Black and White Respondents in Their Commitment to Racial Identity, Political Beliefs and Actions, Beliefs about the Causes of Racial Inequality, and Levels of Support for Racial Policy (PALS and GSS)

Dependent variables	Black and white non-Protestants			Black Protestants and white mainline Protestants			Black Protestants and white evangelicals			Intraracial comparisons		
	Blacks	Whites	B–W[a]	Blacks	Whites	B–W[a]	Blacks	Whites	B–W[a]	BNP–BP[b]	WNP–WP[c]	WMP–WE[d]
Racial Identity[i]												
Treated unfairly[e]	43.4	7.2	**36.2*****	32.2	5.9	26.3***	31.7	10.3	21.4***	11.2	1.3	-4.4*
Aware of race[f]	57.1	17.7	39.4***	54.0	13.0	**41.0*****	53.0	16.0	37.0***	3.1	4.7*	-3.0
Race important[g]	88.1	49.6	38.5***	93.2	52.1	41.1***	92.2	50.3	**41.9*****	-5.1	-2.5	1.8
Close to race[h]	73.8	47.7	26.1***	75.9	48.2	**27.7*****	76.3	49.6	26.7***	-2.1	-0.5*	-1.4
Political Views[j]												
Conservative[j]	13.3	21.9	-8.6*	17.3	35.3	-18.0***	17.9	41.8	**-23.9*****	-4.0	-13.4***	-6.5
Moderate	18.1	29.4	-11.3*	14.7	32.1	**-17.4*****	13.4	22.5	-9.1*	3.4	-2.7	9.6*
Liberal[k]	26.5	27.5	-1.0	22.8	19.4	3.4	21.2	10.3	**10.9*****	3.7	8.1***	9.1***
Republican	6.0	21.9	15.9***	5.3	44.2	**-38.9*****	5.6	40.2	-34.6***	0.7	-22.3***	4.0
Independent	28.9	35.9	-7.0	12.0	22.9	-10.9*	12.3	28.0	**-15.7*****	16.9**	13.0***	-5.1
Democrat	57.1	34.9	22.2***	80.0	29.7	**50.3*****	77.1	27.1	50.0***	-22.9**	5.2*	2.6
Voted in '04 election[e]	53.0	69.4	-16.4**	66.0	84.7	**-18.7*****	65.9	68.9	-3.0	-13.0*	-15.3*	15.8***
Bush	11.6	42.8	-31.2***	14.9	63.6	-48.7***	17.9	74.7	**-56.8*****	-3.3	-20.8***	-11.1
Kerry	76.7	51.1	25.6	77.7	34.6	43.1***	75.0	23.0	**52.0*****	-1.0	16.5***	11.6***
Racial Inequality												
In-born ability[e]	11.3	7.3	4.0	11.4	8.4	3.0	11.3	6.2	**5.1**	-0.1	-1.1	2.2
Motivation[e]	41.2	43.6	-2.4	44.6	50.0	-5.4	41.8	59.2	**-17.4*****	-3.4	-6.4***	-9.2*
Education[e]	56.6	48.3	8.3	46.4	46.6	-0.2	43.8	34.5	**9.3***	10.2	1.7*	12.1**
Discrimination[e]	67.3	32.5	**34.8*****	53.3	26.8	26.5***	55.1	26.4	28.7***	14.0	5.7*	0.4
Racial Policy												
Help blacks[l]	55.6	13.8	**41.8*****	42.6	11.3	31.3***	42.3	9.4	32.9***	13.0	2.5*	1.9
Help minorities[m]	75.3	38.2	37.1***	70.5	37.5	33.0***	70.9	32.3	**38.6*****	4.8	0.7	5.2
Racial preferences[l]	57.2	11.7	**45.5*****	37.3	11.0	26.3***	37.4	8.5	28.9***	19.9*	0.7*	2.5
Reparations[m]	51.3	10.2	41.1***	50.7	6.6	**44.1*****	49.1	6.9	42.2***	0.6	3.6***	-0.3

* p < .05, ** p < .01, *** p < .001

Note: The largest racial gap across the religious-related categories appears in bold (two-tailed tests).

[a] Total difference is the product of blacks' percentage minus whites' percentage; [b] total difference is the product of black non-Protestants' percentage minus black Protestants' percentage; [c] total difference is the product of white non-Protestants' percentage minus white Protestants' percentage; [d] total difference is the product of white mainline Protestants' percentage minus white evangelicals' percentage; [e] percentage who reported at least "nearly every day"; [f] percentage of respondents who reported "yes"; [g] percentage who reported at least "very close"; [h] percentage who reported at least "somewhat important"; [i] all items under this heading contained within the PALS; [j] percentage who reported at least "somewhat conservative"; [k] percentage who reported at least "somewhat liberal"; [l] percentage who reported at least "agree" to or "favor" government action; [m] percentage who reported at least "somewhat agree"

should financially compensate black Americans who are the descendants of slaves." However, only 7% of white Protestants feel this way (see descriptive table B.8E). Our multivariate results confirm this incredibly wide and deep gap: African American Protestants are nearly 14 *times* more likely than white Protestants to support reparations for slavery.

While these findings are powerful, the full thrust of the differences between black and white Protestants does not become evident until we juxtapose them alongside differences between black and white non-Protestants. These results—which are accompanied by an additional set of findings in which we compare black Protestants with white followers of particular Protestant denominations—help to contextualize our awareness of links between race, religion, and identity politics among Protestants.

Table 8.1 displays differences in commitments to identity politics across three religious-related categories: black and white non-Protestants, black Protestants and white mainline Protestants, and black Protestants and white evangelicals. We compare and contrast these religious affiliations across four domains of identity politics: commitments to racial identity, political views, beliefs about racial inequality, and levels of support for racial policy. While we do not discuss commitments to racial identity and political views in detail, these categories help to demonstrate just how wide and deep the gulfs are between black and white Protestants. (Details on how to interpret the findings presented in this table can be found in the note).[18]

In a nutshell, the results in table 8F tell us three things. First, the most frequent and many of the widest differences in commitments to identity politics exist among black Protestants and white evangelicals. Followers of these religious traditions differ most widely on 10 of the 21 items (or 48%). Black Protestants and white mainline Protestants differ most widely on 7 items (or 33%). That means that the least frequent differences tend to occur among black and white non-Protestants. These groups differ most widely on only 4 items (19%, although some of these differences are quite wide as well).

Second, racial differences in commitments to identity politics often either gradually recede or intensify in accordance with whites' affiliation with Protestantism. Across 7 of the 21 items (or 33%), racial differences escalate as we move from white mainline believers to white evangelicals (see the findings for conservative, liberal, voted for Bush in the 2004 election, and the belief that racial inequality results from lack of motivation, for instance). Differences recede on only one item (or 5%; see "treated unfairly") as we move from white mainline Protestants to evangelicals.

There is still more to be learned from this table. To the far right, we have included three columns that provide data on how differences in affiliations with Protestantism shape attitudes *within* racial groups.[19] It appears that the nexus between religious affiliation and identity politics is *not* a major source of ideological conflict among African Americans: black Protestants and non-Protestants differ on only 4 items (or 19%). However, this is not true for whites: white Protestants and non-Protestants differ on 16 items (or 76%). Arguably, what is most telling about our findings for intraracial comparisons is that differences in commitments to identity politics are wider and deeper among white mainline Protestants and white evangelicals than they are among black Protestants and black *non-Protestants*. White Protestants differ among themselves on 7 items (or 33%).

So what do all of these findings mean? The results presented in table 8F demonstrate that race, religion, and identity politics are not only deeply intertwined but operate in dramatically different ways among black and white Americans. For blacks, the consequences of racial minority status are the driving force behind identity politics. The fact that black Protestants and black non-Protestants are largely similar in their commitments to identity politics suggests that racial group membership—not religion or political views—provides the framework that most African Americans use to interpret what they see out in the social world. This finding supports the contention that denominational affiliations are more consequential for white Protestants than for black Protestants. In other words, racial group membership takes precedence over individual denominational affiliations and associations with Protestantism in general in shaping blacks' commitments to identity politics.

For whites, on the other hand, religious affiliations with Protestantism in general and affiliations with particular denominations within Protestantism strongly influence commitments to identity politics. Moreover, it appears that political views are especially critical in shaping non-Protestants commitments to identity politics. These results not only attest to the complex effects of religion and political views among whites[20] but also suggest that earthly matters of identity politics profoundly restrict black and white Protestants' ability to all just get along.

Individualism, Structuralism, and Racial Reconciliation

The idea that black and white Christians must reconcile their differences and live as brothers and sisters in Christ is not new. The racial reconciliation movement was born out of racially oppressive conditions in society such as slavery and segregation. During the 1950s and '60s, a handful of black preachers and political activists who were inspired by the Civil Rights Movement began evangelizing that racial reconciliation is the "message of Christianity."[21] These early pioneers of the movement, such as John Perkins, Tom Skinner, and Samuel Hines, argued that racism is a "sin" that should be viewed in the same way that Christians view other moral transgressions such as murder, theft, and adultery. They also proclaimed that black and white Christians must demonstrate God's power by not only reconciling to one another but also linking arms to fight against inequality and injustice.[22]

The aforementioned leaders argued that three things must happen in order for blacks and whites to reconcile: (1) believers must *admit* that there are problems with race relations, (2) believers must *submit* to God's will in order to solve the problems of race relations, and (3) believers must *commit* to close-knit personal relationships with members of other races.[23] In addition to these larger goals of racial reconciliation, two additional goals emphasized "relocation" and "redistribution." The former called on Christians to pick up and move to parts of the country where they could help with improving race relations, while the latter addressed government and large-scale efforts at improving living conditions and opportunities for minorities.

Despite some early successes, the racial reconciliation movement did not find its stride until the mid 1990s. This second wave of the movement was more popular than the first because white evangelical preachers and activists played a more critical role in the crusade. With support from highly influential clergy such as Rev. Billy Graham and a great number of lesser-known yet deeply respected everyday preachers and believers such as Curtiss DeYoung and former University of Colorado head football coach Bill McCartney (the founder of the Promise Keepers), the racial reconciliation movement peaked: there was a deluge of new organizations, books, musicians, articles, publications, formal apologies, sermons, instructional guides, and religious conferences that addressed the issue. During this time, it was common for more than 50,000 believers to attend Promise Keepers events, which were often held in some of our nation's largest stadiums and arenas.

The second wave of the movement maintained most of the goals and values of the first wave (and even expanded on some of them). For instance, racism was still viewed as a "sin," so the movement maintained a focus on changing the hearts and minds of those believers who possessed prejudiced thoughts or engaged in discriminatory actions. In fact, much of the *reconciliation theology*[24] of admitting, submitting, and committing remained firmly in place. However, the broader interest in *social justice* goals—namely, attention to and support for redistributive policies—was no longer integral to the movement. The followers of the second wave at least indirectly depicted the "race problem" as an individual and cultural problem but not a structural problem. This implied that it could be "solved" by admitting, submitting, and committing but not necessarily *remitting* opportunities for racial minorities. In short, the second wave of the movement dropped the structural items off the reconciliation agenda and redoubled its efforts toward strengthening interpersonal bonds and cultural connections between blacks and whites.

The leaders and laity associated with the second wave passionately believed that they were doing God's will. However, the lack of a structural agenda—something that spoke to the nation's past and present "race problem" beyond individual and cultural differences—undoubtedly explains why many African Americans were less enthusiastic about the second wave of the racial reconciliation movement. The politics of identity go a long way toward explaining why it had nearly fizzled out by the late 1990s: most black Protestants wanted to do more than exchange "tears and hugs and [say] I'm sorry,"[25] while most white Protestants thought that would be enough.

This is because *black and white Protestants profoundly differ in their definitions and understandings of "racial reconciliation."* It could very well be that many white evangelicals were less interested in the first wave of the racial reconciliation movement because it was too structural in orientation, while many black Protestants were less interested in the second wave because it was too individualistic and cultural in orientation. In fact, Rev. Cecil Murray of First A.M.E. Church in Los Angeles advanced a variation of this point in his critique of the second wave. In an article published by the highly influential magazine *Christianity Today*, he declared that successful racial reconciliation efforts must address both individualism and structuralism. He wrote, "White evangelicals need an at-risk gospel. . . . Calling sinners to repentance means also calling societies and structures to repentance—economic, social, educational, corporate, political, religious structures. . . . The gospel at once works with the individual and the individual's society: to change one, we of necessity must change the other."[26]

Most of the high-ranking clergy members whom we interviewed would agree with Rev. Murray's assessment. We feel confident about this since we directly asked them to share their opinions about the possibilities for racial reconciliation. One of the final questions that we asked our interviewees was, "In recent years, there have been calls for racial reconciliation among Christians. Do you think that this is an important issue?" Our interviewees' answers to this question are complex and not easy to categorize. Of the 14 high-ranking clergy members, 6 affirmatively and emphatically responded "Yes" or "Absolutely" when responding to this question. Some of these interviewees then went on to advance a cultural imperative explanation for why they believe that racial reconciliation is "important." However, others recognized the importance of both cultural *and* structural factors. Regardless of whether their answers emphasized culture alone or culture in tandem with structure, these interviewees said that they (a) are not sure how to define "racial reconciliation" and/or (b) do not believe that blacks and whites define "racial reconciliation" in the same way.

Our remaining interviewees advanced epistemological explanations for why they believe that worldly issues of identity politics severely limit black and white Protestants' ability to reconcile. (Many of these clergy members are also unsure about the meaning of racial reconciliation.) While some of these high-ranking clergy members initially stated that racial reconciliation is "important," most of them either communicated (sometimes indirectly) that racial reconciliation is not important or expressed grave concerns about its relevance or ability to happen at all. Moreover, they argued that racial reconciliation efforts can only be successful if they include a social justice agenda that is structural in orientation.

Cultural imperative understandings of "racial reconciliation" emphasize the need for blacks and whites to "talk" with and "get to know" one another. This definition is most consistent with the goals of the second wave of the movement since it is *astructural* in orientation and largely revolves around improved knowledge, communication, and respect for others. We should point out that while these laudable goals are, in fact, consistent with the early pioneers' vision for "racial reconciliation," they say nothing about relocation, redistribution, or remittance.

For example, Rev. Henderson, the senior United Methodist pastor at a congregation in Los Angeles, strongly believes that racial reconciliation would testify to Christianity's power to bring historically divided people together. Her astructural rationale is most consistent with the goals and understandings of the movement's second wave:

> What a religion we would be if we could reconcile! What a statement we would make to this world. What a difference we could make in our communities, cities, regions, this world. Lord have mercy!
>
> It's absolutely necessary for us to reconcile. But we've got to deal with the cultural issues first. Knowing each other and worshiping together means understanding the different types of music, preaching styles, and such.
>
> *Interviewer: How do we do that?*

That's the million-dollar question. Of course, it comes with talking. It comes with laying down our prejudices. It comes with being willing to accept our differences.

Deacon Harris, a Pentecostal director of Christian counseling in New York City, also emphasized the need for improved interracial communication and cultural competence. He believes that blacks and whites must build camaraderie through truth and honesty, as well as a faith-based openness to learning from and about one another. While the thrust of his comment is a cultural imperative in substance and tone, his reference to U.S. President Barack Obama is a subtle reference to identity politics:

I do [believe that racial reconciliation is important] in this sense: it's kind of like the tone of the Obama presidency.[27] Black and white Christians, if we do believe that there is One Church and there's One Church universal, we need to talk to one another. We need to know one another. We should hope to get a view that maybe we've got different gifts and we've got different deficits, and maybe God has put us here together to learn from one another. The best will come out of us by so-called reconciling and talking.

What I mean by that is truth speaking, truth telling—not hiding my presuppositions, my hurts and issues with a white person, and that white person in turn being willing to listen to me, and me be willing to listen to him or her. We must recognize that there are differences and diversity, differences in culture, so let's talk about it.

[Whites should be able to ask us,] "Why do you [blacks in general, Pentecostals in particular] jump up and down while worshiping?" And we should ask them, "Why don't you do?"

If we're going to do better, we're going to need to learn from one another. But we're going to need to learn from one another by not hiding the important issues that we need to talk about.

Both Rev. Henderson and Deacon Harris advanced culturally based individualistic arguments for why and how black and white Protestants might reconcile. Pastor Smith, a young A.M.E. pastor in Fort

Worth, did so as well. While he too believes that blacks and whites should possess positive views of one another and have strong interpersonal relationships, his explanation stands out because he does *not* believe that cultural differences among Christians are a major source of intrafaith tension (some of our other interviewees feel this way as well). To the contrary, he believes that cultural distinctions should be preserved and celebrated as one of the many rich yet exceptional ways that individuals and groups can honor Christ:

> It depends on what we mean by "racial reconciliation." If "racial reconciliation" means all of us sitting together in the same church on Sunday morning, then I would not necessarily agree. The reason that I would not agree is because these cultural differences are unique with respect to how we [black and white Christians] worship and experience God.
>
> Now in terms of us first and foremost setting aside racial differences in the sense that someone is biologically superior or inferior to me—I believe that's *very important*. Race should not be a factor if we are all brothers and sisters who claim that we are Christians. That should have been dispelled as we as individuals started to follow Christ and follow God. The Bible clearly teaches us that there is no distinction between Jew and Gentile. The inference is that there is not a distinction between black and white. We are the Body of Christ, period.
>
> Does that mean that we have to all be in the same church? Not necessarily. I know that we have this problem in America of racial separation on Sunday morning. But I think that has a lot more due to with cultural preference than it does with racial indifference.

The latter part of Pastor Smith's statement is a great example of the ideological split between the first and second waves of the racial reconciliation movement. While all of the high-ranking clergy members whom we interviewed would agree that cultural factors strongly influence how black and white Protestants go about their religious faith, most of them—especially the epistemologists—would profoundly disagree with the idea that "cultural preferences," not "racial indifference," is the primary reason why "11 o'clock on Sunday morning . . . [is] the most segregated hour in this nation."[28] To the contrary, an epistemologist would argue that the consequences of racial minority status—not culture—chiefly explain why blacks and whites typically sit in different pews in different churches on most Sunday mornings. This rationale —which speaks to the continuing significance of racial group membership above and beyond one's religious beliefs—helps to explain why our remaining interviewees expressed indifference, uneasiness, and sometimes even antagonism when asked about the importance of racial reconciliation.

For instance, Rev. Johnson, the senior pastor at a large Baptist congregation in the Dallas–Fort Worth area, is also unsure about precisely what "racial reconciliation" means. However, his point stands out because he was actively involved in the second wave of the racial reconciliation movement. The first part of Rev. Johnson's statement is clearly a cultural imperative. Yet near the end of the statement, he—like Rev. Murray and a few other epistemologists whom we interviewed—suggests that individual and cultural efforts aimed at reconciling the races must be reinforced with structural interventions. Although Rev. Johnson does not provide details, his wonderment about "what's next" implies that "love," "forgiveness," and "building relationships" is not enough to bridge the racial divide between Christians:

> I guess my hesitation has to do with the fact that my feeling and emotion about that question [i.e., the importance of racial reconciliation] has changed over the last 15 years. Had you asked me that exact same question in the 1980s and probably most of the 1990s, my answer would've been, "Absolutely, yes, it's an important issue." And I still think it's a good idea. The only reason we [blacks and whites] are separated is because of our traditions, our cultures. We've made our cultures more important than the Cross by gathering on Sunday along the color line as opposed to our common religious beliefs . . . [*long pause*].
>
> But at the end of the day, every pastor and church has to do their best to practice their faith as they're led by the Spirit, letting the Bible direct them in prayers. And if it results in reconciliation, then you

have to *define what that means*; is it genuine? God be praised, that would be a wonderful thing. But if it is not, I think it's futile to spend a lot of energy and time trying to make something happen that for whatever reason it doesn't happen. If it doesn't fit, don't force it. I think many of us tried to force it in the 1990s. Without very much success too, by the way—obviously.

And I think when God, in His sovereignty, is ready for reconciliation to happen, it will. When we let go and let God, you won't need me, Bill McCartney, Tony Evans, Billy Graham, T. D. Jakes, Rick Warren, or anybody else to lift a finger. So it's no longer at the top of my agenda, though I still I think it's important and valuable.

See, at one point, I think that for many of us, racial reconciliation became the number-one issue that we thought needed to be fixed and addressed. By encouraging whites to repent to blacks for past and present sins of racism—and for blacks to respond with love and forgiveness by encouraging building relationships across racial lines —I think they did a good job with forwarding the agenda of what's often called *racial reconciliation*. But many of us blacks got tired of going because at every meeting a white man would walk up to you to repent for his racism. At some point, we began to wonder, "What's the next step in all of this?" Nothing happened after we forgave them. We forgave them, and they forgave us for our anger and bitterness in responding to their racism. But what's next? The next step never took place.

Rev. Robinson argued the same epistemological point but in a different way. He supports the ideals of the racial reconciliation movement *in principle* because he believes that there is "no place for racial discrimination" among Christians. Yet he expressed major concerns about the way that many white Christians have attempted to improve race relations. More specifically, he questions whether the word *reconciliation* provides cover for a much deeper objective: blacks' "becoming white" (i.e., abandoning their own distinctive faith-based culture and assimilating to the academic manner in which white Protestants go about their religious faith). Furthermore, he believes that white evangelicals are "right" in their attention to personal salvation but "wrong" in their disregard for social justice issues. For him (as well as others), this discrepancy is symptomatic of a wider and deeper racial cleavage in theologically based attitudes: the links between "faith" and "works."

Absolutely, I mean, scripture points to the unity of the human race on many different levels. God has extended His love to all humankind through Christ, so there is no place for racial discrimination.

Reconciliation is a restoration of relationship. First of all, human beings need to be reconciled to God through Christ, and they need to be reconciled to one another. So by all means do I think that the message of reconciliation is an *important* one.

But there are a couple of issues though. Sometimes when one group is talking about reconciliation, what they're really saying is kind of a code word. What they're saying is, "You need to become like me." I think that at least in some expressions of evangelical Christianity, that's what is happening. "Let's all reconcile and be white!" [*laughs*].

So, of course, some people are obviously against that. I believe in a lot of what these people are saying, but they have to also *live it out.* Evangelical Christianity rightly stresses the need for eternal salvation. The problem historically, though, is that the emphasis for many evangelicals has been so strong on personal salvation that many of the social dimensions of the gospel have been neglected. So that's allowed many people to ignore such injustices like slavery or poverty, while reasoning that salvation of the soul is the only thing that matters.

But one must account for the entirety of scripture. For example, Paul talks about faith expressing itself through love. James says that faith without works is dead. He says that genuine religion is this: to take care of the widows and orphans. So if there is a real faith, it's going to express itself in deeds and *actions.* If we truly believe in something, it's going to affect our *behavior.* When we talk about reconciliation, first of all we have to genuinely be reconciled to God. Then there has to be some type of change that occurs on the inside. But there must be changes in society too.

In many ways, our interviewees who advanced epistemological explanations seemed most unsure about how to define "racial reconciliation." Pastor Thomas's comment best captures the intellectual complexity and uncertainly surrounding this topic. He not only repeatedly expressed reservations about what "racial reconciliation" means, but he also addressed potential challenges to racial reconciliation such as denominational differences, the centrality of social justice issues, and the recent emergence of multiracial churches:

> Yes, absolutely, racial reconciliation is an important issue. The question, though, is what does it *mean*? [*laughs*]. For those of us who believe that the Lord is coming back for His church, I don't think that we believe that He's coming back to a black church or a white church. He's coming back for the church in general, so there needs to be racial reconciliation between black and white Christians. But what that means can and does vary widely.
>
> I think it's important that we understand that we are one in Christ and that we are able to come together as Christians in terms of evangelism. But we must also come together in terms of the social gospel and issues of justice so that we become a more just society.
>
> Take the A.M.E. Church, for instance. We started out in the Methodist Episcopal Church. But as we [blacks] increased our numbers, we weren't welcome. So we left that church not because we disagreed with any of the theological issues or even the church structure but because we believe that we should not be treated as second-class citizens at all—but especially not *within* the church.
>
> This tradition has carried on, and the A.M.E. Church has always been an open church. And we welcome anybody of any race, and there are a number of multicultural A.M.E. churches. But one of the interesting things is that, with respect to the growing number of multicultural churches across the country [regardless of denomination]—it's been my observation that African Americans are more likely to attend a multicultural church headed by a white person than white people are to attend a multicultural church headed by a black person. So if that's true, again, I must ask, when you talk about reconciliation, what does *that mean*?

40 Acres and a Mule

Our final group of epistemologists are clearly not very interested in racial reconciliation. To be clear, these high-ranking clergy members believe that black and white Protestants should at least try to get along. However, they also believe that a structurally oriented, race-based social justice agenda must be enacted to complement individual and cultural efforts to mend fences between blacks and whites. But they seriously doubt that this will ever happen, so they do not believe that our nation's longstanding "race problem" will be reconciled anytime soon.

Two Pentecostal pastors' epistemological explanations set the tone for this discussion. Both Rev. Boyd and Rev. Edwards strongly favor race-based redistributive policies—those that are designed specifically to assist African Americans. However, neither of them believes that such policies will ever come into fruition since the white majority tends to oppose them. Thus, both of these high-ranking clergy members (one an older preacher from the South and the other a younger preacher from the Midwest) argued that African Americans should not "wait" for the U.S. government to help improve conditions for blacks in society. Moreover, they believe that African Americans must collectively let go of the possibility of receiving reparations for slavery. Rev. Boyd addressed many blacks' longing for the U.S. government to give them "40 acres and a mule."[29] While his point is largely epistemological, it also includes subtle individualistic overtones:

Regardless of their status in life, every man and woman wants to be respected. We [African Americans] must not let go of that message. But we have to let go of some other things. For instance, a lot of times Caucasians don't want to talk to us because we keep bringing up the fact that we never received our 40 acres and a mule. We [African Americans] must realize that even if they had it—and they do—these people aren't going to give it to us.

The young whites say, "Look, I did not take anything from you." And it's not expedient for them to go all the way back through history and find out how their 40 acres belongs to us. Whites are not trying to find out a way to get rid of the 40 acres. They're trying to find out a way to get 40 more acres! [*laughs*].

So forget about the mule, forget about the 40 acres, and start getting yours based on where you are.

Rev. Edwards agrees with this assessment. The complexity of his point—which is demonstrated by his layering of individualism with structuralism—becomes evident in his critique of a local church-based movement aimed at helping blacks receive their "40 acres and a mule." It is worth noting that he does not believe that blacks have a better chance to receive reparations now that there is an African American president of the United States:

There's a group of people that are fighting for reparations here in Cleveland. They are trying to organize the churches so that we might go to Washington, D.C., and lobby for reparations. They want their 40 acres and a mule.

I think the government knew that they weren't giving us 40 acres and mule when they first said that! [*laughs*]. They probably also didn't think that that would pacify us for as long as it has, either. But too much time has gone by. People's bloodlines have mixed, and black people have started coming here from other parts of the world [i.e., immigrants], so we don't even know whose families were and were not slaves. So I don't believe that type of reconciliation is going to happen. It should, but it's virtually impossible.

Not too long ago, at a church here in Cleveland, a guy from the reparations group I just mentioned locked himself in a cage in front of one of the bigger congregations in the city. He stayed there for two days! He said that he wanted his 40 acres and a mule. Come on now, bruh [*in a sarcastic tone*]. I see blacks working, making money, and living in some of the best neighborhoods in this city. So I had to ask myself, "Does that guy just want an easy way out?" He just has his hand out waiting on something from the government. I believe everybody should get what's coming to them, but the Bible says, "if a man don't work, a man don't eat."

Telling someone that they should give you something because of what was done in the distant past is not a job! That's not working. We have a responsibility to ourselves, and if we don't uphold that responsibility, then we can't expect anyone else to.

The situation really is not going to change all that much once Obama takes office. So in the future, will that brother's [the man in the cage] explanation be, "Oh, they're still trying to keep the black man down"? Or is he gonna finally realize that he's keeping himself down by using that excuse?

Again, I do believe we [African Americans] deserve an apology and reparations, but I don't believe we should sit and wait for it. I don't believe anyone is going to come knock on anyone's door and hand them a big check and say, "Well, sorry for what happened to you. God bless you." *That's not going to happen* [*laughs*].

Rev. Shannon agrees that reparations and government-sponsored racial policies are not "going to happen." However, her comment stands out because she believes that most whites do not want to reconcile because they are afraid of losing political and social power now that a black man has been elected president of the United States. She cited a controversial happening from the 2008 presidential campaign as context for her larger point:

I think that we live in a world where white people are still very busy trying to figure out how they are going to stay on top yet still keep black people down. I could talk until I'm green in the face, and most whites won't hear anything about racial reconciliation.

White people are afraid right now. Do you remember when that white woman at a [Republican presidential nominee John] McCain rally stood up, started talking about Barack Obama? She said to a room full of people (and a lot of them applauded) that she thinks that Obama is "an Arab" and that she's "afraid" of what's going to happen to America if he becomes president. I personally don't think that she was afraid of whether he would be a good president. Her fear, I think, was that she will begin to *lose* some of the privileges that she's gotten accustomed to having if Obama won. Every white person in America gets the benefit of the doubt precisely because they are white. She's afraid of losing her personal part of that power.

So when you talk about reconciliation, you're mostly talking to *the hand* [*in a sarcastic tone*]. Right now, because of Obama, we are nowhere near a situation where white people—especially older whites —want to reconcile. It's going to take some time for them [whites] to realize that Obama might make some changes, but he's not going to make the kind of changes where they lose everything that they have. Personally, though, I'm still not ready to fight the battle to reconcile.

Interviewer: What kind of "battle" will it be?

Yes, reconciliation is going to be a battle. Why? Because we [African Americans] aren't on that Rodney King "Can't we all just get along?" stuff anymore. And I don't mean a violent battle, either. I mean a theological and economic battle. Racial reconciliation is a social battle because one side [i.e., whites] believe that they are in the throes of losing some of what they have historically had, while the other side [i.e., blacks] is in a position of gaining the kind of influence that they have never had before. So, no, I'm not sure if whites really want to reconcile.

Rev. Shannon's point speaks plainly and honestly to the worldly links between race, religion, and identity politics among black and white Christians. However, she was not our only interviewee to argue that Obama's election exposed just how wide and deep the divides are between black and whites in America. Rev. Washington, who possesses a master's degree in divinity, discussed Obama's presidency in a different way: he believes that Obama minimized the problems of race relations in order to get himself elected. Moreover, as with Rev. Robinson, he also attributed whites' reluctance to support social justice issues to their emphasis on "talk" (or faith) rather than "action" (or works).

At the height of the Civil Rights Movement, Dr. James Cone engaged in a great intellectual debate with Dr. J. Deotis Roberts. In essence, Cone's argument was, you can't talk about reconciliation without first

talking about justice, and it is wrong to be talking about reconciliation when our people are being shot down in the streets. And so, like
Cone, I don't think you're going to have racial reconciliation until
blacks and whites have a conversation that does not side step or step
over social justice issues.

See right now, you have Obama going around saying that there's
no such thing as "white America" or "black America"; there're no red
states or blue states, just one America. That's good political rhetoric,
but it's not reality. For example, in the predominantly white eastern
suburb where I live, if I called 911, they'll be at my house in two minutes. But a few Sundays ago, when one of my congregation members
who lives in Cleveland's predominantly black inner city called 911
after an asthma attack, it took EMS a half an hour to get there. That's
pretty black and white to me. And those realities can be enumerated
a million times in a million different ways that black people have to
live with.

So folks can talk that rhetoric of reconciliation, but when there is
no justice in *action*, when all of these issues, disparities, and maltreatment don't motivate people to change conditions in our society, then
you find yourself saying, "Well, why do you want to talk about reconciliation? You want to *talk* about reconciliation 'cause you don't want
to deal with all of these differences—or the redistribution of wealth
and opportunity."

Speaking of Dr. Cone, he, along with Rev. Shannon, Rev. Washington, Rev. Boyd, Rev. Edwards, and several other high-ranking
clergy members whom we interviewed, strongly believes that there
are major epistemologically based obstacles blocking the path toward
racial reconciliation. Moreover, he, like many leaders and support-
ers of both the first and second waves of the racial reconciliation
movement, strongly believes that the best (or only) way to "validate"
Christianity is to bring members of all racial groups together in unity
under its umbrella. However, he has major doubts that racial reconciliation will happen because it requires whites to relinquish some of
their political and social power in establishing a more just and egali-
tarian society.

I absolutely believe that racial reconciliation is *important*. I think the only way the Christian faith can be validated is whether it can create one community for members of all races.

Any time you have an all in-group community, you really have to question who brought it together. Was it was some cultural forces that brought it together, or was it a higher spiritual force? The only way the Christian churches—black and white—can validate themselves and their message is that they have to witness to a cross section of people that transcends race, because race is the most dividing force in the world.

Christians must bring the oppressor and the oppressed together as equals who are fully human with full power. And you must have conversations about power. You can't get reconciliation between the powerful and the powerless unless you disempower the powerful. But whites aren't willing to do that. They will let you come and participate in what they have, but they don't want you to have any power. And so *group* power is essential—not individual power, *group* power. So unless that—you can't get racial reconciliation or any kind of reconciliation unless you have reconciliation with power.

Revisiting the Building Blocks

The findings presented in this chapter provide strong support for our fifth and final *Justice building block of black Protestant faith*. The African American Protestant religious tradition is committed to social justice and equality for individuals and groups in society. Identity politics strongly influence the manner in which black Protestants go about their religious faith. Black Protestants primarily attribute contemporary racial inequality to structural rather than individualistic causes. As a result, they strongly support opportunity-enhancing and outcome-based policies that are specifically designed to assist African Americans with overcoming the problems of racial inequality.

It is worth noting that the *black sacred cosmos*'s commitment to social justice is not only limited to improving conditions for African Americans. Additional survey findings from the PALS and the

GSS reveal that as compared to white Protestants, black Protestants more strongly support race-based policies that target Latinos and class-based policies that target poor people regardless of their race. These results—as well as those from our in-depth interviews with high-ranking clergy—suggest that everyday black believers and their church leaders feel that people-oriented dimensions of Christianity (i.e., the links between "faith" and "works") can help with solving the racial and socioeconomic problems of contemporary inequality.

In contrast, the vast majority of white Protestants neither support government efforts to assist minorities and the poor nor possess a strong commitment to social justice. Disparate ideological commitments to individualism and structuralism are rooted in the highly complex and controversial intersections between racial group membership, religious affiliation, and political views. Consequently, the results presented in this chapter suggest that wide and deep differences in commitments to identity politics severely hinder prospects for racial reconciliation among black and white Protestants.

One final result testifies to the wide and deep differences between black and white Protestants. This finding is especially revealing considering some of our interviewees' argument that blacks and whites must "talk" with and "get to know" one another. Using our PALS survey, we found that 36% of black Protestants and 47% of white Protestants at least "agree" with the statement "One of the most effective ways to improve race relations in the United States is to *stop* talking about race" (see descriptive table B.8F).

Our multivariate results confirm that after controlling for the relevant background factors, black Protestants are less likely than white Protestants to assert that the tensions surrounding race relations will dissipate if we, as individuals and as a society, stop talking about our longstanding "race problem." What is more: racial differences on this item only grow wider and deeper when the comparison group is white evangelicals (this finding echoes the pattern presented in descriptive table 8.1). In other words, black Protestants and white evangelicals are farther apart in their beliefs about whether Americans should be "talking about race" than are black and white non-Protestants.

This result is especially troubling considering that in recent decades, white evangelicals have placed a premium on the ability of blacks and whites to talk with and get to know one another. Furthermore, it suggests that black and white Protestants' "hearts and minds" are more contrary than our research methodology can account for: racial reconciliation cannot happen until a number of very wide and deep structural, cultural, individual, and *interpersonal* communication gaps between black and white Protestants are closed. Thus, although we have come a long way, we still have a long way to go before solving our nation's historic "race problem."

Epilogue
The Race Problem and Beloved Community

The findings presented in this book are clear: black and white Protestants often think about and practice Christianity in vastly dissimilar ways. Results from our survey and in-depth interview data show that racial group membership strongly influences how black and white Protestants go about their religious faith. In conversation with members of our own respective racial groups, we have heard people question whether blacks and whites pray to or believe in the "same God" (you may know people who have wondered this as well). Questions and criticisms of this sort are not baseless, because it is true that black and white Protestants approach faith matters very differently, and faith *matters* very differently to these distinct groups of believers.

But make no mistake about it: the findings presented in chapter 3 strongly suggest that black and white Protestants pray to and believe in the same God. The area of our analysis where there is widespread agreement among the races—and arguably the area of our analysis where there *should* be widespread agreement—concerns Christianity's core tenets. Black and white Protestants are largely of the same mind with respect to their beliefs about the Apostles' Creed.

However, beyond this, the results presented here show that black and white Protestants are committed to distinct models of Christianity. The legacy of racial discrimination and inequality in America has strongly influenced black and white Protestants' *religious sensibilities.* The long shadow of American slavery helps to explain why blacks pray and attend worship services (among other activities) more often than whites do, as well as subscribe to certain faith-based beliefs more strongly than whites. Furthermore, the consequences of past and present racial stratification shed meaningful light on explaining why African Americans remain strongly committed to a racially specific form of Protestantism.

We offered a new framework for understanding how racial group membership color-codes faith-based thoughts and practices among Christians. We established and provided robust empirical support for our *five building blocks of black Protestant faith:* (1) *Experiential,* (2) *Survival,* (3) *Mystery,* (4) *Miraculous, and* (5) *Justice.* These touchstones addressed the nature of black religion by capturing the fundamentally distinct, dynamic, energetic, and at times intricate manner in which African American Protestants go about their religious faith. Moreover, our comprehensive research methodology allowed us to break new ground by presenting fresh theoretical insights, to fill some of the conceptual gaps in established ideas, and to capture the complexity of the *black sacred cosmos.* This study has provided greater quantitative and qualitative detail on black religion than has any other study to date. In many ways, our results challenge Christianity's status as a "universal religion" since different groups think about and practice Christianity in often fundamentally different ways.

In these final pages, we explain how the findings presented in this book supply knowledge relevant to the political, social, and religious functioning of this nation. In chapter 8, we showed how identity politics drive major differences between black and white Protestants' (a) beliefs about the causes of racial inequality, (b) levels of support for redistributive policy, and (c) definitions and understandings of "racial reconciliation." These results are central to our book's climax. To quickly review, black Protestants are more structural in orientation than whites are and tend to favor government efforts to reduce racial inequality. In contrast, white Protestants are more individualistic in orientation and tend to oppose government efforts. As a result, blacks Protestants tend to favor racial reconciliation efforts that include structural interventions, while white Protestants tend to favor efforts that emphasize strengthening interpersonal bonds and cultural connections. These wide and deep differences attest to obstacles we face as a nation with respect to solving our contemporary "race problem." Furthermore, they suggest that Rev. Dr. Martin Luther King, Jr.'s vision of the "Beloved Community"—a spiritually based gathering of people from all walks of life motivated by goodwill and reconciliation—will remain unachievable for the foreseeable future.

What Is the Beloved Community?

Dr. King did not coin the term "Beloved Community." Nor was he the first theologian or philosopher to articulate a vision for the Beloved Community.[1] However, his revelation of this ideal yet achievable appreciation for humanity takes popular precedence over all others. The success of the Civil Rights Movement ensured that Dr. King's views on faith and camaraderie would meaningfully impact millions of people across the American social landscape. His outlook on this topic influences people to this very day.

Dr. King's vision of the Beloved Community involved a dynamic interplay between individualistic, cultural, and structural solutions to the race problem. He devoted his life to building bridges across contentious groups, confronting social problems such as poverty and racism, and ameliorating inequality in society. Dr. King strongly believed that these issues (as well as many others) could be overcome through nonviolent activism buttressed by a steadfast commitment to love, brotherhood, and sisterhood among all people—regardless of their religion or race. He continually reaffirmed his commitment to individualistic and cultural initiatives aimed at "transforming" people's hearts and minds. Take, for instance, a statement that he made in 1956 after the U.S. Supreme Court upheld a ruling that outlawed segregation on public buses in Alabama: "The end is reconciliation; the end is redemption; the end is the creation of the Beloved Community. It is this type of spirit and this type of love that can transform opponents into friends. It is this type of understanding goodwill that will transform the deep gloom of the old age into the exuberant gladness of the new age. It is this love which will bring about miracles in the hearts of men."[2]

As a deeply devoted champion of equality, Dr. King supported the racial reconciliation movement's individualistic and cultural goals (in fact, he was personal friends with some leaders of the first wave). Although he articulated the message differently, he most certainly believed that Christians must (1) *admit* that there are problems with race relations, (2) *submit* to God's will in order to solve the problems of race relations, and (3) *commit* to close-knit personal relationships with members of other races. He not only preached these ideals but practiced them as well. Dr. King consistently and passionately argued that human beings of all colors and creeds—on the basis of their love and respect for all of humankind—must shake hands, exchange greetings, and depart friends. He declared that when conflicts emerge among people and groups, they should be dealt with humanely (i.e., "adversaries cooperating together in a spirit of friendship").[3] In fact, Dr. King directly addressed the links between love, our nation's race problem, and the Beloved Community:

> Love is creative and redemptive. Love builds up and unites; hate tears down and destroys. The aftermath of the "fight with fire" method which you suggest is bitterness and chaos, the aftermath of the love method is reconciliation and creation of the Beloved Community. Physical force can repress, restrain, coerce, destroy, but it cannot create and organize anything permanent; only love can do that. Yes, love —which means understanding, creative, redemptive goodwill, even for one's enemies—is the solution to the race problem.[4]

However, Dr. King did not believe that love and friendship alone would solve the race problem or foster the emergence of the Beloved Community. This is precisely why he placed a premium on *social justice*. Dr. King often said that "injustice anywhere is a threat to justice everywhere."[5] While he most certainly believed that admitting, submitting, and committing are important, he did not just talk about *remitting* but rather *gave his life* in the fight to change discriminatory laws and policies. In fact, he argued that admitting, submitting, and committing could only be successful if they were supported by *structural* interventions. Take, for instance, this passage from Dr. King's classic book *Where Do We Go from Here: Chaos or Community?* (1967):

The fourth challenge we face is to unite around powerful action programs to eradicate the last vestiges of racial injustice. We will be greatly misled if we feel that the [race] problem will work itself out. Structures of evil do not crumble by passive waiting. If history teaches anything, it is that evil is recalcitrant and determined, and never voluntarily relinquishes its hold short of an almost fanatical resistance. Evil must be attacked by a counteracting persistence, by the day-to-day assault of the battering rams of justice.[6]

The first three "challenges" that Dr. King writes about are individualistic or cultural in orientation. However, this "fourth challenge" is meaningful because it provides structural reinforcements for his first three solutions. Dr. King advocated for structural interventions because they provide long-term checks and balances for what could be short-term individualistic and cultural gains. In other words, he knew changing hearts and minds within white America would not ultimately ensure the equality of opportunity for all people (i.e., letting the race problem "work itself out"). A more level playing field through the abolition of unjust laws and "powerful action programs" was essential.

Lastly, Dr. King's attention to structuralism lays the equitable foundation on which the Beloved Community rests. He tirelessly fought for equal rights and the equality of opportunity for all Americans — again regardless of their religion or race. And while the Civil Rights Movement was in many ways a "church movement,"[7] Dr. King did not believe that the Beloved Community was a gathering place for Christians *only*. To the contrary, Christianity provided the basis for a fellowship of humanity that not only emanated a love and appreciation for all people but ultimately drew followers of other faiths *into* the Beloved Community. For example, in his response to a contemptuous letter from a prosegregationist white woman who believed that racial inequality was ordained by God, Dr. King wrote, "It is still true that in Christ [i.e., when someone is a Christian] there is neither Jew nor Gentile (Negro nor white) and that out of one blood God made all men to dwell upon the face of the earth."[8] The point that we are trying to make is that Dr. King supported structural interventions and social justice because he believed that reducing poverty and inequality would set the tone for the fellowship of humanity.

Where Do We Go from Here?

In many ways, black/white race relations in America have reached a crossroad. In chapters 6 and 8, we discussed a host of recent studies showing that racial inequality remains alive and well in the contemporary United States. Although African Americans have made significant gains, they still lag far behind whites across a bevy of quality-of-life indicators such as income, educational attainment, occupational prestige, gainful employment, wealth, home ownership, life expectancy, health outcomes, and family-related factors, to name a few.

Furthermore, our survey findings from the PALS and the GSS showed that black and white American Protestants dramatically differ in their explanations and solutions for reducing these wide and deep differences. Whites are probably correct that individualistic and cultural factors help to perpetuate at least some of the problems of racial inequality. However, blacks are also correct that the aforementioned problems are primarily structural in orientation; virtually all of them existed *before* the Civil Rights Movement, and they have persisted 50 years after its largely successful policies and initiatives were implemented. Racial inequality has been part of the American social fabric since our nation's founding. In fact, Gunnar Myrdal's classic assertion that racial inequality is the product of "the principle of cumulation" —that disadvantages associated with blacks' second-class citizenship have accumulated across different historical epochs and spheres of society[9]—is probably more accurate and relevant now than ever before. This is precisely why we must ask, how can the Beloved Community emerge when there is so much inequality in our society? And how can the Beloved Community emerge when there is not only inequality among Protestants, but black and white Protestants differ more dramatically than black and white non-Protestants in their beliefs about the causes of and solutions for ameliorating inequality? Will we, as a nation, be proactive and *do something* about the problems of inequality? Or will we leave these problems to their own devices and hope that they "work themselves out"? In many ways, we are now discovering the limits of the successes of the Civil Rights Movement. Landmark legislation such as the Civil Rights Acts of 1964 and 1968, the Voting Rights Act of 1965, and equal opportunity policies such as affirmative action help to ensure a level playing field as we move toward *the future*. However, these policies do nothing to redress our nation's ignominious *past*. The *cumulative disadvantages* of slavery and segregation clearly have a lot to do with the problems of contemporary racial inequality. Although blacks are now free to run in the race to success, most of them start toward the back of the pack and have more hurdles to jump over before crossing the finishing line than do whites. As U.S. President Lyndon B. Johnson famously stated in his 1965 commencement address to Howard University, "You do not take a person who, for years, has been hobbled by chains and liberate him, bring him up to the starting line of a race and then say, 'you are free to compete with all the others,' and still justly believe that you have been completely fair. Thus it is not enough just to open the gates of opportunity. All our citizens must have the ability to walk through those gates."[10]

Unfortunately, results from a number of recent studies suggest that most Americans are choosing to let the problems of racial inequality "work themselves out" rather than becoming proactive. For example, we already know that most whites do not favor government efforts to reduce racial inequality. This is important because as with previous periods of American history, whites still hold considerable sway of over solutions to the race problem.

However, it would be unfair solely to blame white America for our contemporary race problem. In recent decades, there has been a notable (and in some cases steep) decline in African Americans' commitment to racially specific structural explanations for inequality.[11] In other words, with the passage of time, blacks are growing less and less committed to the idea that "racial discrimination" explains why they—as a collective group—continue to lag behind whites. African Americans are still far more likely than whites to emphasize the effects of racial discrimination. But as compared to the early 1980s, far fewer African Americans in today's world specifically attribute racial inequality to racial discrimination.[12]

These findings suggest that blacks' and whites' beliefs about the causes of racial inequality are slowly drifting toward a consensus. It could very well be that blacks' and whites' *attitudes* about the causes of racial inequality may not remain at the impasse for long: a few decades from now, it is possible that majorities of both black and white Americans will attribute racial inequality to *motivational individualism* (the idea that some people possess the "right" cultural values or internal drive to succeed). This is partly because as more and more blacks achieve their American dreams, they are growing increasingly likely to blame other blacks for not working "hard enough" to earn their own personal piece of the pie.[13]

We are certain that if Dr. King were alive today, he would be critical of blacks' growing reluctance to explain racial inequality on the basis of persistent racial discrimination. He would also still be critical of many whites' continued resistance to structural interventions and social justice. While Dr. King emphasized the importance of hard work and self-reliance, he also believed it was unfair to "blame the individual" (particularly poor people and minorities) or to hold people within those groupings solely responsible for their predicament. This is precisely why he argued that the "structures of evil do not crumble by passive waiting" and that we must "unite around powerful action programs to eradicate the last vestiges of racial injustice." In other words, he did not believe that the Beloved Community could be built on an individualistic or cultural foundation that is astructural in orientation.

It seems that the answer to Dr. King's rhetorical question is also more relevant now than ever: where do we go from here? The good news is that, among Christians, the successes of the first two waves of the racial reconciliation movement provide a promising individualistic and cultural basis for improving race relations. Don't get us wrong: we strongly believe that blacks and whites must talk, get to know one another, and hopefully build stronger cross-cultural bonds. However, we have argued from the outset of this book that such improvements will have limited success since they do not address the broader structural dynamics that provide the backdrop for—or contextualize —black/white race relations.

The bad news is that in the aftermath of Dr. King's death, racial inequality continues to fester, and too few people seem interested in doing much about it. We believe that all Christians and others who are serious about realizing the Beloved Community must make it of absolute central importance to work for racial equality and social justice. These are in every way spiritual goals to be pursued with passion— they test our mettle with respect to our understanding of the connection between "faith" and "works." The findings presented in this book clearly show that our nation's history is not just a thing of the past; it still lives with us today. In the final analysis, we cannot expect to live in a better world if we do not become actively involved in efforts to eliminate racism, poverty, and injustice.

Appendix A

Sampling Procedures / Sample Characteristics

Portraits of American Life Study Methodology

The Portraits of American Life Study (PALS) is a multilevel study focused on religion in the United States, with a particular focus on capturing ethnic and racial diversity. From April to October 2006, face-to-face interviews were conducted with 2,610 respondents (however, in this study, we analyze data for Protestants only). In this appendix, we describe the sampling methodology, data collection, outcome rates, and data weighting.

PALS Sampling

To obtain a probability sample yet achieve the goal of racially diverse oversamples, a four-stage sampling procedure was used. The sample design and interviews were conducted by RTI International, the second-largest independent nonprofit research organization in the United States. The PALS covers the civilian, noninstitutionalized household population in the continental United States who were 18 years of age or older at the time the survey was conducted and who speak English or Spanish. The sampling frame was based on the use of residential mailing lists supplemented with a frame-linking procedure to add households not included on the lists to the frame. In a recently completed national household survey, RTI estimated that this combined sampling frame accounted for over 98% of the occupied housing units in the United States.

1. In stage one of the sampling, U.S. Census data were used to construct a nationally representative sampling frame of primary sampling

units (PSUs) defined as three-digit zip code tabulation areas. After the frame was constructed, 60 PSUs were sampled with probabilities proportional to a composite size measure that weights PSUs with concentrations of minorities higher than other PSUs with the same number of addresses. The sample of 60 PSUs yielded a variety of local areas from across the country and provided an adequate number of degrees of freedom for variance estimation. While the use of composite size measures reduced screening costs by focusing the sample on PSUs with concentrations of minorities, it should be noted that the coverage of the sample was not adversely affected because PSUs that were mostly "nonminority" had a chance of being selected, as were nonminority households within mostly "minority" PSUs.

2. At the second stage, two five-digit zip codes from each selected PSU (120 zips in all) were selected, again with composite size measures that weight PSUs with concentrations of minorities higher than other PSUs with the same number of addresses.

3. At the third stage, on average, about 100 addresses from each selected zip code were sampled. From these, some addresses were found ineligible because they were not occupied or had no English or Spanish speakers (rarely) or due to physical and mental inability. After the addresses were selected, RTI produced digital maps for a subsample of selected addresses to facilitate the use of the half-open interval (HOI) frame-linking procedure that identified and included housing units that are not on the mailing lists. Housing units may be missing because of new housing units built in the time between frame development and data collection or because of errors in the frame development stage. Field interviewers reported to the home office any missing housing units that were not on the field enumeration. When confirmed by the home office that the units were excluded from the field enumeration, the missed unit was added to the sample to improve coverage.

4. At the fourth stage, one person per selected housing unit was selected for interview. RTI generated a sample selection table for use by the field interviewers at each address to randomly determine which eligible person at the address should be asked to participate in the study.

After data collection was completed, each respondent was assigned a sampling weight that reflected his or her probability of selection at

each stage. The weight was calculated as the inverse of the overall selection probability and can be thought of as the number of persons
in the population that the sample member represents. Moreover, and
importantly, census projections were used to poststratify the weights
of respondents to compensate for differential nonresponse and non-
coverage. Also, due to the design, the data should be analyzed to correct for clustering (by obtaining correct standard errors). Programs
such as STATA or SPSS's Complex Samples are designed for calculat-
ing corrected standard errors and significance tests.

Collecting the Data

To conduct the interviews, advance letters were mailed to all selected households four to five days before interviewers' initial visits to
the sample households. Interviewers then visited sample households
and completed a screening interview, narrowing our sample to meet
the subsample goals as well as to identify English- or Spanish-speaking
adults. The screening was conducted using a paper-and-pencil instru-
ment (PAPI). Upon selecting a respondent from the household and
if the respondent agreed to participate, a questionnaire was adminis-
tered using a laptop computer. Respondents were paid an incentive of
$50 to complete the interview, which took an average of 80 minutes.

A portion of the questionnaire covered sensitive topics such as relationship behaviors and quality, deviance, attitudes about race and
ethnicity, moral attitudes, and religious beliefs and authority. At this
point, the respondent was given a device for audio computer-assisted
self-interviewing (ACASI) to complete about 70 questions. During
this portion of the survey, the respondent wore earphones to hear the
prerecorded questions and entered his or her responses directly into
the computer, apart from the knowledge or aid of the interviewer.

Outcome Rates

We calculated outcome rates—contact rate, screening completion
rate, cooperation rate, and response rate—for the PALS, Wave 1, using
the appropriate formulas based on the definitions provided by the

American Association for Public Opinion Research.[1] Of the homes in which interviewers attempted to reach an eligible respondent, 83% were successfully contacted. Of those contacted persons,[2] 86% were screened. Of the persons screened and selected for an interview, 82% completed an interview. This yielded a response rate of 58% (.83 contact rate × .86 screening completion rate × .82 cooperation rate).[3]

Weighting the Data

By applying the weight variable, the national-level PALS sample closely mirrors the averaged 2005–2006 American Community Surveys (ACS) estimates,[4] considered the gold standard of surveys done between censuses. Table A.1 compares the unweighted and weighted percentages for certain demographics alongside the ACS figures. Once the weight variable is applied, the distributions by race and ethnicity, household income, educational attainment, median age, and marital status for the two sets of data are not significantly different from each other.

TABLE A.1
*Comparison of 2006 PALS and Averaged 2005–2007
American Community Surveys (ACS)*

	PALS		ACS
	Unweighted	Weighted	
Race and Ethnicity			
White, non-Hispanic (%)	48	69	69
Black, non-Hispanic (%)	20	11	11
Hispanic (%)	20	12	13
Asian, non-Hispanic (%)	7	4	4
Married (%)	46	57	53
Median age in years	42	45	45
Household Income			
Less than $30,000 (%)	37	30	30
$30,000 up to $59,999 (%)	30	31	28
$60,000 up to $99,999 (%)	21	24	23
$100,000 and up (%)	12	16	19
Educational Attainment			
Less than high school (%)	14	12	16
HS grad to some college (%)	60	60	59
Bachelor's degree (%)	17	16	16
Advanced degree (%)	10	11	9

Note: Due to rounding, figures may not add to 100%.

TABLE A.2

Percentage Distributions by Race for All Independent Variables in the Portraits of American Life Study (PALS; Black and White Protestants Only)

Independent variables	Blacks	Whites	T-value[a]
Socioeconomic Status			
Income			6.94***
Less than $5,000	9.6	3.1	
$5,000 to $9,999	9.0	3.0	
$10,000 to $14,999	11.7	3.4	
$15,000 to $19,999	4.8	6.0	
$20,000 to $24,999	4.8	5.6	
$25,000 to $29,999	6.9	5.0	
$30,000 to $34,999	5.9	6.1	
$35,000 to $39,999	16.5	14.9	
$40,000 to $49,999	5.3	9.1	
$50,000 to $59,999	4.8	8.5	
$60,000 to $69,999	5.9	6.7	
$70,000 to $79,999	5.9	5.6	
$80,000 to $89,999	2.1	5.6	
$90,000 to $99,999	3.2	3.5	
$100,000 to $124,999	1.6	4.9	
$125,000 to $149,999	1.0	3.6	
$150,000 to $174,999	0.5	1.9	
$175,000 to $199,999	0.5	1.3	
$200,000 and up	0.0	2.2	
Education			3.51***
Less than high school	20.2	10.2	
HS degree or equivalent	52.6	54.8	
Some college	11.7	8.9	
Bachelor's degree	9.6	18.3	
Advanced degree	5.9	7.8	
Sociodemographics			
Age	(43.3)	(48.0)	3.59***
Women	34.7	46.2	−2.98***
Southerners	54.0	39.5	−3.60***

*** p < .001

Notes: Means appear in parentheses. See appendix B, descriptive table B.1A, for data on church attendance by race. Distributions for black and white Protestants across the independent variables in the General Social Survey parallel those presented here. Two-tailed tests.
[a] Scores reflect overall test differences among black and white Protestants on a particular variable.

Data Coding and Analysis Procedures

Due to space constraints, we are unable to publish detailed information regarding our data coding and analysis procedures. However, we will gladly provide this information upon request. With respect to our independent variables, income, education, and age are analyzed as continuous predictors, while gender (women) and region of residence (southerners) are analyzed as dichotomous predictors (see table A.2 for more information.

The dependent variables are coded in a straightforward and conventional way. Some of these items are analyzed as continuous outcomes, others as ordinal outcomes, and still others as dichotomous outcomes. As a result, the data examined in this book are analyzed by way of ordinary least squares regression, ordinal logistic regression, and binary logistic regression (see appendix D for more information).

Appendix B
Descriptive Tables

Chapter 1

Research Methods

TABLE B.1A

Percentage Distributions by Race for Church Attendance (PALS)

Q: How often do you attend worship services at your congregation?

Answer possibilities	Blacks	Whites	T-value
Never	7.3	19.2	
Once or twice a year	12.3	14.5	
Several times a year	12.7	13.8	
Once a month	6.5	5.6	
Two to three times a month	16.0	9.6	
Once a week	23.7	23.9	
Twice a week	15.6	7.5	
Three times a week or more	5.9	5.9	
Total	100.0	100.0	−4.27***

* p < .05, ** p < .01, *** p < .001
Note: T-values assess differences between blacks and whites on the variable overall, not the individual answer possibilities (two-tailed tests).

TABLE B.1B

Percentage Distributions by Race for Church Attendance (GSS)

Q: How often do you attend religious services?

Answer possibilities	Blacks	Whites	T-value
Never	8.9	12.1	
Less than once a year	4.6	7.2	
Once a year	5.3	13.5	
Several times a year	10.6	12.5	
Once a month	6.3	6.9	
Two to three times a month	14.7	8.8	
Nearly every week	6.1	6.4	
Every week	29.6	23.2	
More than once a week	13.9	9.4	
Total	100.0	100.0	−5.47***

* p < .05, ** p < .01, *** p < .001
Note: T-values assess differences between blacks and whites on the variable overall, not the individual answer possibilities (two-tailed tests).

TABLE B.1C
Percentage Distributions by Race for Church Membership (PALS)
Q: Are you an official member of a religious congregation?

Answer possibilities	Blacks	Whites	T-value
No	15.8	25.4	
Yes	84.2	74.6	
Total	100.0	100.0	−2.71**

* p < .05, ** p < .01, *** p < .001
Note: T-values assess differences between blacks and whites on the variable overall, not the individual answer possibilities (two-tailed tests).

Chapter 3

Core Christian Tenets

TABLE B.3A
Percentage Distributions by Race for the Belief in God (PALS)
Q: I definitely believe in God.

Answer possibilities	Blacks	Whites	T-value
Strongly disagree	0.1	0.1	
Somewhat disagree	0.9	0.6	
Neither agree nor disagree	1.7	0.7	
Somewhat agree	0.2	5.6	
Strongly agree	97.1	93.0	
Total	100.0	100.0	0.79

* p < .05, ** p < .01, *** p < .001
Note: T-values assess differences between blacks and whites on the variable overall, not the individual answer possibilities (two-tailed tests).

TABLE B.3B
Percentage Distributions by Race for Beliefs about Creation (PALS)
Q: God created the world in six 24-hour days.

Answer possibilities	Blacks	Whites	T-value
Strongly disagree	18.9	19.2	
Somewhat disagree	4.5	8.1	
Neither agree nor disagree	19.6	24.5	
Somewhat agree	6.9	10.2	
Strongly agree	50.1	38.0	
Total	100.0	100.0	1.99*

* p < .05, ** p < .01, *** p < .001
Note: T-values assess differences between blacks and whites on the variable overall, not the individual answer possibilities (two-tailed tests).

TABLE B.3C
Percentage Distributions by Race for Beliefs about Jesus Christ (PALS)
Q: Which statement best describes your beliefs about Jesus Christ?

Answer possibilities	Blacks	Whites	T-value
He was the Divine, only Son of God	91.1	88.9	
A prophet of God, but not God	3.8	4.5	
A wise man or a good moral teacher, but not God	3.0	5.3	
He was something not described above	1.9	1.3	
Not heard of Jesus Christ	0.2	0.0	
Total	100.0	100.0	−0.40

* p < .05, ** p < .01, *** p < .001
Note: T-values assess differences between blacks and whites on the variable overall, not the individual answer possibilities (two-tailed tests).

TABLE B.3D
Percentage Distributions by Race for Beliefs about the Resurrection of Christ (PALS)
Q: Jesus Christ physically rose from the dead.

Answer possibilities	Blacks	Whites	T-value
Strongly disagree	3.5	0.8	
Somewhat disagree	1.7	1.6	
Neither agree nor disagree	4.9	7.3	
Somewhat agree	4.7	11.7	
Strongly agree	85.2	78.6	
Total	100.0	100.0	0.13

* p < .05, ** p < .01, *** p < .001
Note: T-values assess differences between blacks and whites on the variable overall, not the individual answer possibilities (two-tailed tests).

TABLE B.3E
Percentage Distributions by Race for Beliefs about Heaven (PALS)
Q: I believe in Heaven where people live with God forever.

Answer possibilities	Blacks	Whites	T-value
Strongly disagree	0.5	0.9	
Somewhat disagree	1.0	1.4	
Neither agree nor disagree	4.3	5.0	
Somewhat agree	6.5	11.7	
Strongly agree	87.7	81.0	
Total	100.0	100.0	1.94*

* p < .05, ** p < .01, *** p < .001
Note: T-values assess differences between blacks and whites on the variable overall, not the individual answer possibilities (two-tailed tests).

TABLE B.3F

Percentage Distributions by Race for Beliefs about Hell (PALS)

Q: I believe there is a Hell where people experience pain as punishment for their sin.

Answer possibilities	Blacks	Whites	T-value
Strongly disagree	5.4	6.7	
Somewhat disagree	3.6	6.4	
Neither agree nor disagree	5.8	9.3	
Somewhat agree	12.7	17.5	
Strongly agree	72.5	60.1	
Total	100.0	100.0	2.81**

* p < .05, ** p < .01, *** p < .001
Note: T-values assess differences between blacks and whites on the variable overall, not the individual answer possibilities (two-tailed tests).

TABLE B.3G

Percentage Distributions by Race for Beliefs about the Afterlife (GSS)

Q: Do you believe there is life after death?

Answer possibilities	Blacks	Whites	T-value
No	14.5	11.2	
Yes	85.5	88.8	
Total	100.0	100.0	−1.38

* p < .05, ** p < .01, *** p < .001
Note: T-values assess differences between blacks and whites on the variable overall, not the individual answer possibilities (two-tailed tests).

Religious Centrality

TABLE B.3H

Percentage Distributions by Race for the Importance of God (PALS)

Q: How important is God or spirituality in your life?

Answer possibilities	Blacks	Whites	T-value
Not at all important	0.2	1.2	
Somewhat important	6.2	20.4	
Very important	30.5	27.0	
Extremely important	29.1	23.6	
By far the most important part of your life	34.0	27.8	
Total	100.0	100.0	4.35***

* p < .05, ** p < .01, *** p < .001
Note: T-values assess differences between blacks and whites on the variable overall, not the individual answer possibilities (two-tailed tests).

TABLE B.3I

Percentage Distributions by Race for the Importance of Religious Faith (PALS)

Q: How important is religion or religious faith to you personally?

Answer possibilities	Blacks	Whites	T-value
Not at all important	2.5	3.0	
Somewhat important	10.5	23.8	
Very important	37.1	29.4	
Extremely important	25.7	21.7	
By far the most important part of your life	24.2	22.1	
Total	100.0	100.0	2.64**

* p < .05, ** p < .01, *** p < .001

Note: T-values assess differences between blacks and whites on the variable overall, not the individual answer possibilities (two-tailed tests).

TABLE B.3J

Percentage Distributions by Race for Religiosity (GSS)

Q: To what extent do you consider yourself a religious person? Are you . . .

Answer possibilities	Blacks	Whites	T-value
Not religious at all	3.1	4.7	
Slightly religious	14.4	19.2	
Moderately religious	45.1	50.7	
Very religious	37.4	25.4	
Total	100.0	100.0	3.53***

* p < .05, ** p < .01, *** p < .001

Note: T-values assess differences between blacks and whites on the variable overall, not the individual answer possibilities (two-tailed tests).

TABLE B.3K

Percentage Distributions by Race for Spirituality (GSS)

Q: To what extent do you consider yourself a spiritual person? Are you . . .

Answer possibilities	Blacks	Whites	T-value
Not spiritual at all	2.3	4.8	
Slightly spiritual	12.9	17.5	
Moderately spiritual	41.0	44.6	
Very spiritual	43.8	33.1	
Total	100.0	100.0	3.42***

* p < .05, ** p < .01, *** p < .001

Note: T-values assess differences between blacks and whites on the variable overall, not the individual answer possibilities (two-tailed tests).

Chapter 5

Biblical Perspectives

TABLE B.5A

Percentage Distributions by Race for Beliefs about the Bible (GSS)

Q: Which of these statements comes closest to describing your feelings about the Bible?

Answer possibilities	Blacks	Whites	T-value
The Bible is the actual word of God and is to be taken literally, word for word.	71.4	41.4	
The Bible is the inspired word of God but not everything should be taken literally, word for word.	24.7	49.8	
The Bible is an ancient book of fables, legends, history, and moral precepts recorded by men.	3.9	8.8	
Total	100.0	100.0	−8.58***

* p < .05, ** p < .01, *** p < .001
Note: T-values assess differences between blacks and whites on the variable overall, not the individual answer possibilities (two-tailed tests).

TABLE B.5B

Percentage Distributions by Race for Beliefs about Moral or Religious Errors in the Bible (PALS)

Q: There are errors in your religious text on moral, spiritual, or religious matters.

Answer possibilities	Blacks	Whites	T-value
Strongly disagree	56.7	50.2	
Somewhat disagree	6.3	10.8	
Neither disagree nor agree	23.2	24.1	
Somewhat agree	7.0	11.3	
Strongly agree	6.8	3.6	
Total	100.0	100.0	0.64

* p < .05, ** p < .01, *** p < .001
Note: T-values assess differences between blacks and whites on the variable overall, not the individual answer possibilities (two-tailed tests).

TABLE B.5C
*Percentage Distributions by Race for Beliefs about Scientific or
Historical Errors in the Bible (PALS)*
Q: There are errors in your religious text regarding science or history.

Answer possibilities	Blacks	Whites	T-value
Strongly disagree	53.6	45.5	
Somewhat disagree	8.2	12.4	
Neither disagree nor agree	24.0	27.1	
Somewhat agree	10.2	9.8	
Strongly agree	4.0	5.2	
Total	100.0	100.0	-1.37

* p < .05, ** p < .01, *** p < .001
Note: T-values assess differences between blacks and whites on the variable overall, not the individual answer possibilities (two-tailed tests).

Reading and Studying the Bible

TABLE B.5D
Percentage Distributions by Race for Reading the Bible (PALS)
Q: Outside of religious worship services, have you read any part
of your religious text in the past 12 months?

Answer possibilities	Blacks	Whites	T-value
No	11.2	26.0	
Yes	88.8	74.0	
Total	100.0	100.0	5.39***

* p < .05, ** p < .01, *** p < .001
Note: T-values assess differences between blacks and whites on the variable overall, not the individual answer possibilities (two-tailed tests).

TABLE B.5E
Percentage Distributions by Race for the Frequency of Reading the Bible (PALS)
Q: How often have you typically read your religious text in the past 12 months?

Answer possibilities	Blacks	Whites	T-value
Once	2.5	4.5	
A few times (a year)	23.9	30.8	
Once a month	6.4	8.2	
Two to three times a month	13.1	12.5	
Once a week	9.5	8.8	
A few times a week (but less than every day)	26.5	20.0	
Once a day	10.9	13.0	
More than once a day	7.2	2.2	
Total	100.0	100.0	2.75**

* p < .05, ** p < .01, *** p < .001
Note: T-values assess differences between blacks and whites on the variable overall, not the individual answer possibilities (two-tailed tests).

TABLE B.5F

Percentage Distributions by Race for Participation in a Bible Study Group (PALS)

Q: Are you part of a small group that studies your religious text?

Answer possibilities	Blacks	Whites	T-value
No	64.9	74.9	
Yes	35.1	25.1	
Total	100.0	100.0	−2.62**

* p < .05, ** p < .01, *** p < .001

Note: T-values assess differences between blacks and whites on the variable overall, not the individual answer possibilities (two-tailed tests).

Racial Differences in Prayer

TABLE B.5G

Percentage Distributions by Race for the Frequency of Prayer (PALS)

Q: In the past 12 months, how often have you typically prayed,
not including before meals and at religious services?

Answer possibilities	Blacks	Whites	T-value
Never	2.1	7.9	
A few times a year	7.1	15.6	
Once a month	1.6	3.7	
Two to three times a month	6.6	9.0	
Once a week	4.3	5.3	
A few times a week			
(but less than every day)	16.3	18.2	
Once a day	28.5	18.2	
Two or three times a day	18.5	15.2	
More than three times a day	15.0	6.9	
Total	100.0	100.0	6.76***

* p < .05, ** p < .01, *** p < .001

Note: T-values assess differences between blacks and whites on the variable overall, not the individual answer possibilities (two-tailed tests).

TABLE B.5H

Percentage Distributions by Race for the Frequency of Prayer (GSS)

Q: About how often do you pray?

Answer possibilities	Blacks	Whites	T-value
Never	0.4	4.4	
Less than once a week	3.1	9.5	
Once a week	3.9	6.6	
Several times a week	8.9	11.8	
Once a day	34.1	30.2	
Several times a day	49.6	37.5	
Total	100.0	100.0	6.91***

* p < .05, ** p < .01, *** p < .001

Note: T-values assess differences between blacks and whites on the variable overall, not the individual answer possibilities (two-tailed tests).

TABLE B.5I
Percentage Distributions by Race for the Frequency of
Prayer before Eating a Meal (PALS)
Q: At your meals at home, how often does someone say grace or give thanks aloud?

Answer possibilities	Blacks	Whites	T-value
Never	9.8	20.9	
A few times (a year)	8.9	24.1	
Once a month	2.0	5.7	
Two to three times a month	2.6	4.5	
Once a week	2.5	2.5	
A few times a week (but less than every day)	12.9	13.3	
Once a day	21.7	12.5	
More than once a day	39.6	16.5	
Total	100.0	100.0	9.27***

* p < .05, ** p < .01, *** p < .001
Note: T-values assess differences between blacks and whites on the variable overall, not the individual answer possibilities (two-tailed tests).

Revisiting the Building Blocks

TABLE B.5J
Percentage Distributions by Race for the Frequency of Doubts about
One's Religious Faith (GSS)
Q: Which statement comes closest to expressing what you believe about God?

Answer possibilities	Blacks	Whites	T-value
I don't believe in God.	0.4	0.8	
I don't know whether there is a God and I don't believe there is any way to find out.	0.0	1.1	
I don't believe in a personal God, but I do believe in a Higher Power of some kind.	0.0	5.8	
In find myself believing in God some of the time, but not others.	1.2	3.6	
While I have doubts, I feel that I do believe in God.	5.4	17.8	
I know God really exists and I have no doubts about it.	93.0	70.9	
Total	100.0	100.0	9.21***

* p < .05, ** p < .01, *** p < .001
Note: T-values assess differences between blacks and whites on the variable overall, not the individual answer possibilities (two-tailed tests).

TABLE B.5K

Percentage Distributions by Race for the Respondent's Financial Contribution to His or Her Religious Congregation (PALS)

Q: During the year 2005, what was the total dollar value of all donations, if any, that you and your spouse/partner made to your local congregation? Donations include any gifts of money, assets, or property.

Answer possibilities	Blacks	Whites	T-value
Did not donate	12.7	11.7	
$1 to $100	22.0	22.5	
$101 to $200	5.9	3.6	
$201 to $500	9.7	16.1	
$501 to $1,000	17.2	8.8	
$1,001 to $2,000	11.9	8.4	
$2,001 to $3,000	5.2	9.3	
$3,001 to $5,000	5.8	6.1	
$5,001 to $8,000	6.1	6.4	
$8,001 to $15,000	3.3	4.4	
More than $15,000	0.2	2.7	
Total	100.0	100.0	2.49*

* p < .05, ** p < .01, *** p < .001
Note: T-values assess differences between blacks and whites on the variable overall, not the individual answer possibilities (two-tailed tests).

Chapter 6

Convinced of Purpose but Not What Is Right

TABLE B.6A

Percentage Distributions by Race for Beliefs about the Respondent's Purpose in Life (PALS)

Q: I believe there is some real purpose for my life.

Answer possibilities	Blacks	Whites	T-value
Strongly disagree	0.0	0.0	
Somewhat disagree	0.5	0.7	
Neither agree nor disagree	1.6	5.3	
Somewhat agree	6.9	22.0	
Strongly agree	91.0	72.0	
Total	100.0	100.0	−6.31***

* p < .05, ** p < .01, *** p < .001
Note: T-values assess differences between blacks and whites on the variable overall, not the individual answer possibilities (two-tailed tests).

TABLE B.6B

Percentage Distributions by Race for Beliefs about Breaking Moral Rules (PALS)

Q: It is sometimes okay to break moral rules if it works to your
advantage and you can get away with it.

Answer possibilities	Blacks	Whites	T-value
Strongly disagree	67.7	74.7	
Somewhat disagree	12.2	16.7	
Neither agree nor disagree	7.9	4.2	
Somewhat agree	9.5	3.2	
Strongly agree	2.7	1.2	
Total	100.0	100.0	−3.24***

* p < .05, ** p < .01, *** p < .001
Note: T-values assess differences between blacks and whites on the variable overall, not the individual answer possibilities (two-tailed tests).

TABLE B.6C

*Percentage Distributions by Race for Beliefs about the
Basis of Right and Wrong (PALS)*

Q: For you personally, do you believe that what is morally right or wrong . . .

Answer possibilities	Blacks	Whites	T-value
Should be based on God's law	72.2	59.3	
Should be decided by society	4.3	5.8	
Is a matter of personal conscience	23.5	34.9	
Total	100.0	100.0	3.48***

* p < .05, ** p < .01, *** p < .001
Note: T-values assess differences between blacks and whites on the variable overall, not the individual answer possibilities (two-tailed tests).

TABLE B.6D

Percentage Distributions by Race for Beliefs about the Uncertainty of Morality (GSS)

Q: Right and wrong are not usually a simple matter of black and
white; there are many shades of gray.

Answer possibilities	Blacks	Whites	T-value
Strongly disagree	7.2	9.4	
Somewhat disagree	7.6	11.0	
Somewhat agree	36.7	40.7	
Strongly agree	48.5	38.9	
Total	100.0	100.0	−2.61**

* p < .05, ** p < .01, *** p < .001
Note: T-values assess differences between blacks and whites on the variable overall, not the individual answer possibilities (two-tailed tests).

TABLE B.6E
Percentage Distributions by Race for Beliefs about
Whether Sinners Should Be Punished (GSS)
Q: Those who violate God's rules must be punished.

Answer possibilities	Blacks	Whites	T-value
Strongly disagree	4.9	17.5	
Somewhat disagree	29.2	30.0	
Somewhat agree	33.7	31.4	
Strongly agree	32.2	21.1	
Total	100.0	100.0	−5.56***

* p < .05, ** p < .01, *** p < .001
Note: T-values assess differences between blacks and whites on the variable overall, not the individual answer possibilities (two-tailed tests).

TABLE B.6F
Percentage Distributions by Race for Beliefs about Whether God Has
Punished the Respondent for His or Her Sins (PALS)
Q: In the last three years, how often have you felt that God is punishing you
for your sins or lack of spirituality?

Answer possibilities	Blacks	Whites	T-value
Never	41.6	53.7	
Rarely	18.5	18.8	
Sometimes	32.6	24.6	
Very often	5.6	2.3	
Almost every day	1.7	0.6	
Total	100.0	100.0	−3.53***

* p < .05, ** p < .01, *** p < .001
Note: T-values assess differences between blacks and whites on the variable overall, not the individual answer possibilities (two-tailed tests).

Dealing with Major Problems

TABLE B.6G
Percentage Distributions by Race for Whether the Respondent Has Tried to
Deal with Major Problems in Life on His or Her Own (PALS)
Q: Think about how you have tried to understand and deal with major problems in your
life over the past three years. To what extent did you try to make sense of the situation
and decide what to do on your own?

Answer possibilities	Blacks	Whites	T-value
Not at all	3.1	3.7	
A little	10.2	17.7	
Quite a bit	25.7	33.9	
A great deal	61.0	44.7	
Total	100.0	100.0	−3.66***

* p < .05, ** p < .01, *** p < .001
Note: T-values assess differences between blacks and whites on the variable overall, not the individual answer possibilities (two-tailed tests).

TABLE B.6H

Percentage Distributions by Race for Whether the Respondent Has Tried to Deal with Major Problems in Life by Considering Passages in the Bible (PALS)

Q: Think about how you have tried to understand and deal with major problems in your life over the past three years. To what extent did you consider passages in the Bible?

Answer possibilities	Blacks	Whites	T-value
Not at all	3.7	19.8	
A little	13.3	27.3	
Quite a bit	23.9	25.2	
A great deal	59.1	27.7	
Total	100.0	100.0	−10.78***

* p < .05, ** p < .01, *** p < .001
Note: T-values assess differences between blacks and whites on the variable overall, not the individual answer possibilities (two-tailed tests).

TABLE B.6I

Percentage Distributions by Race for Whether the Respondent Has Tried to Deal with Major Problems in Life by Considering Church Teachings (PALS)

Q: Think about how you have tried to understand and deal with major problems in your life over the past three years. To what extent did you consider church teachings or talk to religious leaders?

Answer possibilities	Blacks	Whites	T-value
Not at all	11.6	26.2	
A little	23.3	33.3	
Quite a bit	24.4	21.1	
A great deal	40.7	19.4	
Total	100.0	100.0	−7.20***

* p < .05, ** p < .01, *** p < .001
Note: T-values assess differences between blacks and whites on the variable overall, not the individual answer possibilities (two-tailed tests).

TABLE B.6J

Percentage Distributions by Race for Whether the Respondent Has Tried to Deal with Major Problems in Life by Talking with Members of His or Her Congregation (PALS)

Q: Think about how you have tried to understand and deal with major problems in your life over the past three years. To what extent did you talk with people in your church?

Answer possibilities	Blacks	Whites	T-value
Not at all	15.7	16.6	
A little	30.0	37.3	
Quite a bit	26.4	28.2	
A great deal	27.9	17.9	
Total	100.0	100.0	−2.06*

* p < .05, ** p < .01, *** p < .001
Note: T-values assess differences between blacks and whites on the variable overall, not the individual answer possibilities (two-tailed tests).

TABLE B.6K

Percentage Distributions by Race for Whether the Respondent Has Tried to Deal with Major Problems in Life by Looking to God (PALS)

Q: Think about how you have tried to understand and deal with major problems in your life over the past three years. To what extent did you look to God or a larger spiritual force for strength, support, and guidance?

Answer possibilities	Blacks	Whites	T-value
Not at all	1.1	3.9	
A little	10.6	20.7	
Quite a bit	16.3	29.6	
A great deal	72.0	45.8	
Total	100.0	100.0	−6.93***

* p < .05, ** p < .01, *** p < .001

Note: T-values assess differences between blacks and whites on the variable overall, not the individual answer possibilities (two-tailed tests).

Revisiting the Building Blocks

TABLE B.6L

Percentage Distributions by Race for Whether the Respondent Has Wondered Whether God Has Abandoned Him or Her (PALS)

Q: In the last three years, how often have you wondered whether God had abandoned you?

Answer possibilities	Blacks	Whites	T-value
Never	58.9	59.3	
Rarely	16.7	22.5	
Sometimes	21.1	16.1	
Very often	2.2	1.8	
Every day	1.1	0.3	
Total	100.0	100.0	1.03

* p < .05, ** p < .01, *** p < .001

Note: T-values assess differences between blacks and whites on the variable overall, not the individual answer possibilities (two-tailed tests).

TABLE B.6M

Percentage Distributions by Race for Whether the Respondent Has Been Angry with God (PALS)

Q: In the last three years, how often have you felt angry at God?

Answer possibilities	Blacks	Whites	T-value
Never	68.9	53.8	
Rarely	16.1	27.9	
Sometimes	12.8	16.9	
Very often	1.1	1.4	
Every day	1.1	0.0	
Total	100.0	100.0	−2.57*

* p < .05, ** p < .01, *** p < .001

Note: T-values assess differences between blacks and whites on the variable overall, not the individual answer possibilities (two-tailed tests).

Chapter 7

Is Being a "Good Person" Good Enough?

TABLE B.7A

Percentage Distributions by Race for Beliefs about Being a Good Person (PALS)

Q: It doesn't much matter what I believe so long as I am a good person.

Answer possibilities	Blacks	Whites	T-value
Strongly disagree	40.2	42.3	
Somewhat disagree	10.9	14.1	
Neither agree nor disagree	5.4	8.7	
Somewhat agree	15.8	19.2	
Strongly agree	27.7	15.7	
Total	100.0	100.0	−2.08*

* p < .05, ** p < .01, *** p < .001

Notes: T-values assess differences between blacks and whites on the variable overall, not the individual answer possibilities (two-tailed tests).

Realm of the Supernatural

TABLE B.7B

Percentage Distributions by Race for Whether the Respondent Believes That an Angel Has Helped Him or Her in a Time of Need (PALS)

Q: An angel has directly helped me in a time of need.

Answer possibilities	Blacks	Whites	T-value
Strongly disagree	6.4	20.4	
Somewhat disagree	4.8	8.0	
Neither agree nor disagree	14.4	24.6	
Somewhat agree	17.6	19.4	
Strongly agree	56.8	27.6	
Total	100.0	100.0	−8.63***

* p < .05, ** p < .01, *** p < .001

Note: T-values assess differences between blacks and whites on the variable overall, not the individual answer possibilities (two-tailed tests).

TABLE B.7C

Percentage Distributions by Race for Whether the Respondent Believes That Evil Spirits Exist (PALS)

Q: The Devil, demons, or evil spirits exist.

Answer possibilities	Blacks	Whites	T-value
Strongly disagree	5.9	8.5	
Somewhat disagree	3.2	4.4	
Neither agree nor disagree	5.9	9.1	
Somewhat agree	13.9	18.2	
Strongly agree	71.1	59.8	
Total	100.0	100.0	−2.75**

* p < .05, ** p < .01, *** p < .001

Note: T-values assess differences between blacks and whites on the variable overall, not the individual answer possibilities (two-tailed tests).

TABLE B.7D

Percentage Distributions by Race for Whether the
Respondent Has Experienced a Miracle (PALS)

Q: I have experienced a supernatural miracle, an event that could not have
happened without the intervention of God or a spiritual force.

Answer possibilities	Blacks	Whites	T-value
Strongly disagree	7.0	18.1	
Somewhat disagree	4.2	6.2	
Neither agree nor disagree	13.4	18.6	
Somewhat agree	11.2	18.7	
Strongly agree	64.2	38.4	
Total	100.0	100.0	−6.78***

* p < .05, ** p < .01, *** p < .001
Note: T-values assess differences between blacks and whites on the variable overall, not the individual answer possibilities (two-tailed tests).

Alignment among the Stars

TABLE B.7E

Percentage Distributions by Race for Whether the Respondent
Has Ever Read His or Her Horoscope (GSS)

Q: Do you ever read a horoscope or your personal astrology report?

Answer possibilities	Blacks	Whites	T-value
No	37.1	45.1	
Yes	62.9	54.9	
Total	100.0	100.0	−1.94*

* p < .05, ** p < .01, *** p < .001
Note: T-values assess differences between blacks and whites on the variable overall, not the individual answer possibilities (two-tailed tests).

TABLE B.7F

Percentage Distributions by Race for Beliefs about the
Scientific Merits of Astrology (GSS)

Q: Would you say that astrology is very scientific, sort of scientific,
or not at all scientific?

Answer possibilities	Blacks	Whites	T-value
Not at all scientific	48.2	72.0	
Sort of scientific	40.5	24.8	
Very scientific	11.3	3.2	
Total	100.0	100.0	−5.64***

* p < .05, ** p < .01, *** p < .001
Note: T-values assess differences between blacks and whites on the variable overall, not the individual answer possibilities (two-tailed tests).

A Far East Influence?

TABLE B.7G
Percentage Distributions by Race for Beliefs about Reincarnation (PALS)
Q: I believe in reincarnation, that people have lived previous lives.

Answer possibilities	Blacks	Whites	T-value
Strongly disagree	32.8	50.3	
Somewhat disagree	8.9	14.4	
Neither agree nor disagree	22.8	18.5	
Somewhat agree	18.9	11.3	
Strongly agree	16.6	5.5	
Total	100.0	100.0	-5.90^{***}

* $p < .05$, ** $p < .01$, *** $p < .001$
Note: T-values assess differences between blacks and whites on the variable overall, not the individual answer possibilities (two-tailed tests).

A Habit of Inclusion: How Far Does It Reach and Why?

TABLE B.7H
Percentage Distributions by Race for Beliefs about Muhammad (PALS)
Q: The founder of Islam, Muhammad, was the Holy Prophet of God.

Answer possibilities	Blacks	Whites	T-value
Strongly disagree	38.0	45.7	
Somewhat disagree	6.4	8.1	
Neither agree nor disagree	36.3	37.0	
Somewhat agree	11.7	6.3	
Strongly agree	7.6	2.9	
Total	100.0	100.0	-3.02^{**}

* $p < .05$, ** $p < .01$, *** $p < .001$
Note: T-values assess differences between blacks and whites on the variable overall, not the individual answer possibilities (two-tailed tests).

May "the Force" Be with You?

TABLE B.7I
Percentage Distributions by Race for Beliefs about Whether
God Is a Personal Being or an Impersonal Force (PALS)
Q: God is not a personal being, but more like an impersonal spiritual force.

Answer possibilities	Blacks	Whites	T-value
Strongly disagree	29.4	43.4	
Somewhat disagree	5.6	8.5	
Neither agree nor disagree	7.2	10.5	
Somewhat agree	11.1	16.9	
Strongly agree	46.7	20.7	
Total	100.0	100.0	-5.45^{***}

* $p < .05$, ** $p < .01$, *** $p < .001$
Note: T-values assess differences between blacks and whites on the variable overall, not the individual answer possibilities (two-tailed tests).

Chapter 8

Beliefs about Racial Inequality

TABLE B.8A

Percentage Distributions by Race for Beliefs about the
Causes of Racial Inequality (GSS)

Q: On the average, African Americans have worse jobs, income, and housing than white people. Do you think these differences are (1) because most African Americans have less in-born ability to learn, (2) because most African Americans just don't have the motivation or will power to pull themselves up out of poverty, (3) because most African Americans don't have the chance of education it takes to rise out of poverty, and/or (4) mainly due to discrimination?

Answer possibilities	Blacks	Whites	T-value
Individual Attributions			
Less in-born ability			
No	88.3	92.9	
Yes	11.7	7.1	
Total	100.0	100.0	−1.69
Lack of motivation			
No	58.1	44.9	
Yes	41.9	55.1	
Total	100.0	100.0	3.06**
Structural Attributions			
Unequal chances in education			
No	55.9	59.7	
Yes	44.1	40.3	
Total	100.0	100.0	−0.93
Racial discrimination			
No	43.7	73.5	
Yes	56.3	26.5	
Total	100.0	100.0	−6.95***

* p < .05, ** p < .01, *** p < .001
Note: T-values assess differences between blacks and whites on the variable overall, not the individual answer possibilities (two-tailed tests).

Support for Racial Policy

TABLE B.8B

Percentage Distributions by Race for Levels of Support for
Racially Specific Opportunity-Enhancing Policy (GSS)

Q: Some people think that African Americans have been discriminated against
for so long that the government has a special obligation to help improve their
living standards. Others believe that the government should not be giving special
treatment to African Americans. Where would you place yourself on this scale,
or haven't you made up your mind on this?

Answer possibilities	Blacks	Whites	T-value
Strongly agree no special treatment	11.0	35.3	
Agree no special treatment	4.1	24.9	
Agree with both	42.4	29.9	
Agree government should help blacks	9.3	5.9	
Strongly agree government should help blacks	33.1	4.0	
Total	100.0	100.0	−12.17***

* p < .05, ** p < .01, *** p < .001
Note: T-values assess differences between blacks and whites on the variable overall, not the individual answer possibilities (two-tailed tests).

TABLE B.8C

Percentage Distributions by Race for Levels of Support for
Racially Specific Opportunity-Enhancing Policy (PALS)

Q: Government should do more to help minorities increase their standard of living.

Answer possibilities	Blacks	Whites	T-value
Strongly disagree	8.2	19.2	
Somewhat disagree	6.5	19.0	
Neither agree nor disagree	14.1	27.6	
Somewhat agree	19.0	23.1	
Strongly agree	52.2	11.1	
Total	100.0	100.0	−10.89***

* p < .05, ** p < .01, *** p < .001
Note: T-values assess differences between blacks and whites on the variable overall, not the individual answer possibilities (two-tailed tests).

TABLE B.8D

Percentage Distributions by Race for Levels of Support for
Racially Specific Outcome-Based Policy (GSS)

Q: Some people say that because of past discrimination, black should be given preference in hiring and promotion. Others say that such preference in hiring and promotion of blacks is wrong because it discriminates against whites. What about your opinion—are you for or against preferential hiring and promotion of blacks?

Answer possibilities	Blacks	Whites	T-value
Strongly oppose	34.8	66.8	
Not strongly oppose	28.7	24.0	
Not strongly favor	8.5	4.5	
Strongly favor	28.0	4.7	
Total	100.0	100.0	-8.23***

* $p < .05$, ** $p < .01$, *** $p < .001$
Note: T-values assess differences between blacks and whites on the variable overall, not the individual answer possibilities (two-tailed tests).

TABLE B.8E

Percentage Distributions by Race for Levels of Support for
Reparations for Blacks (PALS)

Q: The government should financially compensate black Americans
who are descendants of slaves.

Answer possibilities	Blacks	Whites	T-value
Strongly disagree	16.4	73.3	
Somewhat disagree	6.8	10.1	
Neither agree nor disagree	28.2	9.8	
Somewhat agree	19.2	3.1	
Strongly agree	29.4	3.7	
Total	100.0	100.0	-16.71***

* $p < .05$, ** $p < .01$, *** $p < .001$
Note: T-values assess differences between blacks and whites on the variable overall, not the individual answer possibilities (two-tailed tests).

Revisiting the Building Blocks

TABLE B.8F

Percentage Distributions by Race for Beliefs about Not Talking about Race (PALS)

Q: One of the most effective ways to improve race relations in the
United States is to stop talking about race.

Answer possibilities	Blacks	Whites	T-value
Strongly disagree	37.1	16.2	
Somewhat disagree	11.2	15.0	
Neither agree nor disagree	15.7	21.9	
Somewhat agree	10.7	25.5	
Strongly agree	25.3	21.4	
Total	100.0	100.0	3.43***

* $p < .05$, ** $p < .01$, *** $p < .001$
Note: T-values assess differences between blacks and whites on the variable overall, not the individual answer possibilities (two-tailed tests).

Appendix C
Interview Guides

Interview Guide for Religious Clergy

Thank you for participating in our study. We are writing a book about race relations and possibilities for reconciliation among Christians. The purpose of this meeting today is to ask your help with this project. We conducted a national survey of several thousand people. The findings from the survey are very interesting, so interesting that we feel that we need to talk to religious clergy in person in order to help us put our findings in perspective.

This interview should only take about 45 minutes of your time. I am going to ask you 10 questions. There are no right or wrong answers. All that we are asking for is your opinion about why black and white Christians responded to some of the questions on our survey very differently. Do you have any questions? If not, then let's begin!

1. Do you think that there are any differences between black and white Christians in how they go about their religious faith? If so, are these differences important?

2. Nearly 45% of black Christians believe that "it doesn't matter what you believe so long as you are a good person," while only 35% of whites feel this way. Why do you think that black and white Christians differ on beliefs about being a "good person"?

3. The results of our study show that black Christians are more likely to see God as an "impersonal force," while white Christians are more likely to see God as a "personal being." Why do you think some Christians see God differently than others?

a. What does it mean if God is a "personal being"?

b. What does it mean if God is an "impersonal force"?

4. The results of our study show that black Christians go to church more often, read the Bible, pray, and study the Bible more often than white Christians. Why do you think that blacks engage in these religious activities more than whites?

5. Black Christians are more likely than white Christians to say that it is okay to "break the rules if it works to your advantage and you can get away with it." Why do think that is?

6. Our results show that blacks are more likely than whites to agree with the following statement: "God created the world in six 24-hour days." Why do you think that blacks are more likely than whites to feel this way?

7. Our findings indicate that black Christians are more likely than white Christians to agree with the following statement: "I believe in reincarnation, that people have lived previous lives." Why do you think that black Christians are more likely to believe in reincarnation?

8. The results of our study show that black Christians are more likely than white Christians to lean on various aspects of their faith (the Bible, church teachings, and clergy) when facing "major problems" in life. Why do you think that is?

9. In recent years, there have been calls for racial reconciliation among Christians. Do you think that this is an important issue?

I'd like to thank you again, Pastor [*insert name*], for agreeing to be interviewed for this study. Do you have any remaining comments or observations about race relations between black and white Christians?

Interview Guide for Focus Groups

Thank you for participating in our study. We are writing a book about Christian beliefs, values, and religious practices. The purpose of this meeting today is to ask your help with this project. We conducted a national survey of several thousand people. The findings from the survey are very interesting, so interesting that we feel that we need to talk to everyday Christians in person in order to help us put our findings in perspective.

This focus group session should only take about an hour of your time. I am going to ask this group eight questions. There are no right or wrong answers. You do not have to tell any personal information about yourself or your faith. All that we are asking for is your opinion about what other people say and do with respect to their Christian faith.

You do not have to answer each of the questions. Please raise your hand when you are ready to talk, and I will recognize you. Do you have any questions? If not, then let's begin!

1. Most Christians turn to God when facing "major problems" in life. However, the results of our study show that some Christians not only turn to God but also consult church teachings, seek out fellowship with other believers, *and* talk with clergy. Our question is: Why do you think that some Christians rely on many aspects of their faith when facing major problems in life?

2. Nearly 40% of the Christians in our study believe that "it doesn't matter what you believe so long as you are a good person." Why do you think this is—that it doesn't matter what you think as long as you are a good person?

3. The results of our study show that some Christians go to church more often, read the Bible, pray, and study the Bible more often than others. Why do you think that some Christians engage in these religious activities more than others?

4. The results of our study show that some Christians see God as an "impersonal force," while others see God as a "personal being." Why do you think some Christians see God differently than others?
   a. What does it mean if God is a "personal being"?
   b. What does it mean if God is an "impersonal force"?

5. Some Christians believe that it is okay to "break the rules if it works to your advantage and you can get away with it." Why do think that is?

a. Can you think of an example of when it may be okay to break the rules?

6. One finding from our survey shows that Christians are split (50%–50%) on whether "God created the world in six 24-hour days." Why do you think this is so?

   a. [*If directly mentioned or alluded to*]: Why do some Christians read the word of the Bible literally while others do not?

7. One of the results of our study shows that people who say that their race is "important" to them pray, attend worship services, and read their Bibles more often than others. Why do you think that is?

8. One of the findings of our study shows many Christians believe in reincarnation. Is the belief in reincarnation consistent with Christianity?

Appendix D, containing multivariate tables, is available online at http://nyupress.org/shelton/appendixD.pdf

Notes

1. Unless otherwise noted, the names of the individual persons whom we refer to or interviewed for this study have been changed in order to protect their confidentiality and anonymity.

2. A great number of studies could be listed here. However, we cannot do so due to time and space constraints. Some notable studies include Baer (1984), Baer and Singer (1993), Barnes (2005), Battle (2006), Bridges (2001), Calhoun-Brown (1999, 1996), Callahan (2006), Carter (1995), Cone (1975, 1969), Du Bois (1920), Edwards (2009), Ellison and Sherkat (1995), Felder (1991), Frazier (1964), Frederick (2003), F. Harris (1994), Hood (1994), Hunt (2002), P. Johnson (1994), Lincoln and Mamiya (1990), Marsh (2005), Mc-Mickle (2000), Morris (1984), Nelson (2005), Pattillo-McCoy (1998), Pew Research Center (2009b), Pinn (2003, 2002, 1995), Raboteau (1978), Sobel (1979), Taylor et al. (1996), Taylor, Chatters, and Levin (2004), Thurman (1976), Weber (1978), and Wilmore (1973). We will reference other meaningful contributions throughout this text.

3. See Pew Research Center (2008, 2009b), Taylor, Chatters, and Levin (2004), and Hunt and Hunt (2001).

4. See Ellison and Sherkat (1995), Hunt and Hunt (2001), and Taylor et al. (1996).

5. See Battle (2006), Calhoun-Brown (1998), Cone (1975, 1969), Floyd-Thomas and Pinn (2010), Gutierrez (1971), Hopkins (1999), Lincoln and Mamiya (1990), and Wilmore (1973).

6. See Felder (1991), Frederick (2003), Gutierrez (1987), Pinn (2002, 1995).

7. Lincoln and Mamiya (1990).

8. Ibid., 2–3.

9. Ibid., 7.

10. See, for example, Barnes (2011, 2005), Brown and Brown (2003), Calhoun-Brown (1999, 1998), Cavendish, Welch, and Leege (1998), Edwards

(2009), Ellison and Sherkat (1995, 1990), Emerson and Yancey (2008), Frederick (2003), Harrison (2005), Hunt and Hunt (2001), McRoberts (2003), Nelson (2005), Pattillo-McCoy (1998), Sherkat (2002), Stump (1987), Taylor, Chatters, and Levin (2004), and Taylor et al. (1996).

11. The percentage distributions mentioned in this paragraph are based on findings from the Portraits of American Life Survey (PALS) and the General Social Survey (GSS). These distributions are consistent with those of other leading data sources including the Pew Research Center's "U.S. Religious Landscape Survey" (2008).

12. See Chen (2002), Ebaugh (2000), Ecklund (2006), Warner (1998), Waters and Ueda (2007), and Yang and Ebaugh (2001).

13. See, for example, Abbington (2002), Aghahowa (1996), Coleman (2008), Conde-Frazier, Parrett, and Kang (2004), Costen (2004, 1993), Felder (1991), Grant (1989), LaRue (2000), Maynard-Reid (2000), Moyd (1995), Price (2001), Priest and Nieves (2006), Christine Smith (2008), Smith and Jackson (2005), Thistlethwaite and Engel (1998), Thomas (1997), West (1993, 1982), West and Glaude (2003), and Delores Williams (1995).

14. As examples, see Brown (2009), Carpenter (1999), Emerson and Smith (2000), Greeley and Hout (2006), Lindsay (2007), Marsden (1980), Noll (2001), Roof and McKinney (1987), Christian Smith (1998), Wilcox (1990), Wilcox and Robinson (2010), and Daniel Williams (2010).

15. See Calhoun-Brown (1998), Edwards (2009), Hunt and Hunt (2001), Lincoln and Mamiya (1990), Steensland et al. (2000), Roof and McKinney (1987), and Wilcox (1990).

16. As with white Protestants, the distribution of black Baptists, Methodists, and Pentecostals has meaningfully changed in recent decades. The results of most nationally representative surveys show that at least 60% of blacks affiliate with Baptist denominations. Pentecostals are among the fastest growing families, now comprising about 12% of the black Protestant population. The percentage of black Methodists has notably declined due to greater religious mobility (or "switching") across affiliations. A number of recent studies have shown that black Methodists now constitute about 7% of the black Protestant population. See Ellison and Sherkat (1990), Lincoln and Mamiya (1990), Pew Research Center (2009b), Roof and McKinney (1987), Sherkat (2002), Steensland et al. (2000), and Taylor, Chatters, and Levin (2004). Data from the PALS and GSS corroborate this finding as well.

17. For instance, our findings for significant racial differences across church attendance and church membership hold constant even when we

restrict our analysis to specific Protestant denominations such as Baptists, Methodists, and Pentecostals. This result is especially meaningful considering the relatively small number of black respondents in both the PALS and GSS who claimed an affiliation with these particular denominations (and sub-denominations).

18. See Commanger (1945), Cruse (1967), Drake and Cayton (1945), Du Bois (1903/2005), Emerson and Smith (2000), Holt (2002), McKee (1993), Myrdal (1944), Reuter (1927), Steinberg (2007, 1981), Thernstrom and Thernstrom (1997), Tranby and Hartmann (2008), Woofter (1928), Work (1924), and Young (2002).

19. See, for instance, Brown (2009), Edgell and Tranby (2007), Emerson and Hawkins (2007), Emerson and Smith (2000), Hunt (2002), Roof and McKinney (1987), Taylor, Chatters, and Levin (2004), and Tranby and Hartmann (2008).

20. See Pew Research Report (2009b, 7–8).

21. As just a few examples, see Darnell and Sherkat (1997), Ellison and Sherkat (1990), Greeley and Hout (2006), and Steensland et al. (2000).

22. Save for a handful of exceptions, we decided against publishing non-significant multivariate results for racial group membership. This approach saves time, space, and cost. Appendix D, which includes all multivariate tables, is available online at http://nyupress.org/shelton/appendixD.pdf.

23. The qualitative interview data presented in this book have been edited for presentation and clarity. Like most people who engage in casual conversation, our interviewees would sometimes inadvertently repeat themselves (e.g., "I . . . I . . . I, think that . . . ," "uhh, uhh . . . ," "you know, you know . . ."), restart/revisit certain points, and/or dramatically change direction when responding to a question or statement. These revisions were made for the expressed purpose of preserving intelligibility. The thrust of our interviewees' comments, arguments, and sentiments remain intact.

24. The quotations appearing in this paragraph are paraphrased statements from Michael Emerson's field notes.

25. Many of the high-ranking clergy members that we interviewed do not actually preside over congregations in the cities that are specified in the text. For instance, while Rev. Washington is, in fact, a Baptist preacher (we did not change our interviewees denominational affiliation), he may or may not actually preside over a church in Cleveland. We chose (1) to "move around" and (2) to alter the size of our interviewees' congregations in order to further protect their anonymity and confidentiality.

NOTES TO CHAPTER 2

1. This chapter is principally authored by Derek Hicks, a professor of African American religions and theology. He is the Luce Diversity Fellow in Theological Education and teaches at Wake Forest University's School of Divinity.

2. Thurman (1976, 11).

3. See Holifield (2007).

4. See Haynes (2002). Several religious and Biblical scholars have offered in-depth and critical analysis of the Curse of Ham as well as the Curse of Cain, which connects God's "mark" on Cain to that of the curse of black skin. Notwithstanding the fact that, at least in Cain's case, the mark was meant to sustain and even to protect him, the broader question centers on the ways in which these Biblical interpretations set the tone for black identity formation during the antebellum period and after. See Goldenberg (2003), Haynes (2002), and Johnson (2004).

5. See Goldenberg (2003).

6. Blyden (1869, 75).

7. See Johnson (2004).

8. See Gomez (1998).

9. See Mitchell (2004, 1). For a study on the convergence of the conjuring tradition and Christianity in early African American life, see also Chireau (2003).

10. Bibb (1849/1999, 77–78).

11. T. Smith (1994, 3).

12. Raboteau (1978, 128).

13. See Boles (1990).

14. Randolph (1855/2010, 30–31).

15. Quoted in Jordan (1969, 213).

16. See Earl (2003).

17. See Gomez (1998).

18. Jordan (1969, 213).

19. Earl (2003, 46).

20. Hayden (1846/2001, 242).

21. Gronniosaw (1770/2010, 17).

22. Ibid., 20.

23. See Hopkins (2003, 3).

24. Quoted in Faulkner (1977, 54).

25. Emerson and Smith (2000).

26. Cone (1975, xiii).

27. African and African American slaves sought, through literacy, a curative tool equipping them to respond to dehumanization and, when connected to religious sensibilities, full spiritual and/or ontological personhood in the hope of overcoming their oppressive social conditions. See Cornelius (1991).

28. Hopkins (2003, 19–20).

29. Ibid.

30. Ibid.

31. Ibid.

32. Curry (1840/1977, 131).

33. Washington (1995, xxx).

NOTES TO CHAPTER 3

1. At least for Protestants, the term "catholic" is taken to mean the universal Christian church.

2. The Apostles' Creed has slight variations across Christian traditions. For example, some versions say "crucified, dead, and buried," while others say "crucified, died, and buried." Such variations are more differences in wording choice than in meaning.

3. See Roof and McKinney (1987). Findings from both the PALS and the GSS support this claim as well.

4. We designed this survey question so that a wide swath of Americans could respond to it regardless of their religious affiliation—from those who believe in a god to those who do not. That is why the question is worded "God or spirituality."

NOTES TO CHAPTER 4

1. See Abbington (2002), Baer (1984), Barnes (2005), Bibb (1849/1999), Calhoun-Brown (1999), Cone (1992), Edwards (2009), Felder (1991), Frazier (1964), Frederick (2003), Gomez (1998), F. Harris (1994), P. Johnson (1994), Lincoln and Mamiya (1990), Nelson (2005), Pinn (2003, 2002), Raboteau (1978), T. Smith (1994), Sobel (1979), Taylor, Chatters, and Levin (2004), Washington (1995), Webber (1978), West (1982), and Wilmore (1973).

2. See Bobo and Kluegel (1993), Bonilla-Silva (2006), Emerson and Smith (2000), Feagin (1975), Hacker (2003), Huber and Form (1973), Hughes (1997),

Hunt (2007), Kluegel (1990), Kluegel and Smith (1986), Lewis (1968, 1959), Massey and Denton (1993), McKee (1993), Pattillo-McCoy (1998), Shelton and Greene (forthcoming), Steinberg (1981), Swidler (1986), and G. Wilson (1996).

3. See Gordon (1964) and Shelton (2008).

4. See Elijah Anderson (1999), Bonilla-Silva (2006), Cone (1991), Emerson and Smith (2000), Emerson, Smith, and Sikkink (1999), Feagin (1975), Feagin and Sikes (1994), Hacker (2003), Huber and Form (1973), Hunt (2007, 2004, 2002, 1996), Jackman (1996), Kluegel (1990), Kluegel and Smith (1986), Lewis (1968, 1959), Massey (2007), Massey and Denton (1993), McKee (1993), Pinkney (2000), Shapiro (2004), Shelton and Greene (forthcoming), Shelton (2012), Steinberg (2007, 1981), Tuch and Hughes (1996), G. Wilson (1996), and W. Wilson (2009).

5. See Collins (1990), Feagin and Sikes (1994), Hacker (2003), Kennedy (1997), Kozol (1992), Macleod (2008), Massey and Denton (1993), O'Connor, Tilly, and Bobo (2003), Omi and Winant (1994), Pinkney (1984), Quadagno (1996), Shapiro (2004), G. Wilson (2005), and W. Wilson (1996, 1987).

6. Many scholars of black religious studies have advanced or acknowledged variations of this argument as well—particularly blacks' "experiential" understanding of Christianity. See Abbington (2002), Aghahowa (1996), Battle (2006), Bridges (2001), Callahan (2006), Carter (1995), Coleman (2008), Cone (1975, 1969), Cooper-Lewter and Mitchell (1986), Costen (2004, 1993), Douglas (1993), Evans (1993), Felder (1991), Fordham (1975), Frazier (1964), Frederick (2003), Grant (1989), Hood (1994), Hopkins (1999), P. Johnson (1994), Jones (1973), LaRue (2000), Lincoln and Mamiya (1990), McMickle (2000), Moyd (1995), Nelson (2005), Paris (1985), Pinn (2002), Smith and Jackson (2005), T. Smith (1994), Sobel (1979), Thomas (1997), Thurman (1976), Washington (1995), Webber (1978), West (1982), West and Glaude (2003), Delores Williams (1995), and Wilmore (1973).

7. These are major themes across many studies of black religion as well. See the sources cited in note 6.

8. For example, Ninian Smart (1983) argues that all religions must negotiate six faith-based cultural and attitudinal dimensions: experiential, mythical, doctrinal, ethical, ritual, and social. He posits that all religious worldviews address these elements in their own unique way. The results presented in this book support this contention.

9. See Lincoln and Mamiya (1990, 2–3).

10. See Bowen and Bok (2000), Kozol (1992), Macleod (2008), Massey et al. (2006), Orfield and Ashkinaze (1991), and Orfield and Eaton (1997).

11. A good example of this is the longstanding pseudoscientific argument that blacks are biologically/genetically inferior to whites (Gould 1981; Graves 2004; Hannaford 1996; Brace 2005; McKee 1992). Over the past few decades, advances in science and technology have allowed researchers to map the human genome. The results of these studies have shown that there is no biological/genetic basis for racial group membership (please go to the Human Genome Project's website, http://www.ornl.gov/sci/techresources/ Human_Genome/home.shtml, to learn more about this important information). However, just because race is not biologically "real" does not mean that it is not socially "real." In other words, just because blacks and whites are genetically similar on the inside, they still appear different on the outside and so tend to be treated differently in the social world. The findings presented in this book support this conclusion.

12. See Baer (1984), Felder (1991), P. Johnson (1994), and Raboteau (1978).

NOTES TO CHAPTER 5

1. See Pew Research Center (2008). Some of the survey items examined in chapters 5, 6, and 7 are at least similar to those analyzed in other studies—most notably Greeley and Hout (2006). While some of our descriptive results are comparable, our multivariate findings and interpretation often sharply differ.

2. Findings from the PALS also show that black Protestants are more confident in their belief in God than white mainline or evangelical Protestants are.

3. This figure is not immediately apparent from the data presented; it can only be determined by analyzing the raw data.

4. See Farley and Allen (1987), Kerbo (2011), Massey (2007), Shelton and Greene (forthcoming), Shelton and Wilson (2009), Stoll (2005), and Webster and Bishaw (2007).

5. See Conley (1999), Pew Research Center (2011), and Shapiro (2004).

NOTES TO CHAPTER 6

1. Cooper-Lewter and Mitchell (1986, 113–114).

2. Pinn (2003, 179).

3. Ibid., 158.

4. Ibid., 181.

5. The links between social inequality and morality among Americans in general (Merton 1938; Rodman 1963) and blacks in particular (Elijah Anderson 1999; Paris 1985; Valentine 1978; Venkatesh 2006) has remained a longstanding topic of scholarly interest. For instance, Rodman (1963, 205) discusses the concept of "value stretch," by which he means that marginalized people and groups have a "wider range of values, and a lower degree of commitment to these values." By way of illustration of this concept, if the value is to prefer the taste of sweet grapes, but marginalized people have less access to sweet grapes, they will not give up that value but will also learn to value the taste of sour grapes. And because of this value stretch or expansion, they can hold these values simultaneously by being less fully committed to either.

6. See Davis and Smith (2010). The questions used in this analysis were asked in 1983–1984.

7. See Froese and Bader (2010).

8. Elizabeth Anderson (2010, 23).

9. See Corcoran (2001).

10. See West and Sabol (2009, 4), Bonczar (2003, 8), and Western and Wildeman (2009, 231).

11. National Center for Injury Prevention and Control (2006).

12. See Isaacs (2008).

13. See Rugh and Massey (2010).

14. See Helling and Sawicki (2003).

15. See Baer (1984), Battle (2006), Cone (1975, 1969), Cooper-Lewter and Mitchell (1986), Cornelius (1991), Felder (1991), Floyd-Thomas and Pinn (2010), Fordham (1975), Frederick (2003), Gomez (1998), Hopkins (1999), P. Johnson (1994), Nelson (2005), Paris (1985), Parker (2003), Pinn (2003), West (1982), and Wilmore (1973), to name a few.

NOTES TO CHAPTER 7

1. A model including data for *whites only* found that evangelicals are significantly far more likely to "disagree" with the statement than mainline Protestants are. More specifically, 66% of evangelicals at least "disagree" with the statement, while only 29% at least "agree."

2. See Pew Research Center (2009a).

3. See Pew Research Center (2008).

4. See Pew Research Center (2009a).

5. See J. Anderson (2007), Chireau (2003), Long (2001), and Webber (1978).

6. See Alkebulan (2007), Asante (1998, 1988), Dawson (2001), and Karenga (1992).

7. See Barton (1994), Bauval and Brophy (2011), Browder (1992), E. Harris (1998), Lefkowitz (1996) Lefkowitz and Rogers (1996), Mure (1854/2008), Neugebauer (1969), and Witt (1997). Also see "Astrology: The True Religion," Afrocentric Online, http://www.afrocentriconline.com/phpBB2/viewtopic.php ?p=85348&sid=f912dfc4abeb9a4df68931b30dff604e.

8. Bernal (1987), James (2009), Lefkowitz (1996), Lefkowitz and Rogers (1996).

9. See Shelton and Emerson (2010) and Sniderman and Piazza (2002).

10. See Brown and Shaw (2002), Davis and Brown (2002), and Spence, Shaw, and Brown (2005).

11. See McCartney (1992), Pinkney (1976), Shelby (2005), and Van Deburg (1997).

12. See Davis and Smith (2010).

13. See Pew Research Center (2009a). A close inspection of this data suggests that whites are more likely than blacks to find themselves among the minority of Protestants who view yoga as a "spiritual practice." Unfortunately, we are unable to further examine this issue since neither the PALS nor the GSS includes a survey item that specifically concerns beliefs about yoga.

14. Ibid.

15. Some scholars of black religious studies would probably advance this argument as well. See J. Anderson (2007), Long (2001), T. Smith (1994), and Thurman (1976).

16. See Asante (1998, 1988), Bennett (1969), Herskovits (1958), and Karenga (1992).

17. See Pew Research Center (2009a).

18. These analyses were conducted with additional survey items contained within the PALS.

19. See Pew Research Center (2009a).

20. A model with data for *whites only* indicates that evangelicals are significantly more likely than mainline Protestants to "disagree" with this statement. In particular, 60% of evangelicals at least "disagree" with the statement, while only 33% at least "agree."

21. Several of NYU Press's anonymous reviewers were surprised by this finding as well. One reviewer attributed our result to an "emphasis on God as spirit that pervades black Christianity." He or she argued that "the key word here [in the survey statement] is 'force' and not 'impersonal.'" Unfortunately, neither the PALS nor the GSS contain survey items that allow us to assess

racial differences in beliefs about "God as spirit." The reviewer may be correct that black Protestants are more likely to emphasize God as spirit than white Protestants are. However, we cannot speculate beyond the limits of our data.

22. A number of scholars of black religious studies have argued this point (in different ways) as well. See, for example, Calhoun-Brown (1999), Cleage (1972, 1968), Cone (1975, 1969), Douglas (1993), Evans (1993), Grant (1989), Jones (1973), and Thurman (1976).

23. See Turner (1898).

NOTES TO CHAPTER 8

1. See Commanger (1945), Cruse (1967), Du Bois (1903/2005), Emerson and Smith (2000), Holt (2002), McKee (1993), Myrdal (1944), Reuter (1927), Steinberg (1981, 2007), Thernstrom and Thernstrom (1997), Woofter (1928), Work (1924), and Young (2002).

2. Myrdal (1944) did not actually use the phrase "hearts and minds." We choose to use it because it is common parlance in today's world. To be clear, Myrdal argued that the "American Negro problem is a problem in the hearts of the Americans" (xlvi). He described it as discrepancy between (a) the nation's ideals about equality among people and (b) its persistent refusal to grant blacks full citizenship and participation rights. He wrote, "From the point of view of the American Creed, the status accorded the Negro in America represents nothing more and nothing less than a century-long lag in public morals. In principle, the Negro problem was settled long ago; in practice the solution is not effectuated" (24).

3. See Gould (1981), Graves (2004), Hannaford (1996), Brace (2005), McKee (1993) and Steinberg (2007, 1981).

4. See Conley (1999), Farley and Allen (1987), Farley and Bianchi (1985), Massey (2007), Shapiro (2004), G. Wilson (2005), and W. Wilson (1996, 1987, 1978).

5. Dickens (1859/2010).

6. See Feagin (1975), Huber and Form (1973), Hunt (2007, 2004, 2002, 1996), Kluegel (1990), Kluegel and Smith (1986), Shelton and Greene (forthcoming), and Sigelman and Welch (1991).

7. See Feagin (1975) Hunt (2007, 2004, 2002, 1996), Kluegel (1990), Kluegel and Smith (1986), and Shelton and Greene (forthcoming). Some Americans also advance *fatalistic* attributions (Feagin 1975, Hunt 2005, Kluegel and Smith 1986). However, we do not assess these explanations since

"luck" and "chance" have been shown to be less consequential to Americans' beliefs about the causes of poverty.

8. See Feagin (1975), Huber and Form (1973) Kluegel and Smith (1986), and Shelton and Wilson (2006).

9. See Feagin (1975), Hunt (2007), Kluegel and Smith (1986) and G. Wilson (1996).

10. See Hunt (2007) and G. Wilson (1996).

11. See, for example, Brimeyer (2008), Cobb (2009), Edgell and Tranby (2007), Emerson, Smith, and Sikkink (1999), Hinojosa and Park (2004), Hunt (2007, 2002), Tranby and Hartmann (2008), and J. Wilson (1999).

12. See Hunt (2007) and Kluegel (1990).

13. See, for example, Brimeyer (2008), Cobb (2009), Edgell and Tranby (2007), Emerson, Smith, and Sikkink (1999), Hinojosa and Park (2004), Hunt (2007, 2002), Tranby and Hartmann (2008), and J. Wilson (1999).

14. See the studies cited in note 13.

15. See Bobo (1991), Bobo and Kluegel (1993), Gilliam and Whitby (1989), Hughes (1997), Hughes and Tuch (2000), Jackman (1996), Kluegel and Bobo (2001), Shelton and Wilson (2009), Tuch and Hughes (1996), Tuch and Sigelman (1997), and G. Wilson (2001).

16. See, for example, Brown (2009), Edgell and Tranby (2007), Taylor and Merino (2011), and Tranby and Hartmann (2008).

17. See Bobo (1991), Bobo and Kluegel (1993), Brown (2009), Brown and Brown (2003), Edgell and Tranby (2007), Shelton and Wilson (2009), Sigelman and Welch (1991), and G. Wilson (2001).

18. The most important columns are those marked *B-W* (blacks' percentage minus whites' percentage on a particular survey item). If a result appears in bold, it signals that the difference between blacks and whites within that particular religious-related category is larger than those found elsewhere. For example, the first row of data assesses the extent to which blacks and whites differ in their beliefs about whether they have been "treated unfairly" because of their race: 43.4% of black non-Protestants say that they have experienced racial discrimination, while only 7.2% of white non-Protestants say that they have done so. The resulting figure in bold, **36.2** (i.e., the product of *B–W*), tells us that this is the largest difference across the three religious-related categories. As you can see, the *B–W* gap gets noticeably smaller (although remains statistically significant) as we move across the columns: the difference between black Protestants and white mainline Protestants is 26.3, and the difference between black Protestants and white evangelicals is 21.4.

See the PALS codebook and data file (http://www.PALS.org/) for more information on the survey questions/statements and answer categories for the "racial identity" and "political views" items.

19. *BNP–BP* = black non-Protestants minus black Protestants; *WNP–WP* = white non-Protestants minus white Protestants (whether mainline or evangelical); *WMP–WE* = white mainline Protestants minus white evangelicals.

20. See Alumkal (2004), Carpenter (1999), Emerson and Hawkins (2007), Lindsay (2007), Marsden (1980), Roof and McKinney (1987), Wilcox (1990), Wilcox and Robinson (2010), Daniel Williams (2010), and Wood (1999).

21. Emerson and Smith (2000, 54).

22. See Emerson and Smith (2000), Emerson and Yancey (2008), and Yancey (2001).

23. See Perkins and Rice (2000).

24. See Yancey (2001).

25. Emerson and Smith (2000, 67).

26. Murray (1993, 20).

27. Many of our interviews with high-ranking clergy were conducted in the weeks just before and after Barack H. Obama was inaugurated the 44th president of the United States.

28. This quote was delivered in a speech by Rev. Dr. Martin Luther King, Jr., at Western Michigan University in 1963. See Western Michigan University Libraries, "Dr. Martin Luther King's 1963 WMU Speech Found," http://www.wmich.edu/library/archives/mlk/q-a.html.

29. In 1865, during the latter stages of the Civil War, General William T. Sherman issued Special Field Orders No. 15. This directive granted some newly freed blacks in parts of Georgia, South Carolina, and Florida "40 acres and a mule" so that they could establish their own family farm as recompense for slavery. The orders only remained in effect for one year, as President Andrew Johnson revoked the policy and returned the land to its previous white owners.

NOTES TO THE EPILOGUE

1. See Lischer (1997), Luker (2002), and Royce (1968).

2. Quoted in the King Center's online essay "The King Philosophy" at http://www.thekingcenter.org/history/the-king-philosophy/.

3. Quoted in ibid.

4. This is a very popular quote from Dr. King that can be easily found across a wide variety of books, magazines, and websites such as http://mlk

-kppo1.stanford.edu/kingweb/liberation_curriculum/pdfs/transformation handout.pdf.

5. See Dr. King's famous "Letter from a Birmingham Jail" (April 16, 1963) and the Martin Luther King Jr. Center for Nonviolent Social Change website: http://www.thekingcenter.org/history/quotations/.

6. See King (1967, 128).

7. See Baer (1984), Barnes (2005), Battle (2006), Bennett (1969), Brown and Brown (2003), Calhoun-Brown (1996), Cone (1991), Dawson (2001), F. Harris (1994), Lincoln and Mamiya (1990), Marsh (2005), McCartney (1992), Morris (1984), Pinn (2002), and West and Glaude (2003).

8. See King (1956/1997, 373).

9. See Myrdal (1944, 1065–1070).

10. A transcript of the speech is available at http://www.lbjlib.utexas.edu/johnson/archives.hom/speeches.hom/650604.asp.

11. See Hunt (2007), Shelton (2012), and Shelton and Greene (forthcoming).

12. See Hunt (2007), Shelton (2012), and Shelton and Greene (forthcoming).

13. See Shelton (2012) and Shelton and Greene (forthcoming).

NOTES TO APPENDIX A

1. AAPOR (2009).

2. The number of persons contacted was adjusted to exclude an estimated number of refusals that would not have met the PALS screening criteria. This estimate was based on the ratio of the actual count of persons not selected for interview (2,109) to the total number of completed screenings (5,689) and applied to the number of refusals at the screening stage.

3. Outcome rates for the PALS Wave 1 were calculated using the appropriate formulas based on the definitions provided by the American Association for Public Opinion Research (AAPOR, 2009). For the contact rate, we used Contact Rate 2 (CON2), which is calculated as $((I+P)+R+O)/((I+P)+R+O+NC+e(U+UO))$, where I = completed screening, P = partial screening, R = refusal and break-offs, NC = noncontacts, O = other contacts, e = estimated proportion of cases of unknown eligibility that are eligible, UH = unknown if household occupied, and UO = other unknown. Using the proportional allocation, or CASRO, method, the estimated eligible cases were calculated by applying the proportion of all persons screened of the determined eligible cases to the number of unknown eligibility cases. A screening

completion rate was calculated to reflect the nonresponse during the screening phase. This rate is the proportion of completed screenings to the adjusted number of persons contacted. For the interview rate, or cooperation rate, we used AAPOR's Cooperation Rate 2 (COOP2), as (I+P)/(I+P)+R+O, where I = completed interview, P = partial interview, R = refusal and break-offs, and O = other contacts. Because the data collection involved a two-stage process of screening in order to meet race subsample targets and then interviewing those persons, we present a response rate based on taking the product of the contact rate, a screening completion rate (reflecting refusals before the screening), and the cooperation rate, specifically, 83% × 86% × 82% = 58%. AAPOR recognizes this approach for a multistage design, because we are able to demonstrate that the PALS sample is representative of the U.S. population, using the 2005–2007 American Community Survey as the comparison. At the end of the data collection period, a sample of 620 households was opened and work was begun on contacting them (preliminary letters sent out, in some cases an initial contact made) but not concluded. These cases were excluded from all of the outcome rate calculations. If we include those households in the potential sample, the contact rate is 82%, the screening completion rate is 84%, the cooperation rate remains 82%, and the response rate becomes 56% (.82 × .84 × .82).

4. U.S. Census Bureau (2009).

References

Abbington, James, ed. 2002. *Readings in African American Church Music and Worship*. Chicago: Gia.

Aghahowa, Brenda Eatman. 1996. *Praising in Black and White*. Cleveland: United Church Press.

Alkebulan, Adisa. 2007. "Defending the Paradigm." *Journal of Black Studies* 37(3): 410–427.

Alumkal, Antony. 2004. "American Evangelicalism in the Post-Civil Rights Era: A Racial Formation Theory Analysis." *Sociology of Religion* 65(3): 195–213.

American Association for Public Opinion Research (AAPOR). 2009. *Standard Definitions: Final Dispositions of Case Codes and Outcome Rates for Surveys, Revised 2009*. http://www.aapor.org/AM/Template.cfm?Section=Standard_Definitions1&Template=/CM/ContentDisplay.cfm&ContentID=1814.

Anderson, Elijah. 1999. *Code of the Street: Decency, Violence, and the Moral Life of the Inner City*. New York: Norton.

Anderson, Elizabeth. 2010. *The Imperative of Integration*. Princeton: Princeton University Press.

Anderson, Jeffrey E. 2007. *Conjure in African American Society*. Baton Rouge: Louisiana State University Press.

Asante, Molefi Keti. 1998. *The Afrocentric Idea*, rev. and exp. ed. Philadelphia: Temple University Press.

———. 1988. *Afrocentricity: The Theory of Social Change*. Trenton, NJ: Africa World.

Baer, Hans A. 1984. *The Black Spiritual Movement: A Religious Response to Racism*. Knoxville: University of Tennessee Press.

Baer, Hans A., and Merrill Singer. 1993. *African-American Religion in the Twentieth Century: Varieties of Protest and Accommodation*. Knoxville: University of Tennessee Press.

Barnes, Sandra L. 2011. "Black Megachurches: Social Gospel Usage and Community Empowerment." *Journal of African American Studies* 15(2): 177–198.

Barnes, Sandra L. 2005. "Black Church Culture and Community Action." *Social Forces* 84:967–994.

Barton, Tamysn. 1994. *Ancient Astrology*. New York: Routledge.

Battle, Michael. 2006. *The Black Church in America: African American Christian Spirituality*. Malden, MA: Blackwell.

Bauval, Robert, and Thomas Brophy. 2011. *Black Genesis: The Prehistoric Origins of Ancient Egypt*. Rochester, VT: Bear.

Bennett, Lerone, Jr. 1969. *Before the Mayflower: A History of Black America*. New York: Penguin Books.

Berger, Peter L. 1967. *The Sacred Canopy: Elements of a Sociological Theory of Religion*. New York: HarperPerennial.

Bernal, Martin. 1987. *Black Athena: The Afroasiatic Roots of Classical Civilization*. New Brunswick: Rutgers University Press.

Bibb, Henry. 1849/1999. "Conjuration and Witchcraft." In *African American Religious History: A Documentary Witness*, edited by Milton C. Sernett. Durham: Duke University Press.

Blyden, Edward. 1869. "The Negro in Ancient History." *Methodist Quarterly Review* 52:62–78.

Bobo, Lawrence. 1991. "Social Responsibility, Individualism, and Redistributive Policies." *Sociological Forum* 6:71–92.

Bobo, Lawrence, and James Kluegel. 1993. "Opposition to Race-Targeting: Self-Interest, Stratification Ideology, or Racial Attitudes?" *American Sociological Review* 58:443–464.

Boles, John B., ed. 1990. *Masters and Slaves in the House of the Lord: Race and Religion in the American South, 1740–1870*. Lexington: University Press of Kentucky.

Bonczar, Thomas. 2003. *Prevalence of Imprisonment in the U.S. Population 1974–2001, Special Report NCJ 197976*. Washington, DC: Bureau of Justice Statistics. http://www.ojp.usdoj.gov/bjs/pub/pdf/piusp01.pdf.

Bonilla-Silva, Eduardo. 2006. *Racism without Racists: Colorblind Racism and the Persistence of Racial Inequality in the United States*. Lanham, MD: Rowman and Littlefield.

Bowen, William, and Derek Bok. 2000. *The Shape of the River: Long-Term Consequences of Considering Race in College and University Admissions*. Princeton: Princeton University Press.

Brace, C. Loring. 2005. *"Race" Is a Four-Letter Word: The Genesis of the Concept*. New York: Oxford University Press.

Bridges, Flora Wilson. 2001. *Resurrection Song: African American Spirituality*. Maryknoll, NY: Orbis Books.

Brimeyer, Ted M. 2008. "Research Note: Religious Affiliation and Poverty Explanations: Individual, Structural, and Divine Causes." *Sociological Focus* 41(3): 226–237.

Browder, Anthony T. 1992. *Nile Valley Contributions to Civilization*. Washington, DC: Institute of Karmic Guidance.

Brown, Khari R. 2009. "Denominational Differences in Support for Race-Based Policies among White, Black, Hispanic, and Asian Americans." *Journal for the Scientific Study of Religion* 48(3): 604–615.

Brown, Khari R., and Ronald E. Brown. 2003. "Faith and Works: Church-Based Social Capital Resources and African American Political Activism." *Social Forces* 82:617–641.

Brown, Robert, and Todd C. Shaw. 2002. "Separate Nations: Two Attitudinal Dimensions of Black Nationalism." *Journal of Politics* 64(1): 22–44.

Calhoun-Brown, Allison. 1999. "The Image of God: Black Theology and Racial Empowerment in the African American Community." *Review of Religious Research* 40:197–212.

———. 1998. "While Marching to Zion: Otherworldliness and Racial Empowerment in the Black Community." *Journal for the Scientific Study of Religion* 37:427–439.

———. 1996. "African American Churches and Political Mobilization: The Psychological Impact of Organizational Resources." *Journal of Politics* 58:935–953.

Callahan, Allen D. 2006. *The Talking Book*. New Haven: Yale University Press.

Carpenter, Joel. A. 1999. *Revive Us Again: The Reawakening of American Fundamentalism*. New York: Oxford University Press.

Carter, Harold A. 1995. *The Prayer Tradition of Black People*. Baltimore: Gateway.

Cavendish, James C., Michael R. Welch, and David C. Leege. 1998. "Social Network Theory and Predictors of Religiosity for Black and White Catholics: Evidence of a 'Black Sacred Cosmos'?" *Journal for the Scientific Study of Religion* 37 (3): 397–410.

Chen, Carolyn. 2002. "The Religious Varieties of Ethnic Presence: A Comparison between a Taiwanese Immigrant Buddhist Temple and an Evangelical Christian Church." *Sociology of Religion* 63:215–238.

Chireau, Yvonne. 2003. *Black Magic: Religion and the African American Conjuring Tradition*. Berkeley: University of California Press.

Cleage, Albert. 1972. *Black Christian Nationalism: New Directions for the Black Church*. New York: Morrow.

———. 1968. *The Black Messiah*. New York: Sheed and Ward.

Cobb, Ryon Jayson. 2009. "*Still* Divided By Faith? Race, Protestantism, and Beliefs about Black/White Economic Inequality, 1985–2008." Unpublished manuscript.

Coleman, Monica. 2008. *Making a Way Out of No Way: A Womanist Theology*. Minneapolis: Fortress.

Collins, Patricia Hill. 1990. *Black Feminist Thought: Knowledge, Consciousness, and the Politics of Empowerment*. New York: Routledge.

Commanger, Henry S. 1945. "The Negro Problem in Our Democracy." *American Mercury* 60:755.

Conde-Frazier, Elizabeth, Gary A. Parrett, and S. Steve Kang. 2004. *A Many Colored Kingdom: Multicultural Dynamics for Spiritual Formation*. Grand Rapids, MI: Baker Academic.

Cone, James H. 2011. *The Cross and the Lynching Tree*. Maryknoll, NY: Orbis Books.

———. 1992. *The Spirituals and the Blues: An Interpretation*. Maryknoll, NY: Orbis Books.

———. 1991. *Martin and Malcolm and America: A Dream or a Nightmare?* Maryknoll, NY: Orbis Books.

———. 1975. *God of the Oppressed*. New York: Seabury.

———. 1970. *A Black Theology of Liberation*. Philadelphia: Lippincott.

———. 1969. *Black Theology and Black Power*. San Francisco: Harper and Row.

Conley, Dalton. 1999. *Being Black, Living in the Red*. Berkeley: University of California Press.

Cooper-Lewter, Nicholas, and Henry Mitchell. 1986. *Soul Theology: The Heart of American Black Culture*. San Francisco: Harper and Row.

Corcoran, Mary. 2001. "Mobility, Persistence, and the Consequences of Poverty for Children: Child and Adult Outcomes." In *Understanding Poverty*, edited by Sheldon Danziger and Robert Haveman, 127–161. New York: Russell Sage.

Cornelius, Janet Duitsman. 1991. *"When I Can Read My Title Clear": Literacy, Slavery, and Religion in the Antebellum South*. Columbia: University of South Carolina Press.

Costen, Melva Wilson. 2004. *In Spirit and in Truth: The Music of African American Worship*. Louisville: Westminster John Knox Press.

———. 1993. *African American Christian Worship*. Nashville: Abingdon.

Cruse, Harold. 1967. *The Crisis of the Negro Intellectual*. New York: Quill.

Curry, James. 1840/1977. "Narrative of James Curry." In *Slave Testimony: Two Centuries of Letter, Speeches, Interviews, and Autobiographies*, edited by John W. Blassingame. Baton Rogue: Louisiana State University Press.

Darnell, Alfred, and Darren F. Sherkat. 1997. "The Impact of Protestant Fundamentalism on Educational Attainment." *American Sociological Review* 62:306–315.

Davis, Darren, and Ron Brown. 2002. "The Antipathy of Black Nationalism: Behavioral and Attitudinal Implications of an African American Ideology." *American Journal of Political Science* 46(2): 239–252.

Davis, James A., and Tom W. Smith. 2010. *General Social Surveys, 1972–2008: Cumulative Codebook.* Chicago: University of Chicago, National Opinion Research Center.

Dawson, Michael C. 2001. *Black Visions: The Roots of Contemporary African American Political Ideologies.* Chicago: University of Chicago Press.

Dickens, Charles. 1859/2010. *A Tale of Two Cities.* Calgary, AB: Qualitas.

Douglas, Kelley Brown. 1993. *The Black Christ.* Maryknoll, NY: Orbis Books.

Douglass, Frederick. 1845/1985. "Slaveholding Religion and the Christianity of Christ." In *Afro-American Religious History: A Documentary Witness*, edited by Milton C. Sernett. Durham: Duke University Press.

Drake, St. Clair, and Horace R. Cayton. 1945. *Black Metropolis.* Chicago: University of Chicago Press.

Du Bois, W. E. B. 1920. *Darkwater: Voices from within the Veil.* New York: Harcourt Brace.

———. 1903/2005. *The Souls of Black Folk.* New York: Simon and Schuster.

Earl, Riggins. 2003. *Dark Symbols, Obscure Signs: God, Self, and Community in the Slave Mind.* Knoxville: University of Tennessee Press.

Ebaugh, Helen R. F. 2000. Introduction to *Religion and the New Immigrants: Continuities and Adaptations in Immigrant Congregations*, edited by Helen R. F. Ebaugh and Janet Chafetz, 13–28. Walnut Creek, CA: AltaMira.

Ecklund, Elaine Howard. 2006. *Korean American Evangelicals: New Models for Civic Life.* New York: Oxford University Press.

Edgell, Penny, and Eric Tranby. 2007. "Religious Influences on Understandings of Racial Inequality in the United States." *Social Problems* 54(2): 263–288.

Edwards, Korie L. 2009. "Race, Religion, and Worship: Are Contemporary African-American Worship Practices Distinct?" *Journal for the Scientific Study of Religion* 48 (1): 30–52.

Ellison, Christopher G., and Darren E. Sherkat. 1995. "The 'Semi-Involuntary Institution' Revisited: Regional Variations in Church Participation among Black Americans." *Social Forces* 73:1415–1437.

———. 1990. "Patterns of Religious Mobility among Black Americans." *Sociological Quarterly* 31:551–568.

Emerson, Michael O., and J. Russell Hawkins. 2007. "Viewed in Black and White: Conservative Protestantism, Racial Issues, and Oppositional Politics." In *Religion and American Politics: From the Colonial Period to the Present*, edited by Mark A. Noll and Luke E. Harlow, 327–344. New York: Oxford University Press.

Emerson, Michael O., and Christian Smith. 2000. *Divided by Faith: Evangelical Religion and the Problem of Race in America*. New York: Oxford University Press.

Emerson, Michael O., Christian Smith, and David Sikkink. 1999. "Equal in Christ, but Not in the World: White Conservative Protestants and Explanations of Black/White Inequality." *Social Problems* 46:398–417.

Emerson, Michael O., and George Yancey. 2008. "African Americans in Interracial Congregations: An Analysis of Demographics, Social Networks, and Social Attitudes." *Review of Religious Research* 49(3): 301–318.

Evans, James H., Jr. 1993. *We Have Been Believers: An African-American Systematic Theology*. Minneapolis: Augsburg Fortress.

Farley, Reynolds, and Walter R. Allen. 1987. *The Color Line and the Quality of Life in America*. New York: Oxford University Press.

Farley, Reynolds, and Suzanne Bianchi. 1985. "Social Class Polarization: Is It Occurring among Blacks?" *Research in Race and Ethnic Relations* 4:1–31.

Faulkner, William J. 1977. *The Days When Animals Talked: Black American Folktales and How They Came to Be*. Chicago: Follett.

Feagin, Joe R. 1975. *Subordinating the Poor*. Englewood Cliffs, NJ: Prentice Hall.

Feagin, Joe R., and Melvin P. Sikes. 1994. *Living with Racism: The Black Middle-Class Experience*. Boston: Beacon.

Felder, Cain Hope, ed. 1991. *Stony the Road We Trod: African American Biblical Interpretation*. Minneapolis: Fortress.

Floyd-Thomas, Stacey, and Anthony Pinn. 2010. *Liberation Theologies in the United States: An Introduction*. New York: NYU Press.

Fordham, Monroe. 1975. *Major Themes in Northern Black Religious Thought, 1800–1860*. Hicksville, NY: Exposition.

Frazier, E. Franklin. 1964. *The Negro Church in America*. New York: Schocken Books.

Frederick, Marla. 2003. *Between Sundays: Black Women and Everyday Struggles of Faith*. Berkeley: University of California Press.

Froese, Paul, and Christopher Bader. 2010. *America's Four Gods: What We Say about God—and What That Says about Us*. New York: Oxford University Press.

Gilliam, Franklin, and Kenny Whitby. 1989. "Race, Class, and Attitudes toward Social Welfare Spending: An Ethclass Interpretation." *Social Science Quarterly* 70:89–99.

Goldenberg, David M. 2003. *The Curse of Ham: Race and Slavery in Early Judaism, Christianity, and Islam.* Princeton: Princeton University Press.

Gomez, Michael A. 1998. *Exchanging Our Country Marks: The Transformation of African Identities in the Colonial and Antebellum South.* Chapel Hill: University of North Carolina Press.

Gordon, Milton. 1964. *Assimilation in American Life.* New York: Oxford University Press.

Gould, Stephen Jay. 1981. *The Mismeasurement of Man.* New York: Norton.

Grant, Jacquelyn. 1989. *White Women's Christ and Black Women's Jesus: Feminist Christology and Womanist Response.* Atlanta: American Academy of Religion.

Graves, Joseph L., Jr. 2004. *The Race Myth: Why We Pretend Race Exists in America.* New York: Plume.

Greeley, Andrew M., and Michael Hout. 2006. *The Truth about Conservative Christians: What They Think and What They Believe.* Chicago: University of Chicago Press.

Gronniosaw, James. 1770/2010. *A Narrative of the Most Remarkable Particulars in the Life of James Albert Ukawsaw Groniosaw.* Memphis: General Books.

Gutierrez, Gustavo. 1987. *On Job: God-Talk and the Suffering of the Innocent.* Maryknoll, NY: Orbis Books.

———. 1971. *A Theology of Liberation: History, Politics, and Salvation.* Maryknoll, NY: Orbis Books.

Hacker, Andrew. 2003. *Two Nations: Black and White, Separate, Hostile, and Unequal.* New York: Scribner.

Hannaford, Ivan. 1996. *Race: The History of an Idea in the West.* Baltimore: John Hopkins University Press.

Harris, Eleanor. 1998. *Ancient Egyptian Divination and Magic.* Newburyport, MA: Red Wheel.

Harris, Fredrick. 1994. "Something Within: Religion as a Mobilizer of African American Political Activism." *Journal of Politics* 56:42–68.

Harrison, Milmon F. 2005. *Righteous Riches: The Word of Faith Movement in Contemporary African American Religion.* New York: Oxford University Press.

Hayden, William. 1846/2001. "Narrative of William Hayden." In *African American Slaves Narrative: An Anthology,* vol. 1, edited by Sterling L. Bland, Jr. Westport, CT: Greenwood.

Haynes, Stephen R. 2002. *Noah's Curse: The Biblical Justification of American Slavery*. New York: Oxford University Press.

Helling, Amy, and David Sawicki. 2003. "Race and Residential Accessibility to Shopping and Services." *Housing Policy Debate* 14(1–2): 69–101.

Herskovits, Melville. 1958. *Myth of the Negro Past*. Boston: Beacon.

Hinojosa, Victor, and Jerry Z. Park. 2004. "Religion and the Paradox of Racial Inequality Attitudes." *Journal for the Scientific Study of Religion* 43:229–238.

Holifield, E. Brooks. 2007. *The Gentlemen Theologians: American Theology in Southern Culture, 1795–1860*. Eugene, OR: Wipf and Stock.

Holt, Thomas. 2002. *The Problem of Race in the Twenty-First Century*. Cambridge: Harvard University Press.

Hood, Robert E. 1994. *Begrimed and Black: Christian Traditions on Blacks and Blackness*. Minneapolis: Fortress.

Hopkins, Dwight. 2003. "Slave Theology in the 'Invisible Institution.'" In *Cut Loose Your Stammering Tongue: Black Theology in the Slave Narrative*, edited by Dwight N. Hopkins and George C. L. Cummings. Louisville, KY: Westminster John Knox Press.

———. 1999. *Introducing Black Theology of Liberation*. Maryknoll, NY: Orbis Books.

Huber, Joan, and William H. Form. 1973. *Income and Ideology: An Analysis of the American Political Formula*. New York: Free Press.

Hughes, Michael. 1997. "Symbolic Racism, Old-Fashioned Racism, and Whites' Opposition to Affirmative Action." In *Racial Attitudes in the 1990's*, edited by Steven Tuch and Jack Martin. Westport, CT: Praeger.

Hughes, Michael, and Steven A. Tuch. 2000. "How Beliefs about Poverty Influence Racial Policy Attitudes: A Study of Whites, African Americans, Hispanics, and Asians in the United States." In *Racialized Politics: The Debate about Racism in America*, edited by David. O. Sears, Jim Sidanius, and Lawrence Bobo. Chicago: University of Chicago Press.

Hunt, Larry, and Matthew O. Hunt. 2001. "Race, Region, and Religious Involvement: A Comparative Study of Whites and African Americans." *Social Forces* 80(2): 605–631.

Hunt, Matthew O. 2007. "African American, Hispanic, and White Beliefs about Black/White Inequality, 1977–2004." *American Sociological Review* 72:390–415.

———. 2004. "Race/Ethnicity and Beliefs about Wealth and Poverty." *Social Science Quarterly* 85(3): 827–853.

———. 2002. "Religion, Race/Ethnicity, and Beliefs about Poverty." *Social Science Quarterly* 83(3): 810–831.

———. 1996. "The Individual, Society, or Both? A Comparison of Black, Latino, and White Beliefs about the Causes of Poverty." *Social Forces* 75(1): 293–322.

Isaacs, Julia. 2008. "Economic Mobility of Black and White Families." In *Getting Ahead or Losing Ground: Economic Mobility in America*, edited by Ron Haskings, Julia Isaacs, and Isabel Sawhill. Washington, DC: Brookings Institute.

Jackman, Mary. 1996. "Individualism, Self-Interest, and White Racism." *Social Science Quarterly* 77:760–769.

James, George G. M. 2009. *Stolen Legacy.* New York: Classic House Books.

Johnson, Paul E., ed. 1994. *African American Christianity: Essays in History.* Berkeley: University of California Press.

Johnson, Sylvester. 2004. *The Myth of Ham in Nineteenth-Century American Christianity: Race, Heathens, and the People of God.* New York: Palgrave Macmillan.

Jones, William R. 1973. *Is God a White Racist? A Preamble to Black Theology.* Boston: Beacon.

Jordan, Winthrop D. 1969. *White over Black: American Attitudes toward the Negro, 1550–1812.* Baltimore: Penguin Books.

Karenga, Maulana. 1992. *Introduction to Black Studies.* Los Angeles: University of Sankore Press.

Kennedy, Randall. 1997. *Race, Crime, and the Law.* New York: Pantheon Books.

Kerbo, Harold. 2011. *Social Stratification and Inequality: Class Conflict in the United States.* New York: McGraw-Hill.

King, Martin Luther King, Jr. 1956/1997. "To Sally Canada." In *The Papers of Martin Luther King, Jr.*, vol. 3, *Birth of a New Age*, edited by Clayborne Carson, Stewart Burns, Susan Carson, Peter Holloran, and Dana Powell. Berkeley: University of California Press.

———. 1967. *Where Do We Go from Here: Chaos or Community?* New York: Harper and Row.

Kluegel, James R. 1990. "Trends in Whites' Explanations for the Black/White Gap in Socioeconomic Status, 1977–1989." *American Sociological Review* 55(4): 512–525.

Kluegel, James R., and Lawrence Bobo. 2001. "Perceived Group Discrimination and Policy Attitudes: The Sources and Consequences of the Race and Gender Gaps." In *Urban Inequality: Evidence from Four Cities*, edited by Alice O'Connor, Chris Tilly, and Lawrence Bobo. New York: Russell Sage Foundation.

Kluegel, James R., and Eliot R. Smith. 1986. *Beliefs about Inequality: Americans' Views of What Is and What Ought to Be.* New York: Aldine de Gruyter.

Kozol, Jonathan. 1992. *Savage Inequalities: Children in America's Schools.* New York: HarperPerennial.

LaRue, Cleophus J. 2000. *The Heart of Black Preaching.* Louisville, KY: Westminster John Knox Press.

Lefkowitz, Mary. 1996. *Not Out of Africa: How Afrocentrism Became an Excuse to Teach Myth as History.* New York: Basic Books.

Lefkowitz, Mary, and Guy M. Rogers, eds. 1996. *Black Athena Revisited.* Chapel Hill: University of North Carolina Press.

Lewis, Oscar. 1968. *La Vida: A Puerto Rican Family in the Culture of Poverty —San Juan and New York.* New York: Knopf.

———. 1959. *Five Families: Mexican Case Studies in the Culture of Poverty.* New York: Basic Books.

Lincoln, C. Eric, and Lawrence H. Mamiya. 1990. *The Black Church in the African American Experience.* Durham: Duke University Press.

Lindsay, D. Michael. 2007. *Faith in the Halls of Power: How Evangelicals Joined the American Elite.* New York: Oxford University Press.

Lischer, Richard. 1997. *The Preacher King: Martin Luther King, Jr. and the Word That Moved America.* New York: Oxford University Press.

Long, Carolyn Morrow. 2001. *Spiritual Merchants: Religion, Magic, and Commerce.* Knoxville: University of Tennessee Press.

Luker, Ralph E. 2002. "Kingdom of God and Beloved Community in the Thought of Martin Luther King, Jr." In *The Role of Ideas in the Civil Rights Movement,* edited by Ted Ownby. Jackson: University Press of Mississippi.

Macleod, Jay. 2008. *Ain't No Makin' It: Aspirations and Attainment in a Low-Income Neighborhood.* Boulder, CO: Westview.

Marsden, George. 1980. *Fundamentalism and American Culture.* New York: Oxford University Press.

Marsh, Charles. 2005. *The Beloved Community: How Faith Shapes Social Justice, from the Civil Rights Movement to Today.* New York: Basic Books.

Massey, Douglas. 2007. *Categorically Unequal: The American Stratification System.* New York: Russell Sage Foundation.

Massey, Douglas, Camille Z. Charles, Garvey Lundy, and Mary J. Fischer. 2006. *The Source of the River: The Social Origins of Freshmen at America's Selective Colleges and Universities.* Princeton: Princeton University Press.

Massey, Douglas S., and Nancy A. Denton. 1993. *American Apartheid: Segregation and the Making of the Underclass.* Cambridge: Harvard University Press.

Maynard-Reid, Pedrito U. 2000. *Diverse Worship: African American, Caribbean, and Hispanic Perspectives.* Downers Grove, IL: InterVarsity.

McCartney, John T. 1992. *Black Power Ideologies: An Essay in African-American Political Thought.* Philadelphia: Temple University Press.

McKee, James B. 1993. *Sociology and the Race Problem: The Failure of a Perspective.* Urbana: University of Illinois Press.

McMickle, Marvin A. 2000. *Preaching to the Black Middle Class: Words of Challenge, Words of Hope.* Valley Forge, PA: Judson.

McRoberts, Omar M. 2003. *Streets of Glory: Church and Community in a Black Urban Neighborhood.* Chicago: University of Chicago Press.

Merton, Robert K. 1938. "Social Structure and Anomie." *American Sociological Review* 3:672–682.

Mitchell, Henry H. 2004. *Black Church Beginnings: The Long-Hidden Realities of the First Years.* Grand Rapids, MI: Eerdmans.

Morris, Aldon D. 1984. *The Origins of the Civil Rights Movement: Black Communities Organizing for Change.* New York: Free Press.

Moyd, Olin P. 1995. *The Sacred Art: Preaching and Theology in the African American Tradition.* Valley Forge, PA: Judson.

Mure, William. 1854/2008. *A Dissertation on the Calendar and the Zodiac of Ancient Egypt.* Charleston, SC: BiblioBazaar.

Murray, Cecil. 1993. "Needed: An At-Risk Gospel." *Christianity Today* 37:20.

Myrdal, Gunnar. 1944. *An American Dilemma: The Negro Problem and Modern Democracy.* New York: Harper and Brothers.

National Center for Injury Prevention and Control. 2006. *WISQARS Injury Mortality Reports, 1999–2006.*

Nelson, Timothy J. 2005. *Every Time I Feel the Spirit: Religious Experience and Ritual in an African American Church.* New York: NYU Press.

Neugebauer, Otto. 1969. *The Exact Sciences in Antiquity.* New York: Dover.

Noll, Mark A. 2001. *American Evangelical Christianity: An Introduction.* Malden, MA: Blackwell.

O'Connor, Alice, Chris Tilly, and Lawrence Bobo, eds. 2003. *Urban Inequality: Evidence from Four Cities.* New York: Russell Sage Foundation.

Omi, Michael, and Howard Winant. 1994. *Racial Formation in the United States: From the 1960s to the 1990s.* New York: Routledge.

Orfield, Gary, and Carole Ashkinaze. 1991. *The Closing Door: Conservative Policy and Black Opportunity.* Chicago: University of Chicago Press.

Orfield, Gary, and Susan Eaton. 1997. *Dismantling Desegregation: The Quiet Reversal of Brown v. Board of Education.* New York: New Press.

Paris, Peter J. 1985. *The Social Teaching of the Black Churches*. Philadelphia: Fortress.

Parker, Evelyn. 2003. *Trouble Don't Last Always: Emancipatory Hope among African American Adolescents*. Cleveland: Pilgrim.

Pattillo-McCoy, Mary. 1998. "Church Culture as a Strategy of Action in the Black Community." *American Sociological Review* 63:767–784.

Perkins, Spencer, and Chris Rice. 2000. *More Than Equals: Racial Healing for the Sake of the Gospel*. Downers Grover, IL: InterVarsity.

Pew Research Center. 2011. "Wealth Gaps Rise to Record Highs between Whites, Blacks, and Hispanics." Report by Rakesh Kochhar, Richard Fry, and Paul Taylor. July. http://pewsocialtrends.org/files/2011/07/SDT-Wealth -Report_7-26-11_FINAL.pdf.

———. 2009a. "Many Americans Mix Multiple Faiths: Eastern, New Age Beliefs Widespread." Pew Forum report. December. http://pewforum.org/ Other-Beliefs-and-Practices/Many-Americans-Mix-Multiple-Faiths.aspx.

———. 2009b. "A Religious Portrait of African Americans." Pew Forum report by Neha Sahgal and Greg Smith. January. http://pewforum.org/ A-Religious-Portrait-of-African-Americans.aspx.

———. 2008. "U.S. Religious Landscape Survey: Religious Beliefs and Practices: Diverse and Politically Relevant." June. http://religions.pewforum .org/pdf/report2-religious-landscape-study-full.pdf.

Pinkney, Alphonso. 2000. *Black Americans*. Upper Saddle River, NJ: Prentice Hall.

———. 1984. *The Myth of Black Progress*. New York: Cambridge University Press.

———. 1976. *Red, Black, and Green: Black Nationalism in the United States*. New York: Cambridge University Press.

Pinn, Anthony B. 2003. *Terror and Triumph: The Nature of Black Religion*. Minneapolis: Fortress.

———. 2002. *The Black Church in the Post–Civil Rights Era*. Maryknoll, NY: Orbis Books.

———. 1995. *Why, Lord? Suffering and Evil in Black Theology*. New York: Continuum Books.

Price, Frederick. 2001. *Race, Religion, and Racism*, vol. 2, *Perverting the Gospel to Subjugate a People*. Los Angeles: Faith One.

Priest, Robert, and Alvaro Nieves, eds. 2006. *This Side of Heaven: Race, Ethnicity, and Christian Faith*. New York: Oxford University Press.

Quadagno, Jill. 1996. *The Color of Welfare: How Racism Undermined the War on Poverty*. New York: Oxford University Press.

Raboteau, Albert J. 1978. *Slave Religion: The "Invisible Institution" in the Antebellum South*. New York: Oxford University Press.

Randolph, Peter. 1855/2010. *Sketches of Slave Life: Illustrations of the "Peculiar Institution."* Forgotten Books.

Reuter, Edward Byron. 1927. *The American Race Problem: A Study of the Negro*. New York: Thomas Y. Crowell.

Rodman, Hyman. 1963. "The Lower-Class Value Stretch." *Social Forces* 42(2): 205–215.

Roof, Wade Clark, and William McKinney. 1987. *American Mainline Religion: Its Changing Shape and Future*. New Brunswick: Rutgers University Press.

Royce, Josiah. 1968. *The Problems of Christianity*. Chicago: University of Chicago Press.

Rugh, Jacob S., and Douglas S. Massey. 2010. "Racial Segregation and the American Foreclosure Crisis." *American Sociological Review* 75(5): 629–651.

Shapiro, Thomas M. 2004. *The Hidden Cost of Being African American: How Wealth Perpetuates Inequality*. New York: Oxford University Press.

Shelby, Tommie. 2005. *We Who Are Dark: The Philosophical Foundations of Black Solidarity*. Cambridge: Belknap Press of Harvard University Press.

Shelton, Jason E. 2012. "Black Middle Class Beliefs about Racial Inequality." Unpublished manuscript.

———. 2008. "The Investment in Blackness Hypothesis: Toward Greater Understanding of Who Teaches What during Racial Socialization." *Du Bois Review: Social Science Research on Race* 5(2): 235–257.

Shelton, Jason E., and Michael O. Emerson. 2010. "Extending the Debate over Nationalism versus Integration: How Cultural Commitments and Assimilation Trajectories Influence Beliefs about Black Power." *Journal of African American Studies* 14:312–336.

Shelton, Jason E., and Anthony D. Greene. Forthcoming. "Get Up, Get Out, and Git' Sumthin': How Race and Class Influence African Americans' Attitudes about Inequality." *American Behavioral Scientist*.

Shelton, Jason E., and George Wilson. 2009. "Race, Class, and the Basis of Group Alignment: An Analysis of Support for Redistributive Policy among Privileged Blacks." *Sociological Perspectives* 52(3): 385–408.

———. 2006. "Socioeconomic Status and Racial Group Interests among Black Americans." *Sociological Spectrum* 26:184–204.

Sherkat, Darren E. 2002. "African-American Religious Affiliation in the Late 20th Century: Cohort Variations and Patterns of Switching, 1973–1998." *Journal for the Scientific Study of Religion* 41:485–493.

Sigelman, Lee, and Susan Welch. 1991. *Black Americans' Views of Racial Inequality*. New York: Cambridge University Press.

Smart, Ninian. 1983. *Worldviews: Crosscultural Explorations of Human Beliefs*. New York: Scribner.

Smith, Christian. 1998. *American Evangelicalism: Embattled and Thriving*. New York: Oxford University Press.

Smith, Christine Marie. 2008. *Preaching Justice: Ethnic and Cultural Perspectives*. Eugene, OR: Wipf and Stock.

Smith, Efrem, and Phil Jackson. 2005. *The Hip-Hop Church: Connecting with the Movement Shaping Our Culture*. Downers Grove, IL: InterVarsity.

Smith, Theophus H. 1994. *Conjuring Culture: Biblical Formations of Black America*. New York: Oxford University Press.

Sniderman, Paul, and Thomas Piazza. 2002. *Black Pride and Black Prejudice*. Princeton: Princeton University Press.

Sobel, Mechal. 1979. *Trabelin' On: The Slave Journey to an Afro-Baptist Faith*. Westport, CT: Greenwood.

Spence, Lester, Todd C Shaw, and Robert Brown. 2005. "True to Our Native Land: Distinguishing Attitudinal Support for Pan-Africanism from Black Separatism." *Du Bois Review: Social Science Research on Race* 2(1): 91–111.

Steensland, Brian, Jerry Z. Park, Mark D. Regnerus, Lynn D. Robinson, W. Bradford Wilcox, and Robert Woodberry. 2000. "The Measure of American Religion: Toward Improving the State of the Art." *Social Forces* 79: 291–318.

Steinberg, Stephen. 2007. *Race Relations: A Critique*. Stanford: Stanford University Press.

———. 1981. *The Ethnic Myth*. Boston: Beacon.

Stoll, Michael. 2005. "African Americans and the Color Line." In *The American People: Census 2000*, edited by Reynolds Farley and John Haaga. New York: Russell Sage Foundation.

Stump, Roger. 1987. "Regional Contrasts with Black Protestantism: A Research Note." *Social Forces* 66(1): 143–151.

Swidler, Ann. 1986. "Culture in Action: Symbols and Strategies." *American Sociological Review* 51:273–286.

Taylor, Marylee C., and Stephen M. Merino. 2011. "Race, Religion, and Beliefs about Racial Inequality." *Annals of the American Academy of Political and Social Science* 634:60–77.

Taylor, Robert Joseph, Linda M. Chatters, Rukmalie Jayakody, and Jeffrey S. Levin. 1996. "Black and White Differences in Religious Participation: A

Multisample Comparison." *Journal for the Scientific Study of Religion* 35(4): 403–410.

Taylor, Robert Joseph, Linda M. Chatters, and Jeff Levin. 2004. *Religion in the Lives of African Americans: Social, Psychological, and Health Perspectives.* Thousand Oaks, CA: Sage.

Thernstrom, Stephan, and Abigail Thernstrom. 1997. *America in Black and White.* New York: Touchstone.

Thistlethwaite, Susan Brooks, and Mary Potter Engel. 1998. *Lift Every Voice: Constructing Christian Theologies from the Underside.* Maryknoll, NY: Orbis Books.

Thomas, Frank. 1997. *They Like to Never Quit Praisin' God: The Role of Celebration in Preaching.* Cleveland: Pilgrim.

Thurman, Howard. 1976. *Jesus and the Disinherited.* Boston: Beacon.

Tranby, Eric, and Douglas Hartmann. 2008. "Critical Whiteness Theories and the Evangelical 'Race Problem': Extending Emerson and Smith's Divided by Faith." *Journal for the Scientific Study of Religion* 47(3): 341–359.

Tuch, Steven, and Michael Hughes. 1996. "Whites' Racial Policy Attitudes." *Social Science Quarterly* 77:723–745.

Tuch, Steven, and Lee Sigelman. 1997. "Race, Class, and Black/White Differences in Social Policy Views." In *Understanding Public Opinion*, edited by Barbara Norrander and Clyde Wilcox. Washington, DC: CQ Press.

Turner, Henry McNeal. 1898. "God Is a Negro." *Voice of Missions* (African Methodist Episcopal Church).

U.S. Census Bureau. 2009. "American Community Survey 3-Year Estimates: 2005–2007." January 16. http://factfinder.census.gov/servlet/DatasetMain PageServlet?_program=ACS&_submenu Id=&_lang=en&_ts=.

Valentine, Bettylou. 1978. *Hustling and Other Hard Work: Lifestyles in the Ghetto.* New York: Free Press.

Van Deburg, William. 1997. *Modern Black Nationalism: From Marcus Garvey to Louis Farrakhan.* New York: NYU Press.

Venkatesh, Sudhir A. 2006. *Off the Books: The Underground Economy of the Urban Poor.* Cambridge: Harvard University Press.

Warner, R. Stephen. 1998. "Immigration and Religious Communities in the United States." In *Gatherings in the Diaspora: Religious Communities and the New Immigration*, edited by R. Stephen Warner and Judith Wittner, 3–34. Philadelphia: Temple University Press.

Washington, James Melvin. 1995. Introduction to *Conversations with God: Two Centuries of Prayers by African Americans*, edited by James Melvin Washington. New York: HarperCollins.

Waters, Mary, and Reed Ueda, with Helen Marrow. 2007. *The New Americans: A Guide to Immigration since 1965*. Cambridge: Harvard University Press.

Webber, Thomas. 1978. *Deep like the Rivers*. New York: Norton.

Webster, Bruce, and Alemayehu Bishaw. 2007. "Income, Earnings, and Poverty Data from the 2006 American Community Survey." U.S. Department of Commerce, Economics and Statistics Administration, U.S. Census Bureau.

West, Cornel. 1993. *Race Matters*. Boston: Beacon.

———. 1982. *Prophesy Deliverance! An Afro-American Revolutionary Christianity*. Louisville, KY: Westminster John Knox Press.

West, Cornel, and Eddie S. Glaude Jr., eds. 2003. *African American Religious Thought: An Anthology*. Louisville, KY: Westminster John Knox Press.

West, Heather, and William Sabol. 2009. *Prisoners in 2007, NCJ 224280*. Washington, DC: Bureau of Justice Statistics. http://www.ojp.usdoj.gov/bjs/pub/pdf/p07.pdf.

Western, Bruce, and Christopher Wildeman. 2009. "The Black Family and Mass Incarceration." *Annals of the American Academy of Political and Social Science* 621(1): 221–242.

Wilcox, Clyde. 1990. "Religion and Politics among White Evangelicals: The Impact of Religious Variables on Political Attitudes." *Review of Religious Research* 32(1): 27–42.

Wilcox, Clyde, and Carin Robinson. 2010. *Onward Christian Soldiers? The Religious Right in American Politics*. Boulder, CO: Westview.

Williams, Daniel. 2010. *God's Own Party: The Making of the Christian Right*. New York: Oxford University Press.

Williams, Delores. 1995. *Sisters in the Wilderness: The Challenge of Womanist God-Talk*. Maryknoll, NY: Orbis Books.

Wilmore, Gayraud S. 1973. *Black Religion and Black Radicalism: An Interpretation of the Religious History of African Americans*. Garden City, NY: Anchor/Doubleday.

Wilson, George. 2005. "Race and Job Dismissal: African American/White Differences in Their Sources during the Early Work Career." *American Behavioral Scientist* 48(9): 1182–1199.

———. 2001. "Support for Redistributive Policies among the African American Middle Class: Race and Class Effects." *Research in Social Stratification and Mobility* 18:97–115.

———. 1996. "Toward a Revised Framework for Examining Beliefs about the Causes of Poverty." *Sociological Quarterly* 37(3): 413–428.

Wilson, J. Matthew. 1999. "'Blessed Are the Poor': American Protestantism and Attitudes toward Poverty and Welfare." *Southeastern Political Review* 27(3): 421–437.

Wilson, William. 2009. *More Than Just Race: Being Black and Poor in the Inner City*. New York: Norton.

——. 1996. *When Work Disappears: The World of the New Urban Poor*. New York: Knopf.

——. 1987. *The Truly Disadvantaged: The Inner City, the Underclass, and Public Policy*. Chicago: University of Chicago Press.

——. 1978. *The Declining Significance of Race*. Chicago: University of Chicago Press.

Witt, Reginald E. 1997. *Isis in the Ancient World*. Baltimore: Johns Hopkins University Press.

Wood, Richard L. 1999. "Religious Culture and Political Action." *Sociological Theory* 17:307–332.

Woofter, Thomas J., ed. 1928. *Negro Problems in Cities*. New York: Doubleday.

Work, Monroe N. 1924. "The Race Problem in Cross Section: The Negro in 1923." *Social Forces* 2:245–252.

Yancey, George. 2001. "Color Blindness, Political Correctness, or Racial Reconciliation: Christian Ethics and Race." *Christian Ethics Today* 35(7): 1–5.

Yang, Fenggang, and Helen Rose Ebaugh. 2001. "Religion and Ethnicity among New Immigrants: The Impact of Majority/Minority Status in Home and Host Countries." *Journal for the Scientific Study of Religion* 40:367–378.

Young, Alford. 2002. "The 'Negro Problem' and the Character of the Black Community: Charles Johnson, E. Franklin Frazier, and the Constitution of a Black Sociological Tradition, 1920–1935." In *Confronting the American Dilemma of Race: The Second Generation of Black American Sociologists*, edited by Robert E. Washington and Donald Cunnigen. Lanham, MD: University Press of America.

Index

Academic model of Christianity: defined, 68; overview of, 67; Rev. Robinson on, 74

Academic-versus-experiential dichotomy: and black and white Protestants views of God, 159; in relation to being a "good person" (Rev. Boyd), 137–138; in relation to blacks' commitment to a far-reaching faith (Dr. Cone), 156; level of operation, 69; tested across range of religious actions and beliefs, *see* chapter 5; as widely accepted and deeply rooted, 78;

Affirmative action, 13, 171, 178, 205

African American (Old Negro) spirituals, 45–46

African culture: and black Protestantism, 7, 33, 37, 61, 66, 114, 128–129, 166–167; in relation to blacks' beliefs about "reincarnation," 148–153. *See also* Voodoo

African Methodist Episcopal Church (A.M.E.): as first Protestant denomination founded by blacks, 19, 190; our interviewees' beliefs about reflective thinking, 95–99; religious affiliation of pastor interviewed in this study, 23, 26, 81, 96, 98, 117, 130, 185; requirements for ordination, 79. *See also* Turner, Henry McNeal

Africanisms, 149

Afrocentrism, 146

Afterlife, 53

An American Dilemma (Myrdal), 169

Ancient Egyptians, 146, 150

Anderson, Elizabeth, 125

Apostles' Creed: beliefs associated with, 11, 53; and explanation for racial differences in religious sensibilities (Dr. Cone), 76; importance of, 48–49; longer form, 48; strongest tie binding black and white

Protestants, 56, 57, 199. *See also* Survey findings

Astrology: church teachings about, 145; defined, 144; explanation for blacks' attention to, 147

Atlanta, 111

Bader, Christopher, 122

Baptist, 12, 13, 20, 24, 28, 58, 60, 61, 69, 92, 95, 97, 111, 116, 117, 159, 187

"Beloved Community," Martin Luther King Jr.'s vision of, 4, 9, 200–204; challenges to, 204–207

Berger, Peter, 113

Bibb, Henry, 37

Big Bang Theory, 91

Big Momma, 73, 90, 104, 153

Black and white Protestants, explanation for research focus, 9–10

The Black Codes, 170

Black Nationalism: defined, 146; habit of inclusion among blacks, 155–157, 167

Black Power Movement, 146–147

Black sacred cosmos: Africanisms and, 149; in relation to the afterlife, 53, 154; and building blocks of black Protestant faith, 8, 28, 200; defined, 6–7; expanded commitment to social justice, 196–197; 169; in relation to blacks' faith-based open-mindedness and tolerance for others, 167; in relation to blacks' faith-based tolerance and open-mindedness, and the limits of, 157–166; and identity politics, 169; as theologically broad and definitive, 134, 167

Blyden, Edward, 36

Broad and definitive: defined and applied to the black sacred cosmos, 134, 167; definitive, as pertaining to Biblical

Broad and definitive (*continued*)
perspectives, 88; theologically, the
African American Protestant religious
tradition as, 30, 137, 140
Brown, Simon, 43
Brown v. Board of Education, 171
Buddhism: as a universal religion, 3; as
related to yoga, 148

Canaan, 35
Catholics, 10
Christianity as a universal religion, 3
Civil Rights Act of 1964, 171, 205
Civil Rights Act of 1968, 171, 205
Civil Rights Movement: and the African
American Protestant religious tradition,
33; and America's "race problem," 171,
176; and King's "Beloved Community,"
201; as a "church movement," 129, 203;
as referenced by our interviewees, 22,
129, 146–147, 194; and the racial reconciliation movement, 181; limits to success of, 205
Civil War, 169, 170
Cleveland, Ohio, 17, 20, 21, 98, 107, 117, 120,
158, 192, 195
Complex subjectivity, 114–115, 131
Cone, James H.: on Black Nationalism and
commitment of blacks to a far-reaching
faith, 156; on blacks' beliefs about miracles, 143–144; on blacks' emphasis on
God as an "impersonal force," 165–166;
on blacks' "Jesusology," 154, 166; career
overview, 19; on God as a "liberator," 44;
on "purpose" in black religion, 114, 115;
on racial differences in religious sensibilities, 76–78; on racial discrimination
and the African American Protestant
religious tradition, 27; on racial identity
and religious affiliation, 20; on racial
reconciliation, 195–196; as references by
our interviewees, 194; relevance to the
study, 19, 29
Conjure, cultural tradition of, 37
Cooper-Lewton, Nicholas, 114
Creation, in six 24-hour days: references
of interviewees to survey finding,
80, 90–91, 94, 97, 98. *See also* Survey
findings
Cultural factors: and the

academic-versus-experiential dichotomy, 84–85; description of, 59:
differences among followers of the same
faith, 2–3, 11, 59; as pertaining to epistemological explanations, 66–67; as pertaining to racial differences in religious
sensibilities, 62; in relation to interpreting the Bible (Pastor Smith), 97–98;
Cultural imperatives: criticisms of, 64;
defined, 59; prevalence in the United
States, 59–60
Curry, James, 46
Curse of Ham, 35–36; referenced by an
interviewee, 103. *See also* 242n4

Dallas-Fort Worth, Texas, 17, 24, 62, 71, 81,
90, 96, 116, 185, 187
David, 119
Deacon Harris: on black Christianity as
"survival focused," 143; on blacks' beliefs
about reincarnation, 152–153; on blacks'
emphasis on how a person "lives their
life," 138; on blacks' need for a more
academic understanding of Christianity, 80; on blacks' reliance on multiple
faith-based sources for solving "major
problems," 126; on "encountering God"
and praise and worship methods among
blacks, 161–162; on God's Rules versus
Man's Rules, 119–120; on perceived
cultural differences between black and
white Protestants, 60–62; on racial
reconciliation, 185; on religious identity
among blacks, 106–107
Definitive. *See* Broad and definitive
De jure segregation, 170
Denominational affiliations: importance
among white Protestants, 12; lesser
importance among black Protestants,
12–13, 58–60. *See also* 240n14
DeYoung, Curtiss, 182
Dickens, Charles, 171
Dominant ideology, individualism as, 73

Earl, Riggins, 41–42
Education: and the African American
Protestant religious tradition, 78–81;
and weakening religious sensibilities,
93. *See also* Reflective thinking
Emerson, Michael, 17, 44, 49, 174

Epistemological explanations, defined, 65–67

Ethiopians, 105

Evangelical: term not fullest way of expressing African American Christianity, 37; as "white term used by white people" (Rev. Johnson), 90; and whiteness (Rev. Robinson), 189

Evans, Tony, 188

Exodus story, 38

Experiential building block, 8, 53, 57, 83, 86, 108

Experiential model of Christianity, 67; and blacks' beliefs about reincarnation, 149; and blacks' emphasis on how a person "lives their life," 139; defined, 68; as explained by Rev. Robinson, 74; how devotees think about what they find in the Bible, 101

Faith, as supernatural call for help, 4–5, 86, 107, 132

"Faith and works," relationship between: argument for racial differences in religious sensibilities (Dr. Cone), 77; and blacks' emphasis on how a person "lives their life," 139; as explained by Rev. Robinson, 75–76; as explained by Pastor Smith, 81–83; and social justice, Rev. Robinson on, 188–189; and social justice, Rev. Washington on, 194–195

Five building blocks of Black Protestant Faith, 8–9; overview of, 5, 137; and racial differences in religious sensibilities, 27–29, 200; research goals, 3

Focus group members: black female, highly educated, 87–88, 120, 158–159; black male, age 30-something, 92, 120, 158; black male, fun-loving yet quirky, 22–23; blacks' reliance on multiple faith-based sources for solving "major problems," 130; white female confused about survey finding, 18

Folk theology, 81; defined (Pastor Smith), 82; understanding of Christianity complicated by (Pastor Smith), 98

"40 acres and a mule," 250n29; as mentioned by interviewees, 191, 192

Franklin, Aretha, 73

Froese, Paul, 122

General Social Survey (GSS), 10–11; discussion of survey results, 14, 15, 55, 88, 101–102, 109, 121, 122, 145, 147, 174, 177, 197, 204

Genesis, book of, 51

Glass ceiling, 105

God: black and white Protestants' view, contrast in attributes of, 122; but for the grace of, 20–27, 102–108, 143; as liberator and "worth-giver," 41, 44–46; will "show up" when needed, 25, 73, 160, 161. *See also* Man's rules versus God's rules; Survey findings

Gomez, Michael, 36,

Graham, Billy, 182, 188

Gronniosaw, James Albert, 42

Great Awakenings, 12, 16, 33, 38, 40, 41

Habit of inclusion, 154–157; as defined by Pastor Jenkins, 154

Harvard University, 73

Hayden, William, 42

Haynes, Stephen, 35

Heaven, 11, 37, 44, 48, 52–53, 70, 157. *See also* Survey findings

Hell, 11, 22, 48, 52–53. *See also* Survey findings

Hicks, Derek, 29, 31–32, 123, 125, 241n1

Hinduism: and blacks' beliefs about "reincarnation," 148–153; yoga and, 148

Hines, Samuel, 181

Holy Spirit: as aspect of the Apostles' Creed, 56, 247n21; as emphasized among Pentecostals, 61, 161–163; as part of the Holy Trinity, 23, 63, 74, 158

Houston, Texas, 2

Howard University, 205

Human Genome Project, 245n11

Hunter, Jeffery, 24–25

"I Am Somebody" (poem), 115

Identity politics, 4, 168; beliefs about racial inequality and, 30, 200; beliefs about role of government and, 13, 30, 200; black and white Protestant religious sensibilities and, 179–181, 196–197; and racial reconciliation, 13, 30, 200

Income inequality, 110

Individualism: and cultural imperatives, 64; as factor influencing beliefs about

Individualism (*continued*)
the role of government, 30, 168, 175–176, 196–197; as factor influencing contemporary racial inequality, 13, 24, 30, 168, 197. *See also* Stratification beliefs
"Invisible Institution," 39
Isaiah, book of, 105
Islam, 3. *See also* Nation of Islam; Survey findings
Israelites, 38, 45

Jackson, Jesse, 115
Jakes, T. D., 188
James, book of, 75, 77, 189
Japheth, 35
Jesus Christ, 23, 38, 41, 44–46, 51–52, 60, 94, 106, 107–108, 118–119, 136, 137, 140, 152, 154, 157, 158, 163, 165, 166, 189; Eurocentric depictions of, 161, 163–165, 186. *See also* Survey findings
Jim Crow segregation, 22, 33, 117
Johnson, Andrew, 250n29
Johnson, Lyndon B., 205
Jordan, Winthrop, 41
Judaism, 3
Justice building block, 9, 168–169, 196

Kentucky, 37
King, Martin Luther King, Jr.: as leader in the Civil Rights Movement, 171; on goals of the racial reconciliation movement, 201–202; referenced by interviewees, 105, 117, 120; on social justice, 202–204; and vision of the "Beloved Community," 4, 9, 200–204
King, Rodney, 194

Liberation theology: and the African American Protestant religious tradition, 36, 46; and black religious studies, 6, 29; Deacon Harris (focus group member) on, 120; defined, 6; man's rules versus God's rules and, 119–120
Lincoln, Abraham, 144
Lincoln, C. Eric, 6, 20, 69, 129; on the black sacred cosmos, 7–8
Los Angeles, 17, 22, 32, 60, 117, 130, 140, 150, 157, 184
Louisiana, 32, 71, 104

Malcolm X, 156
Mamiya, Lawrence, 6, 20, 69, 129; on the black sacred cosmos, 7–8
Manifest destiny, 34, 41
Man's rules versus God's rules, 118–123, 131
Marshall, Thurgood, 171
McCain, John, 193
McCartney, Bill, 182, 188
Methodist, 12, 13, 18, 19, 28, 58, 85, 92, 95, 117, 159. *See also* African Methodist Episcopal Church; United Methodist Church
Michelangelo, 165
Middle Passage, 37
Miraculous building block, 8, 25, 134, 166
Mitchell, Henry, 37, 114
Moses, 38, 45
Motivational individualism, 174–175, 206
Muhammad. *See* Survey findings
Multiracial/multicultural churches, 69, 161, 190
Murphy, Eddie, 123–124
Muslims, 141, 154. *See also* Nation of Islam
Myrdal, Gunnar, 169, 204, 248n2
Mystery building block, 8, 21, 53, 84, 114, 133–134, 166

Nation of Islam, 155–156
Native Americans, ix, 169
"Never Would Have Made It" (gospel song), 26
New immigrants, 10
New Testament, 35, 74, 98
New York City, 17, 26, 60, 96, 119, 123, 138, 185
Noah, 35, 103
North Carolina, 46,
Numerology, 147

Obama, Barack, 185, 192–195
Old Testament, 35, 94, 98, 99
Opportunity-enhancing policies, 176–179, 196
Outcome-based policies, 176–179, 196

Parks, Rosa, 171
Pastor Jenkins: on Biblical literalism among blacks, 91; on blacks' attention to astrology, 146–147; on blacks' beliefs about reincarnation, 150–151;

on breaking moral rules, 117; defining blacks' habit of inclusion, 157
Pastor Smith: on Biblical literalism and women in society, 96–98; on folk theology, 81–83; on racial reconciliation, 185–187
Pastor Thomas: on the basic teachings of the African American Protestant religious tradition, 26; on blacks' faith-based open-mindedness and tolerance, 155–156; on blacks' reliance on multiple faith-based sources for solving "major problems," 126, 130; on Eurocentric depictions of Christ, 163–165; on a perceived "theological training" gap among black pastors, 79–80; on racial reconciliation, 190; on reflective thinking as a "sign of a lack of faith," 96; on survival and morality among black Protestants, 118
Paul, the Apostle, 81, 97, 98, 189
Payne, Daniel, 79
Pentecostal, 12, 13, 21, 22, 28, 58, 60, 61, 71, 73, 90, 91, 92, 95, 107, 117, 130, 157, 159, 161, 163, 185, 191
Perkins, John, 181
Pew Research Center: "Many Americans Mix Multiple Faiths," 144–145, 151, 156–157; "U.S. Religious Landscape Survey," 6, 14, 16, 99, 100, 105, 141
Pinn, Anthony, 111, 114, 115
Planter class, 34
Plessy v. Ferguson, 170
Pontius Pilate, 48
Portraits of American Life Study (PALS), 10–11; discussion of survey results, 14–16, 50, 52, 92, 99, 100, 101–102, 109, 113; 126, 134, 141, 148, 158, 177, 196, 197, 204
"Principle of cumulation," 204, 205. *See also* Myrdal, Gunnar
Promise Keepers, 182
Protestant: percentages of racial and ethnic groups who identify as, 10
Psalms, book of, 105

Qualitative research methodology: on the decision to "move around" interviewees, 241n25; overview of in-depth interviews and focus groups, 16–20
Quantitative research methodology:

analysis procedures, 14–16; multivariate tables available online at http://nyupress.org/shelton/appendixD.pdf. *See also* General Social Survey; Portraits of American Life Study

Raboteau, Albert, 38
"The race problem," 169–172; and identity politics, 13, 168, 200; and religion, 13
Racial reconciliation: black and white Protestants' contrasting definitions of, 182–183; history of and goals of the movement, 181–183; and identity politics, 13, 30, 184, 200; and the Civil Rights Movement, 181. *See also* chapter 8
Randolph, Peter, 39
Reconstruction Era, 33, 170
Reflective thinking: and education, 90; and a literal interpretation of the Bible, 92–99; as pertaining to blacks' emphasis on God as an "impersonal force," 161–163
Reincarnation: growing influence among American Christians, 148. *See also* Survey findings
Relationalism, 174
Religious sensibilities: defined, 4; and the five building blocks of black Protestant faith, 5, 27–28, 199–200; racial oppression and privilege and, 21, 199–200; theoretical framework for racial differences in, 57–85
Research methodology (in general): comparing black and white Protestants, 5; contributions to the literature, 9. *See also* Qualitative research methodology; Quantitative research methodology
Rev. Boyd: on blacks' commitment to Biblical literalism as a family-based tradition, 90; on blacks' not being "reflective enough," 151–152; on the institutional centrality of the black church, 104; on racial differences in religious sensibilities, 71–73; on racial reconciliation, 191–192; on why being a "good person" is not good enough, 136–137
Rev. Davis: on blacks' emphasis on how a person "lives their life," 139; on changing views of God among blacks, 161; on

Rev. Davis (*continued*)
racial differences in religious sensibilities, 69–71
Rev. Edwards: on Jesus using parables, 94; on racial oppression and the African American Protestant religious tradition, 21–22; on racial reconciliation, 192–193
Rev. Henderson: on blacks' faith-based open-mindedness and tolerance, 140; on perceived cultural differences between black and white Protestants, 60, 139; on racial reconciliation, 184–185
Rev. Johnson: on black and white Protestants' views of God, 159–160; on blacks' beliefs about reincarnation, 149–150; on blacks' commitment to Biblical literalism as a family based tradition, 90–91; on blacks' reliance on multiple faith-based sources for solving "major problems," 128–129; on breaking moral rules, 116–117; on everyday practical concerns and the institutional centrality of the black church, 24–25; on how "problems in society" shape black and white Protestants religious sensibilities, 104–106; on perceived cultural differences between black and white Protestants, 62–63; on racial reconciliation, 187–188; on why being a "good person" is not good enough, 136
Rev. Robinson: on Biblical literalism and reflective thinking, 94–95; on blacks' attention to the power of God, 162–163; on blacks' commitment to an experiential model of Christianity, 152; on blacks' literal interpretation of the Bible, 88; on "faith and works," 75–76; on how Christianity helped blacks get through slavery, 103; on perceived contradictions among white evangelicals, 74–75; on racial differences in religious sensibilities, 73–74; on racial reconciliation, 188–189; on survival and morality among black Protestants, 118–119. *See also* Tortured exegesis
Rev. Shannon: on breaking moral rules, 117; on how power influences religious sensibilities, 23; on non-Christians being "good people," 137; on racial reconciliation, 193; on reflective thinking

and blacks' literal interpretation of the Bible, 98; on reincarnation and becoming a more "knowledgeable Christian," 152; on the Bible as blacks' "dictionary," 99; on white Christians having more sources for solving "major problems," 130; on white Protestant modes of praise and worship, 63–64
Rev. Washington: on blacks' emphasis on God as an "impersonal force," 159–160; on blacks' reliance on multiple faith-based sources for solving "major problems," 129; on Eurocentric depictions of Christ, 165; on how Biblical literalism influences blacks' views of God, 160; on perceived contradictions among white evangelicals, 71; on racial differences in religious sensibilities, 20–21; on racial reconciliation, 194–195; on religious identity among blacks, 106; on survival and morality among black Protestants, 118
Roberts, J. Deotis, 194
Rodman, Hyman, 246n5

The Sabbath, Rev. Robinson on Jesus and, 119
The Sacred Canopy (Berger), 113
Sapp, Marvin, 26–27
Satan: as pertaining to folk theology, 83; as referenced in an Old Negro spiritual, 46
Saturday Night Live, 123
"Separate but equal," 170–171
Sharon (candidate for administrative assistant position), 2
Shelton, Jason, 17, 49
Shem, 35
Sherman, William T., 250n29
Sister Anderson, 107
Sistine Chapel, 165
Skinner, Tom, 181
Slave class, 34
Slave testimonials, 37, 39, 42–43
Slavery: and the African American Protestant religious tradition, 21–23, 31–47, 70, 75; Biblical justifications for, 35–36; helped to foster an open-mindedness and tolerance for others among blacks, 139; reparations for, *see* Survey findings
Smart, Ninian, 244n8

Smith, Christian, 44, 174
Smith, Theophus, 37
Social heritage: defined, 59; and structuralism, 65, 67
Social justice: and the African American Protestant religious tradition, 43; and "faith and works," Rev. Robinson on, 188–189; and "faith and works," Rev. Washington, 194–195; Martin Luther King, Jr. on, 202–204; and the racial reconciliation movement, second wave of, 182
Soul Theology (Cooper-Lewter and Mitchell), 114
Southern California, 91, 161
Star Wars (movie), 163
Stratification beliefs, 172–175
Structuralism: and changes in blacks' beliefs about the causes of racial inequality, 205–206; and epistemological explanations, 65–67, 84–85; as a factor influencing contemporary racial inequality, 24, 196; as an ideological challenge to cultural imperatives, 64–67; and the role of government, beliefs about, 175–176, 196–197; and social heritage, 65. *See also* Stratification beliefs
Supernatural, realm of the, 141–147. *See also* Faith; Pew Research Center, "U.S. Religious Landscape Survey"
Suppressor effect, 53, 121
Supreme Court rulings, 144, 201
Survey findings, on: afterlife, 53; the basis of what is morally right and wrong, 120; belief in God, 50; beliefs about angels, 142; beliefs about astrology, 145–146; beliefs about being a good person, 134–135; beliefs about causes of racial inequality, 174–175; beliefs about errors within the Bible, 92; beliefs about Heaven, 52–53; beliefs about Hell, 52–53; beliefs about how the Bible should be interpreted, 88–89; beliefs about Jesus Christ, 51–52; beliefs about miracles, 142–143; beliefs about Muhammad, 154; beliefs about reincarnation, 148; beliefs about whether God has abandoned him or her, 131; breaking moral rules, 116; chances of dissipation

of issues of race relations if conversation about them stops, 197–198; church attendance, 14; church membership, 16; creation in six 24-hour days, 51, 89; doubts about one's religious faith, 109; faith-based sources for dealing with "major problems" in life, 126–128; financial contributions to one's church, 109; God as a "personal being" or "impersonal force," 158; God inflicting personal punishment, 121; morally right and wrong as not always simply black and white, 121; participation in a Bible study group, 100; punishment for violation of God's rules, 121; purpose for one's life, 113; reading the Bible, 99–100; religious centrality, 54–55; resurrection of Jesus Christ, 52; support for opportunity-enhancing policy, 177; support for outcome-based policy, 177–179; whether one has ever been angry with God, 131
Survival building block, 8, 25, 86, 101, 108, 112, 117, 131, 143

Tennessee, 72
Terror and Triumph (Pinn), 114
Theology of suffering and evil, 6; and black religious studies, 6, 29
Thurman, Howard, 32
Timothy, book of, 81
Tortured exegesis, 94, 95
Transcendental meditation, 147
Trinity, 23, 74, 77, 158, 162, 165
Turner, Henry McNeal, 164–165
Turner Theological Seminary, 79

United Methodist Church, 60, 140, 184. *See also* Methodist
United States: distribution of racial and ethnic groups by religious affiliation, 10; history of black/white race relations, 33, 169–172
Universal religions, 3; challenges to Christianity's status as, 56, 200
University of California at Berkeley, 73

Valley of the Shadow of Death, and the academic-versus-experiential dichotomy, 74
Virginia, 39, 46

Voodoo, 156–157
Voting Rights Act of 1965, 171

Warren, Rick, 188
Washington, D.C., 192
Washington, James Melvin, 46
Watts (Los Angeles), 32
"We Shall Overcome" (song), 147
Where Do We Go From Here: Chaos or Community? (King), 202–203
White evangelicals: as impassioned believers, 12; relevance to our quantitative research methodology, 13, 15–16

White male Methodist pastor who declined to participate in the study, 18, 85
White privilege, 87, 193
Whitfield, George, 40–41
Wilson, Sherita, 111–112, 121
Womanism, 23
World Pentecostal Conference, 61
World War II, 170

Yoga, 147, 148, 247n13

Zephaniah, book of, 105
Zodiac signs, 147

About the Authors

Jason E. Shelton is Assistant Professor of Sociology at the University of Texas at Arlington. He publishes research on the sociology of religion as well as the impact of social class and cultural differences among African Americans in the post–Civil Rights Era.

Michael O. Emerson is the Allyn and Gladys Cline Professor of Sociology at Rice University, where he also serves as Co-Director of the Kinder Institute for Urban Research. He is the author of several books, including *Against All Odds: The Struggle for Integration in Religious Organizations* (also available from NYU Press).